BETWEEN FIVE EYES

50 Years of Intelligence Sharing

ANTHONY R. WELLS

CASEMATE
Oxford & Philadelphia

Published in Great Britain and the United States of America in 2020 by
CASEMATE PUBLISHERS
The Old Music Hall, 106–108 Cowley Road, Oxford OX4 1JE, UK
and
1950 Lawrence Road, Havertown, PA 19083, USA

Hardback Edition: ISBN 978-1-61200-900-1
Digital Edition: ISBN 978-1-61200-901-8

A CIP record for this book is available from the British Library

Printed and bound in the United States of America by Sheridan

Typeset by Versatile PreMedia Service (P) Ltd

For a complete list of Casemate titles, please contact:

CASEMATE PUBLISHERS (UK)
Telephone (01865) 241249
Email: casemate-uk@casematepublishers.co.uk
www.casematepublishers.co.uk

CASEMATE PUBLISHERS (US)
Telephone (610) 853-9131
Fax (610) 853-9146
Email: casemate@casematepublishers.com
www.casematepublishers.com

Front cover images: (top left) The seal of the CIA (Wikimedia Commons); (top right) The Sentinel Space Telescope (Wikimedia Commons); (middle left) The joint Australia/US communications facility at Pine Gap near Alice Springs in Central Australia (Wikimedia Commons); (middle right) New Zealand's Government Communications Security Bureau facility in Waihopai (Wikimedia Commons); (bottom) The UK's GCHQ in Cheltenham, Gloucestershire (Ministry of Defence).

Contents

Dedication

This book is dedicated to the men and women of the Five Eyes intelligence community who since World War II have composed the bedrock intelligence agencies and departments for sustaining freedom and democracy in our fragile world. The trust and relationships built between the individuals of each member nation has been the single most important factor for the continuing success of the "Special Relationship" in the provision of timely, accurate, and unvarnished actionable intelligence to their individual national leaderships, and the collective good of the five nations. Those relationships, built so successfully over the decades since World War II, will endure because of the quality, commitment, and loyalty of each serving individual. We all have reason to be grateful for their service. They are the continuity that in an age of global political uncertainly provides the bedrock foundations for modern society's security. May intelligence cooperation between the United States, the United Kingdom, Canada, Australia, and New Zealand continue onwards and upwards, and provide the bedrock security for future society.

This is their story.

The men and women of UK and US intelligence have always sought, and will continue to seek, the best for not just their collective good and the wellbeing of their individual nations, but a much wider vision for the safe and secure future of planet Earth. The words below of the distinguished American astronomer Carl Sagan (1934–1996) say much that embrace the spirit and substance of the people to whom my book is dedicated, their mission, and their sense of a commitment of always doing the "right thing" through the provision of excellent intelligence.

These words were inspired by an image taken, at Carl Sagan's suggestion, by Voyager 1 on February 14, 1990, as the spacecraft left our planetary system for the fringes of the solar system. The spacecraft was turned one last time to look at planet Earth. Voyager 1 was about 4 billion miles from Earth and approximately 32 degrees above the ecliptic plane when it captured a portrait of our world, a pale blue dot. The Earth was caught in the center of scattered light rays, appearing as a tiny point of light, a crescent only 0.12 pixels in size.

"Look again at that dot. That's here. That's home. That's us. On it everyone you love, everyone you know, everyone you ever heard of, every human being who ever was, lived out their lives. The aggregate of our joy and suffering, thousands of confident religions, ideologies, and economic doctrines, every hunter and forager, every hero and coward, every creator and destroyer of civilization, every king and peasant, every young couple in love, every mother and father, hopeful child, inventor and explorer, every teacher of morals, every corrupt politician, every 'superstar,' every 'supreme leader,' every saint and sinner in the history of our species lived there—on a mote of dust suspended in a sunbeam.

The Earth is a very small stage in a vast cosmic arena. Think of the endless cruelties visited by the inhabitants of one corner of this pixel on the scarcely distinguishable inhabitants of some other corner, how frequent their misunderstandings, how eager they are to kill one another, how fervent their hatreds. Think of the rivers of blood spilled by all those generals and emperors so that, in glory and triumph, they could become the momentary masters of a fraction of a dot.

Our posturings, our imagined self-importance, the delusion that we have some privileged position in the Universe, are challenged by this point of pale light. Our planet is a lonely speck in the great enveloping cosmic dark. In our obscurity, in all this vastness, there is no hint that help will come from elsewhere to save us from ourselves.

The Earth is the only world known so far to harbor life. There is nowhere else, at least in the near future, to which our species could migrate. Visit, yes. Settle, not yet. Like it or not, for the moment the Earth is where we make our stand.

It has been said that astronomy is a humbling and character-building experience. There is perhaps no better demonstration of the folly of human conceits than this distant image of our tiny world. To me, it underscores our responsibility to deal more kindly with one another, and to preserve and cherish the pale blue dot, the only home we've ever known."

– Carl Sagan: *The Pale Blue Dot* (1994)

Foreword by Lord West

Qualified as a warfare officer in the 1970s, I was fully aware of the plethora of documents detailing capabilities of Soviet equipment, and the RN Fighting Instructions telling us how the Soviet Navy would fight and how they could be defeated; but had never pondered how we had such information.

It wasn't until 1988 when, as a captain straight from destroyer command, I was appointed to the Defence Intelligence Staff as DI3Navy, a post descended from the old Director of Naval Intelligence, that I became fully aware of the Five Eyes intelligence community and their crucial role in safeguarding the free world.

I became privy to an amazing secret world and network of impressive individuals working assiduously for our greater good. Once a member you become part of a special family and my involvement continued, as Chief of Defence Intelligence and Deputy Chairman of the Joint Intelligence Committee 1997–2000, as Commander in Chief Fleet, First Sea Lord and lastly as government security minister 2007–2010.

It is only recently that the Five Eyes intelligence community has received much media attention, in relation to possible decisions over use of Huawei telecoms equipment in the new 5G array. But there is almost no understanding of what it is, its history and relevance. Anthony Wells, with his deep involvement in the community and the intelligence world more generally, has put that right. I could think of no one better to explain the complex relationships and their development over some 75 years.

By 1945 the most destructive war in history had just been fought and won.

The winners were the English-speaking peoples and the Soviets. The Soviet Union had ripped the guts out of the Wehrmacht but could not have stood alone against Germany, and it was the supply of limitless US materiel that had enabled her tank armies to roll into Germany.

The British Empire and its dominions had stood alone against Hitler for over a year but it was the United States joining the war in December 1941 that enabled the western maritime nations to mobilise their full potential against Germany and Japan, and it was the complete dominance of the maritime that enabled Germany and Japan to be defeated. The only real winner by 1945 was the US, the richest and most powerful country in the world.

What became clear was that one of the Allies' trump cards and a key war-winning capability was intelligence. The UK official histories estimated that Bletchley Park and US intelligence had shortened the war by several years.

The UK's pre-eminence in codebreaking was recognised by the US and as a result, emerging from an informal agreement related to the 1941 Atlantic Charter, a formal treaty, the 1943 BRUSA, was signed and officially enacted on March 5, 1946 by the United Kingdom and the United States. In the following years, it was extended to encompass Canada, Australia, and New Zealand. The Five Eyes community had been born. There is often much talk about the "Special Relationship" but the reality is that it was these agreements that were the bedrock.

Post war, the English-speaking peoples, US, British Empire and dominions took the lead in establishing a new world order. An order that was accepted and has lasted until relatively recently despite tensions and challenges. What is interesting is that the combined British Commonwealth and North American maritime model for wealth and stability proved more durable than the land-based continental power of the Soviets.

It rapidly became clear that the Soviet Union did not want a world of free nations, pursuing their own goals and growing in wealth. The Soviets established a hegemony over Eastern Europe, suppressed freedom of thought and threatened Western Europe.

In March 1946 Churchill made his famous "Iron Curtain" speech, and NATO was formed in 1949.

The Five Eyes intelligence community was key to our ability to avoid war with the Soviet Union and finally win the Cold War. It has also stood the test of time and evolved to confront changes to the world order such as collapse of the Soviet Union and growth of other threats, be they rogue states, China, terrorism and even to an extent narcotics and crime.

This book is a timely and fitting recognition of an organisation that has helped ensure our freedom for 75 years.

Admiral the Right Honourable Lord West of Spithead GCB DSC PC
May 23, 2020

Introduction

This book constitutes 50 years (1968–2018) working for the UK–US intelligence community, where I have been in a unique position to enjoy "dual intelligence nationality" by the very nature of the special UK–US intelligence relationship. I have been honored to have served in and witnessed the inner workings at the highest security levels of both British and US intelligence in a strictly national sense in addition to both countries being integral and lead members of the Five Eyes intelligence community (the United States, the United Kingdom, Canada, Australia, and New Zealand). Parallel to the above I also had the great honor to serve in the Royal Navy and, while in the Royal Navy, to serve with the US Navy both in Washington DC and at sea in the nuclear powered cruiser USS *Bainbridge* in the Third Fleet, US Pacific Fleet. One of my cherished possessions is the commendation that I received in 1977 from the Chief of Naval Operations, Admiral James L. Holloway the Third, for services to the United States Navy.

On returning to the United States permanently in 1983 I have also served in a civilian capacity on USS *Coronado* and USS *Florida*, as well as short visits and assignments to many US Navy units and entities. For just two examples from many, I attended the senior officers Top Gun course at Naval Air Station Fallon, Nevada, and at US Pacific Fleet Headquarters in Makalapa, Pearl Harbor, Hawaii, and Commander Submarine Forces Pacific Fleet in Pearl Harbor. As well as other elements of the US Navy that I will discuss, I have spent decades in and out of a wide variety of parts of the Department of Defense, in multiple capacities, as well as three key agencies of the US national intelligence community, the Central Intelligence Agency, the National Reconnaissance Office, and the National Geospatial Agency. In addition, I have enjoyed reciprocity with both the National Security Agency and the National Maritime Intelligence Center and various echelons and special programs associated with US naval intelligence and the Office of the Secretary of Defense. While a British citizen I enjoyed across-the-board access to a wide community, including, for example, the US Air Force at such locations as Wright Patterson Air Force Base in Dayton, Ohio, as well as all the key echelons of Canadian, Australian, and New Zealand intelligence.

UK–US intelligence and the wider Five Eyes community is primarily, in my opinion, about one main thing—relationships. These encompass decades (since

World War II) of personnel exchanges (such as my own in the mid-1970s), constant round the clock 24/7 exchange of intelligence and assessments, and regular informal and formal gatherings to plan and execute joint intelligence strategy and plans, from collection operations to analysis and the provision of unvarnished, accurate, and timely actionable intelligence to the respective national political leaderships in the US and the UK. I have been privileged to serve both prime ministers and presidents giving me a unique perspective.

This book is in chronological order, beginning in 1968 when I was first introduced to the intelligence community by Sir Harry Hinsley, one of the finest members of the World War II UK–US community, who was at Bletchley Park, and later a grand old man of British intelligence and the official UK government historian of the history of British intelligence in World War II. From 1968 through to 2018, 50 years of change, turmoil, intense challenges, successes and failures, abiding Five Eyes relationships and a great many wonderful friendships, I trace the development of institutions that I firmly believe have sustained and indeed may have saved the free world and Western democracies and their allies from the odious tyranny of not just communism but all the evil attributes of those ill-disposed to the value system and culture of our nations.

This book does not profess at all to be all-seeing and all-knowing. That would be both preposterous and pretentious. This is not another book that seeks to tell laypersons about intelligence. My hope and indeed ideal is that through my 50 years' experience readers can enter into a dialogue with me, make their own observations, draw their own conclusions, and come away with informed, educated, and non-biased and most certainly non-politicized views on intelligence in the modern era.

As a fully trained and accredited security officer for two US intelligence organizations, there is nothing in this book that violates any security regulations or programs of either the United States or the United Kingdom, or their Five Eyes allies, or other affiliated intelligence organizations of other nations. This book is, by definition, an open source dependent publication. I have relied on my own extensive unclassified collection of papers, personal notes, diaries, as well as my family library for source material. These were augmented by the secondary sources listed in the bibliography. I have also referred to various unclassified source material from UK and US government reports and these are annotated in the bibliography.

CHAPTER I

Foundations of the UK–US Special Relationship, 1968–74

Why the "Special Relationship" and why the Five Eyes? The history of why is complex at one level and simple in another. Above all else this relationship was born from the crucible not just of war, but survival during World War II as demonstrated by the historic meeting of Winston Churchill and Franklin Roosevelt on board HMS *Prince of Wales* in Placentia Bay, off Newfoundland, in August 1941.

The Five Eyes are people from five nations united in a common purpose. Critical for survival over the decades has been the exchange and integration of personnel in each nation's intelligence agencies. Each nation's embassies in London, Washington, Ottawa, Canberra, and Wellington have significant Five Eyes liaisons with each other's intelligence affiliates from all the various intelligence agencies and departments. However, outside the normal embassy staff structure of each nation there has been a continuous flow of exchange personnel working side by side with each other nation's intelligence specialists within the agencies. This continuum of relationships is crucial for understanding why the Five Eyes is such a powerful international diplomatic force, and undoubtedly the most successful intelligence organization ever in the world. The Soviet Union and the Warsaw Pact paled in comparison, split by divisive cultures and the occupation of east European countries by Soviet forces, none of which enhanced the kind of cooperation and loyalty that abides to this day in the Five Eyes.

A Moment in Time: Winston Churchill and Franklin Roosevelt

The meeting that took place between Winston Churchill and Franklin Roosevelt on board the battleship HMS *Prince of Wales* in August 1941, a few months before the Japanese attack on Pearl Harbor, was not just about a grand maritime strategy for defeating Hitler. It was about the sharing of the most sensitive intelligence about Germany and Japan based on communications intercepts, in the great tradition of Admiral Reginald "Blinker" Hall and Room 40 (see Appendix). Canada, Australia, and New Zealand would subsequently be invited into this highly secret and secure club as the war progressed and there was not just the exchange of intelligence but the crucial exchange of personnel and equipment. These aspects persist to this day and into the future. The *Prince of Wales* meeting between these two great statesmen was, in retrospect, the birth of the special relationship and the later Five Eyes.

Almost all of what happened within this community during and after World War II was kept secret by the British government, until in 1974 a limited amount of information of the ULTRA secrets of World War II and the ENIGMA code, together with the existence of Bletchley Park, were made known to the British public and the world. Within a few years the data that was released in very slow order changed completely our understanding of World War II, as embodied in Sir Harry Hinsley's masterful volumes published by the British government on the history of British intelligence in World War II. The point is self-evident. There is much that many national security and international relations professionals and those associated with the political-military process do not always know or have considered. This is no one's fault. It is the nature of the highly secure way in which the burgeoning Five Eyes community conducted business both during and after World War II as the Cold War's temperature went lower and lower. Over the eight

Winston Churchill, Franklin D. Roosevelt, Admiral Stark, and Admiral King on board HMS *Prince of Wales* in Placentia Bay off Newfoundland, August 10, 1941. (IWM A 4816)

decades since the momentous meeting at sea off Newfoundland there have been monumental technical changes, undersea cable cutting, brilliant cryptanalysis and deception. The digital revolution alone is in retrospect quite mind boggling. When Alan Turing made his revolutionary applications of basic computer technology at Bletchley Park, with the ENIGMA machine and the ULTRA data, and Captain Joseph John Rochefort, United States Navy, and his colleagues in the US Office of Naval Intelligence, made their extraordinary contributions to victory with the MAGIC data during World War II they were all in the van of technology that will see no slowing down beyond current cloud, cyber, and digital communications and signal processing technologies in the coming decades. How should we best exploit these emerging technologies for the strategic and tactical benefit of the Five Eyes nations and their closest allies, and that fit optimally to their national security needs? Will we need to repeat the monumental achievements, but in a different form, of Captain Rochefort at Station HYPO, working closely with British cryptographers from the British Far East Combined Bureau, first in Singapore, and then in Kenya and Colombo after the fall of Singapore? The victory at Midway may seem like a piece of great naval history and strategy, but is it simply this? The new technologies that still bind the Five Eyes and the strategic necessities of the current world may indeed require another Midway in different form, and for different reasons, with the singularity of the binding power of Five Eyes cooperation ever paramount.

The Atlantic Charter that Churchill and Roosevelt fathered on board HMS *Prince of Wales* laid the foundations for the monitoring of communications of the Soviet Union and the Warsaw Pact, embodied initially in a networked communications intercept system called ECHELON that has expanded with both the nature of communications and the threats that the Five Eyes collectively perceived. The data collected, analyzed and distributed has been at the Top Secret codeword level since inception. Shared intelligence expanded beyond signals intelligence (SIGINT and ELINT) to include HUMINT, satellite imagery intelligence (IMINT) and various forms of geospatial intelligence (GEOINT). Each of the Five Eyes formed separate agencies to manage and work the various types of intelligence sources and methods. The first major agreement after the August 1941 Atlantic Charter was the BRUSA Agreement signed on May 17, 1943 between the UK Code and Cipher School (pre-GCHQ) and the US War Department (pre-National Security Agency). On March 5, 1946 a secret treaty was signed between the UK and US. This treaty forms the basis for all subsequent signals intelligence cooperation between the UK (GCHQ) and the US (NSA).

In 1948 the treaty was extended to include Canada, Australia, and New Zealand. A newer amended version of the UK–US agreement created in effect the Five Eyes in 1955. The Five Eyes began the task of collecting massive amounts of government, private, and commercial communications across all frequencies and bandwidths, such as telephone calls, faxes, and later emails and other visual and data traffic, whether via satellite transmissions, telephone networks, and other more sensitive means. Later technology firms such as Google, Apple and Microsoft cooperated with the Five Eyes, together with existing historic relationships with communications companies. There have been numerous Five Eyes major programs over the decades since World War II, and these continue to this day.

The Earliest Origins of the Special Relationship

Before radio telegraphy became both a science and then a commercial technology, Western European countries had relied mainly on human intelligence (HUMINT) and mail intercepts to procure intelligence. Commander Mansfield Cumming, Royal Navy, became the first head of MI6 (the British Secret Intelligence Service or SIS) upon its founding in 1909. The same year the British Security Service, MI5, was founded, responsible for domestic counterintelligence and internal security. It was not until after World War I that the UK established what was known as the Government Code and Cipher School (GCCS). This latter organization was known under this name until 1946, when Bletchley Park became the Government Communications Headquarters (GCHQ), established near Cheltenham, England. These successive organizations were responsible for communications and signals intercept. They were driven continuously by the need to keep abreast and ideally ahead of communications technology of all descriptions. The British Naval Intelligence Division (NID) founded in 1912, before World War I quickly realized that high-frequency communications predicated transnational intercepts, together with telephonic intercepts, whether via landlines or undersea cables. The British became very much the early masters of communications intelligence. The British Naval Intelligence Department was the intelligence arm of the Admiralty from 1887 until 1912 when significant changes were made and the new name implemented.

The history of UK–US intelligence and the Five Eyes collectively has a direct lineal connection to the development of the British Government Code and Cipher School, Bletchley Park, and then GCHQ. As we will observe, the founding of the United States' capabilities—predominantly through the auspices of the United States Navy and the critical connections established between Bletchley Park and the United States Office of Naval Intelligence, and their key station HYPO in Hawaii—marked the true beginnings of both the UK–US "Special Relationship" and the Five Eyes. The exchange of HUMINT data and the operations of the British Special Operations Executive and the United States Office of Strategic Services (OSS), the precursor to the Central Intelligence Agency (CIA), were all important during World War II, marking the beginning of Five Eyes HUMINT and other related clandestine operations. However, with the benefit of hindsight—plus great research since the 1970s by distinguished wartime professionals such as Sir Harry Hinsley, who later went back to academia and were able to present accurate historical records with full British government approval and total access to the wartime Bletchley Park records—the true nature of what was accomplished by GCHQ in the UK and ONI (Office of Naval Intelligence) in the US became not only apparent, but significantly changed the interpretation of World War II history.

In the immediate post-war years, the US National Security Act of 1947 and the amendment to that Act in 1949 created the US national defense establishment as we know it. The offices of Secretary of Defense and Deputy Secretary of Defense were created, with the Secretary of the Navy becoming subordinate to the Secretary of Defense in the chain of command. The 1947 Act also created the US Air Force, separating it from the US Army. The first Secretary of Defense, James Forrestal, had been Secretary of the Navy prior to the Act and he had opposed the changes. Since 1947 the Office of the Secretary of Defense has multiplied many times with a large number of political appointees.

In 1986 the Goldwater–Nichols Defense Reorganization Act strengthened the statutory framework created by the 1947 and 1949 Acts. Joint service for aspiring general and flag officers effectively became mandatory. However, the office of the Secretary of the Navy, the offices of the Chief of Naval Operations, and the Commandant of the Marine Corps remained intact and their staffs remained unimpaired. The Secretary of Defense sits on the National Security Council, unlike the Secretary of the Navy. Until 1949 the Secretary of the Navy was a member of the President's Cabinet and after the changes became third in the Secretary of Defense succession, highlighting the historic position of the Secretary of the Navy.

The US National Security Act of 1947 also created the Central Intelligence Agency (CIA) and the National Security Council. The Director of Central Intelligence (DCI) was both head of the CIA and the US intelligence community until April 21, 2005 when the DCI lost his community head role with the creation of the Director of National Intelligence (DNI) and his staff. The new DNI also replaced the DCI as the principal intelligence advisor to the President. The DNI also became a member of the National Security Council. The CIA director continues to manage all aspects of the work of the CIA and is responsible for the clandestine operations of the CIA through the National Clandestine Service that replaced the former CIA Directorate of Operations. When the Five Eyes formed from the special UK–US relationship the other three nations (Canada, Australia, and New Zealand) melded into this new US structure in terms of intelligence cooperation.

Although the US Navy, instituted by Congress in 1798 as a key national security entity, lost the preeminent position that it enjoyed at the end of World War II, with the considerable changes made by the 1947 US National Security Act, US naval intelligence persisted virtually unchanged.

In the UK change was also on the way. The Ministry of Defence as we know it today was formed in 1964, based on a perception that there was a requirement for greater cooperation and coordination between the three British armed services – the

Royal Navy, the British Army, and the Royal Air Force. The Royal Navy has always been regarded in the UK as the senior service and is referred to as such. The Royal Marines are part of the Royal Navy and the Commandant of the Royal Marines enjoys the same status and prestige as the Commandant of the US Marine Corps. However, the Royal Marines have always been a fraction of the size of the US Marine Corps and therefore have not enjoyed the level of national recognition rightfully enjoyed by the Marine Corps in the US. A British Chiefs of Staff committee had been formed much earlier in 1923, though the idea of a unified ministry was rejected by Prime Minister David Lloyd George in 1921.

In 1936 a British Cabinet-level position of Minister for the Co-ordination of Defence was created to provide oversight for rearmament in light of growing Nazi aggression. When Winston Churchill became Prime Minster in 1940, he created the office of Minister of Defence in order to better coordinate defense matters and to have direct control over the Chiefs of Staff Committee. It is important to note that Winston Churchill had been First Lord of the Admiralty (the civilian political head of the Royal Navy equivalent to the US Secretary of the Navy) 1911–1915, and 1939–1940 (the famous "Winston is back" period after war was declared in September 1939) before he became Prime Minister. Winston Churchill assumed the joint role of Prime Minister and Minister of Defence for the duration of World War II. In 1946 the government of Clement Attlee (the Labor party won the 1945 general election) introduced into the House of Commons and passed the 1946 Ministry of Defence Act. Prior to this the First Lord of the Admiralty was a member of the Cabinet. The new Minister of Defence supplanted the First Lord, the Secretary of State for War (political head of the Army) and the Secretary of State for Air (the political head of the Royal Air Force) in the British Cabinet. Between 1946 and 1964 there was a hybrid organization in the UK with five separate departments of state running defense—the Admiralty, the War Office (Army), the Air Ministry (Royal Air Force), the Ministry of Aviation, and the nascent Ministry of Defence in an infancy stage. The change in 1964 was therefore monumental. Although the aforementioned departments were all merged in a single Ministry of Defence and the historically powerful position of First Lord of the Admiralty was abolished, the intelligence community continued to function within the (by now well-established) orbit of the Five Eyes.

One final event occurred in 1971 when the Ministry of Aviation Supply became part of the Ministry of Defence, but this had zero effect on Five Eyes intelligence. The first Secretary of State for Defence was Peter Thorneycroft who was short lived in office, from April to October 1964, in the Conservative government of Sir Alec Douglas-Home, and with the new Labor government of Harold Wilson the position was occupied by Denis Healey from October 1964 to June 1970, a very significant period, and he was followed by Lord Carrington in the Conservative government of Edward Heath from June 1970 to January 1974. The ten-year period from 1964 to 1974 witnessed the full solidification of British defense policy under a single minister and a very large bureaucracy. No changes occurred within the Five Eyes relationships. In fact, as the Cold War intensified, intelligence sharing and personnel exchanges increased.

***

Like many young boys in Britain I was brought up on the great voyages of exploration, with Captain James Cook as my personal hero, the Nelson tradition, and the great technological revolution from the age of sail to steam power and then nuclear power. I was simply fascinated by the whole process and the finer detail of why and how all these changes occurred. I was motivated by being a career naval officer but also by a much deeper abiding connection with the sea, maritime history in the wider sense, and how the Royal Navy and the United States Navy had evolved into the powerhouses they became during World War II.

Professor Bryan Ranft at the Royal Naval College, Greenwich, where he was head of Naval History and International Affairs, told me in 1968 that he wanted me to meet someone who had offered to help and guide me in my research. He knew this person well and told me that he had read my study of German public opinion in the 1930s and liked it. He was, as far as Bryan Ranft was concerned, one of the most knowledgeable persons on the purpose and practice of intelligence, and in particular naval intelligence.

This conversation changed my life.

The person he was referring to was Professor Sir Harry Hinsley at St. John's College, Cambridge University. Bryan Ranft had already set up a meeting in Cambridge, and he had cleared this with my official supervisor, Professor Laurence Martin. I worked on my research with Professor Hinsley while also performing my duties as a Royal Navy Lieutenant at a highly secure facility at Upper Lodge, in Bushy Park. The Royal Navy fully supported and funded my research. Little did I realize in the very early days that a small group of hugely experienced World War II intelligence specialists were to become my mentors and supporters of my work.

Between 1969 and 1972 I spent many hours ensconced with Professor Hinsley in his room in St. John's, cluttered with an unbelievable collection of papers, books, original documents, and students' essays. I learned so much in that room about World War II. One day he said to me that he wanted to introduce me to some very special material that very few people knew about. He said no more, except to meet him in London at a building very close by the main British Foreign Office, just off Parliament Square. He took me deep below ground level to a highly secure vault space, well guarded. Access was limited to just a very select few. I became aware that the current foreign office staff and virtually all of the current serving British intelligence community had little or no knowledge of the existence let alone content of this vault.

The ENIGMA and ULTRA Data

What I was able to study in this vault was World War II ENIGMA and ULTRA data. It was a gold mine. Over the ensuing months I would take leave from Upper Lodge and travel to London and study the material. Several aspects were made very clear to me. I could never ever reveal the existence and contents of the ENIGMA data to anyone, and the implications and impact on World War II. Furthermore, I could never mention the people involved and that there was a secret place called Bletchley Park whose work changed the nature and outcome of World War II.

So what was the value to my research, and why did Harry Hinsley open my eyes and mind to ENIGMA and ULTRA and all the reciprocal US highly classified data, the MAGIC, together with all the relationships, the organization, the US connections, the Washington Agreements, and a host of things that I had to remain sworn to secrecy about under the British Official Secrets Act? Some of the material is still classified, for reasons to do with sources, methods, trade craft and, most importantly, for political reasons that are in the best national interests of the United States and the United Kingdom. Certain things that transpired between Prime Minister Winston Churchill and President Franklin Roosevelt, because of both sources and methods issues, and political aspects, based on Bletchley data, are undoubtedly best left for much later generations for very good security reasons. What Harry Hinsley wanted me to understand was that all the research that I had done on British Naval Intelligence from 1880 to 1945 was not quite complete without me at least knowing about Bletchley, all that went on there, the material, and its impact. At one level he wanted to educate me and at another he wanted me, in due course, to be a champion of the Bletchley Park war winners, of whom he was a most distinguished alumnus.

Fast forward to 1974 and the release by the British government under Prime Minister Harold Wilson of a book published by a World War II Royal Air Force Wing Commander Frederick William Winterbotham (1897–1990), who had supervised the distribution of Bletchley product to the small group of recipients who were given access to ULTRA. In effect he managed the couriers through "Special Liaison Units" but he did not have access to any of the detailed technical code-breaking, operations analysis, and fine data. His book, *The Ultra Secret*, was the first that the British public knew of the existence of Bletchley Park and its likely product, however it had many inaccuracies and was severely criticized for its errors of both fact and interpretation. What the British government did not permit was the release of the detailed product. This product included the actual raw intelligence material, and the analysis and reports that were produced, and the actions that were taken and the impact on plans, policies and operations during World War II.

In effect Winterbotham opened Pandora's Box. The British government had now excited considerable interest in all domains of educated British public opinion, in and out of government circles and employees, in academia, and obviously inside the intelligence community. The United States intelligence community was both surprised and taken aback.

Official release and declassification of much, but by no means all of the material, happened much later when Professor Hinsley was commissioned by the government, with the direct permission of the Prime Minister, to begin writing the official history of British intelligence in World War II. The history was published in a number of volumes under the auspices of Her Majesty's Stationery Office.[1] They are remarkable for the sheer scope of the material and the conclusions drawn. These volumes changed the interpretation of what happened before, during, and after World War II. Hinsley made the bold conclusion that Bletchley Park and US intelligence had shortened the war by several years. The impact on the understanding of naval operations in particular was quite dramatic. However, what was even more dramatic were the revelations about the intense close cooperation between the US and the UK, and by association, with Canada, Australia, and New Zealand throughout the war after the various agreements made between Winston Churchill and Franklin Roosevelt. These agreements constituted the beginning of the "Special Relationship," a simple phrase that underscores one critically intrinsic fact.

The Americans and the British shared vital intelligence at all levels and from all sources, and in particular the golden product from the US MAGIC data source and the UK ENIGMA data sources. It is vital to note that at this time the most significant connection in this chain of cooperation and data exchange were the intelligence organizations of the United States Navy and the Royal Navy, and the immediate close working relationship of the latter with the Royal Canadian Navy, the Royal Australian Navy, and the Royal New Zealand Navy. The management of Bletchley Park was largely in the hands of the Royal Navy, and the US Navy was lead for the MAGIC data. Both Winston Churchill and Franklin Roosevelt had direct personal control and influence over whom, how, and when material from these special sources should or should not be used or exploited. Neither leader naturally ever wanted the special sources to be compromised. They decreed that security and other operational costs should not be a factor.

On the operational side, they decreed that material must not be exploited if the risk of revelation to the enemy was too high, even though this may involve serious losses. Short term gain could not stand in the way of long-term benefits. That culture, tradition and the security structure that underpinned their policies endured well after their passing, and still to this day persist within the Five Eyes. No British Prime Minister or US President has ever deliberately or inadvertently divulged, or given away by accidental default, substantive classified information about the nature of the still continuing special relationship of the Five Eyes. Of all the American and British intelligence organizations and departments of state none have been so closely bound and shared such sensitive data as the United States Navy and the Royal Navy, and its sister navies in Canada, Australia, and New Zealand. Since the Five Eyes' inception the Five navies have remained closely knit in all matters of intelligence. At the operational level of intelligence, the overall picture has been one of almost total harmony.

Meanwhile I was working flat out at my regular Navy career at Upper Lodge. Alongside this, in London, I was conducting research for my PhD, in the underground secret vaults, the Public Record Office, the Naval History Library, the British Museum Library, the National Maritime Museum, in numerous interviews of key players, and analyses of private collections, diaries, and memorabilia. As I delved deeply into the origins and detailed development of British intelligence since 1880 and witnessed daily some of the UK's most sensitive intelligence collection operations and analysis, I realized I was a mere "dot," just an individual in what was a huge continuum of political–military intelligence developments since the end of the 19th century. I was cognizant that I was part of this process, just one individual amongst thousands of others who make up the past, the present, and indeed the future, given that in 1969 I was merely 25 years old and ostensibly had a career ahead of me. I had acquired knowledge and information that no one before had assembled in quite the way I had, and I was humbled to be part of a community that had such a wonderful history and heritage.

I realized that my research had to be nothing but the very best. The sacrifices of which I became aware and the sheer genius of many of the people I had researched made me motivated and energized, and every day seemed like a day to do better than the day before. I was just a mere Lieutenant, Royal Navy, but I was surrounded by people, civilian and uniformed, who were not rank conscious and in any way overbearing. They were fine leaders because they nurtured, helped, and encouraged people like me, just a 25-year-old "dot" in the intelligence cosmos of the Cold War. Taking on the Soviet Union, the Warsaw Pact, and others less favorable to the United Kingdom, the Five Eyes, NATO, and our other allies was a challenge, an opportunity, a duty, and commitment to do one's very best.

The British Public and Intelligence in the 1960s

Most British citizens in the late 1960s knew very little about the key British intelligence organizations. They knew their names and that was about it. They knew that MI6 was the spy agency, the organization that supposedly produced Bond-like figures if you believed the movies, and they may have known through various arrests and trials for espionage that MI5 was the counterintelligence organization tasked to ferret out traitors while also locating and tracking foreign agents. The famous spy scandals of the 1950s and 1960s had focused the public mind, with Philby, Burgess, McLean, Blunt, and Cairncross (the "Cambridge Five") at the top of the list of betrayers, the five traitors that gave so much away to the Soviet Union, betraying their own generation, and causing the demise of many British agents.

Three of them defected before being apprehended, Burgess and McLean in May 1951, and Philby in 1963.

Others included the Admiralty spies at Portland in Dorset, where highly sensitive underwater warfare research was conducted. They were illegal residents, operating undercover without the protection of diplomatic protection by the Soviet Embassy in London. They included Harry Houghton, Ethel Gee, Gordon Lonsdale, and Morris and Lona Cohen (also known as Peter and Helen Kroger). MI5 and Scotland Yard's Special Branch tracked them down and they were all arrested. The UK had its share of "Atomic" spies, with Klaus Fuchs, the German-born theoretical physicist who worked on the Manhattan Project as part of the British delegation, and Alan Nunn May, a British citizen who had worked on the Manhattan Project and was betrayed by a Soviet defector in Canada in 1946, and perhaps the most successful of all—undetected until 1999—Melita Norwood, who had spied for the Soviet Union since at least 1938. This lady is generally regarded as the most effective female agent recruited by the Soviet Union. She was revealed by Vasili Mitrokhin, a KGB First Directorate alumnus who defected to the United Kingdom in 1992 (1922–2004). Only through the media, parliamentary questions and debates, and trials did the public become familiar with her treacherous wrongdoing, but the details of MI5 and MI6 were a total blur. For example, the very locations of these entities were classified, naturally, for very good reasons. I can now safely write that MI6 was housed at Century House in Waterloo, on the Thames south bank, before it was transferred to its much more impressive edifice, which today is public knowledge and has been in several movies, including the Bond movie *Skyfall*, further up the Thames on the south side.

Century House was a closely guarded secret. GCHQ's existence, roles and missions were highly classified and buried in secrecy. MI5 was recognized in law in 1989, and "there shall continue to be a Secret Intelligence Service" were the words that officially announced to the world that GCHQ and MI6 actually existed, embodied in the 1994 Intelligence Services Act.

What went on inside Upper Lodge was nothing to do with either MI6 or MI5, based on sound "need-to-know principles," with a clear policy not to let those in other parts of the community have knowledge of things that they did not need to know, and could possibly betray. On a daily round-the-clock basis Upper Lodge absorbed, analyzed, and produced some of the most sensitive and valuable intelligence of the Cold War. The people who helped collect these key intelligence nuggets also operated side-by-side with the analysts. The former were part of a wider operational plan that comprised sensitive assets that went places often only with the sole approval of the Prime Minister. Risks were high and only the best, the most trusted, and highly vetted were part of this discreet and secure club.

While working with Professor Hinsley I was also working in my Navy appointment with one of the most interesting groups within Upper Lodge's grounds, the Applied

Psychology Unit (APU for short). My earlier insights and research into the mindset of the Nazis, and working alongside Harry Hinsley and other World War II veterans, gave me an unusual psychological perspective on our Cold War adversaries. The unit was headed by a distinguished senior civilian, Edward Elliott, a graduate of University College, London University. Edward was my boss, and I had as a working colleague a most wonderful gentleman, Dr. Eon Williams, a Welshman, former Royal Air Force World War II pilot and, like Edward, a University College alumnus. He and I worked closely together, with me very much the junior partner in all regards. However, Eon was the perfect older and much more experienced colleague, never overbearing and always willing to share thoughts and ideas and work as a team. It was a magic time, intellectually stimulating and quite demanding in terms of performance and product. Nothing but the best was demanded, no more, no less. We needed additional outside help, and we traveled extensively both to meet others and also to collect data.

In the late 1960s and early 1970s one of the UK's or indeed the world's most distinguished psychologists was Professor Hans Eysenck (born in Berlin and naturalized British citizen, 1916–1997), who had been a doctoral graduate under the British psychologist Professor Sir Cyril Burt (1883–1971). Hans Eysenck specialized in intelligence and personality and was at my own alma mater's specialist school at King's College London, the Institute of Psychiatry, a part of King's College Hospital Medical School. Eon and I visited Hans Eysenck many times at King's. He was extraordinarily helpful and provided us with insights and stimulating leads that helped fashion our approaches and the structure of our product. We traveled all over the planet. On one visit, to Copenhagen, on a highly specialist liaison, I became aware for the first time at a very personal level of interaction with the Soviet Union's intelligence agencies, in this case a KGB operative. I was located by one of their surveillance teams and clearly one operative seemed to have the sole task of keeping tabs on me 24/7 in Copenhagen. I succeeded in losing him on most occasions or leading him down blind alleys. However, what I did realize was quite simple—I was a target. My counterintelligence training was to stand me in good stead about six months later, as I learned just how hot the Cold War was, and how persistent and insidious Soviet penetration was.

In early 1972 I left the secret enclave at Upper Lodge in Bushy Park. I had anticipated a sea appointment but was both surprised and delighted when my "appointer" (the senior officer responsible for managing my career and appointments) called me and told me my fate. I was quite astonished. I was to be appointed a Senior Lecturer and Tutor at the Royal Naval College Greenwich. In the spring of 1972, I was a senior lieutenant and it was unheard of for a mere lieutenant to be given such a position. It transpired that Professor Bryan Ranft and the Admiral President of Greenwich, Rear Admiral Edward Ellis, CBE (September 6, 1918–January 13, 2002) had specifically asked that I be appointed to replace an officer who was retiring from the service and who was legendary amongst graduates of Greenwich.

Succeeding an officer 25 years senior to me seemed overwhelmingly challenging when my appointer explained the nature of the position and the courses that I would teach. I spent a day at Greenwich meeting with Bryan Ranft. I was to teach on several courses, my most favorite being the Lieutenants Greenwich Course (the LGC), the Special Duties Officers Course, the Royal Naval Staff Officers Course, and as an occasional visiting lecturer on intelligence to the Naval War College (the most senior course at Greenwich, solely for Royal Navy captains and equivalent ranks from the other two services, the Army and the Royal Air Force).

I enjoyed the teaching, both lecturing and tutoring small groups, typically no more than six officers. I specialized in those domains where it was considered that I had expertise. The latter covered the history of intelligence and the role of intelligence in strategy, policy making, and the detailed interface with naval operations. I covered the waterfront on intelligence and I soon appreciated, how much I knew and could impart to those with zero or little knowledge. None of the Greenwich uniformed or academic staff knew what I knew, so I soon built up my self-confidence and ability to hold my own with senior commanders and captains. It was all knowledge based, plus the experience I gained by continuing to do research and provide advice to the intelligence community. I travelled regularly into central London to visit both the Ministry of Defence and the intelligence community. I wanted to extend my research, increase my knowledge base for the benefit of my students, and be completely up to date with current intelligence. Contacts that I had made during my research at King's now became quintessential.

My students were all exceptional in each and every individual way. Many went on to distinguished careers, and most would fight in the Falklands conflict and later be in senior positions during the Gulf Wars. It was an honor to sit in my study in the King Charles building[2] and have the cream of the Royal Navy sitting together sharing thoughts and ideas in ways that would shape the future.

Historical Antecedents Set the Stage for Cold War UK–US Intelligence

The historical antecedents in World War II set the stage for why and how intelligence between the five countries developed during the Cold War and since. The dialogue between hard technical and scientific intelligence and the development of foreign military capabilities is not just axiomatic—it is at the heart of why each member state developed very specific capabilities, force structures, deployment strategies, bases, and logistics to meet the emergence of various threats to the Five Eyes key national security interests. The World War II intelligence organizations of each country were lean and mean. Growth occurred in the US after the emergence of the Soviet Union and its Warsaw Pact allies. In the UK the crown jewels during the war rested with the brilliant minds at the code-breaking center at Bletchley Park. In the US the latter's opposite numbers were in the Office of Naval Intelligence. The hugely significant roles of both entities have been extensively documented. Signals intelligence and the key code breaking associated with reading the enemy's traffic was central to the Allies' victories. The Canadians, Australians, and the New Zealanders joined the club a little later, but their roles were significant. The work of the OSS (the US Office of Strategic Services) in the US and the SIS (Secret Intelligence Service or MI6) and SOE (Special Operations Executive) in the UK was geared to human intelligence (HUMINT) and to clandestine operations to thwart the enemy in multiple ways on the ground in highly sensitive covert operations, often linked to collaboration with the various European and Asian resistance organizations and groups. The leaders of these wartime organizations, such as Sir Harry Hinsley, R. V. Jones and J. C. Masterman, influenced the various reorganizations after 1945. They trained the postwar recruits in the UK and US, and influenced the other three nations' intelligence organizations in the various intelligence arts and sciences so that by the time the Cuban Missile Crisis occurred in 1962 all five countries had very capable cadres who were a mixture of those with great wartime experience and the new generation. The older generation was there to guide the new generation.

Personnel recruited in the 1960s have now largely retired with a few exceptions. I am one of the survivors from the 1960s—mentored by stalwarts like Sir Harry Hinsley and Vice Admiral Sir Norman "Ned" Denning. Harry Hinsley was at Bletchley Park working on ENIGMA for predominantly naval operations and Denning was in the Royal Navy's famous Room 39 at the heart of operational intelligence. Countless Americans, Canadians, Australians, and New Zealanders in their respective intelligence organizations who are part of my generation enjoyed the same extraordinary benefit of being trained and mentored by World War II intelligence veterans.

One change was the creation of the Defense Intelligence Agency in the US on October 1, 1961 and the Defence Intelligence Staff in the UK on April 1, 1964. The various existing UK–US departments and agencies were kept separate based on functionality—primarily SIGINT, HUMINT, counterespionage, and later space-based intelligence systems and operations. These functionalities corresponded to the National Security Agency (NSA) and the Government Communications Headquarters (GCHQ—the lineal successor to Bletchley Park), to the Central Intelligence Agency (CIA) and the Secret Intelligence Service (SIS or MI6—exactly the same entity), to the Federal Bureau of Investigation's counter-espionage department and the Security Service (or MI5). Above all, the other three Five Eyes nations were fully integrated through extensive exchange programs, embassy liaisons, and 24/7 intelligence data exchange via highly secure links. Later the unique US organization, the National Reconnaissance Office (NRO), would be established in the US as the only truly unacknowledged intelligence organization in the US until relatively recently. The existence of the NRO was classified for many years. Within the above organizational milieu lay the naval intelligence organizations of each of the five navies headed by a Director of Naval Intelligence. There were distinctive parallels in each of the five navies and the cooperation between all five never faltered. The extraordinarily strong relationship between GCHQ and NSA, and their sister organizations in Canada, Australia, and New Zealand has been simply outstanding. The working relations at the personal level, the cooperation developed, and the abiding friendships made by successive staffs ensured success. The latter speaks volumes for the bedrock created by their World War II predecessors.

On the naval side the only main organizational difference between the US and the other four naval intelligence organizations was that the non-US navies did not recruit and train specialist intelligence officers. The other four navies selected their intelligence officers from what the Royal Navy calls the General List—the equivalent of full career unrestricted line officers in the US Navy. The British and their Commonwealth naval colleagues argued that their naval intelligence officers should have a wide naval background before being recruited to intelligence and should in due course return to the regular Royal Navy. The US Navy by contrast had during and after World War II specific separate personnel structures and career paths for designated intelligence and cryptographic officers. The same applied to the four navies' ratings and US Navy enlisted personnel—the Commonwealth navies chose from the broad manpower base while the US Navy had specialists trained within designated personnel codes. The US Navy considered the value of deeply trained and experienced personnel to be greater than the British system where intelligence officers were in post for relatively short periods compared with the US Navy. By contrast the Royal Navy believed that a too institutionalized intelligence personnel structure would possibly encourage a too ingrained view of key intelligence issues and a personnel structure that was separate from the main line Navy, with the danger that what happens behind the green door is the preserve of just a few. The Royal Navy liked its intelligence officers to be grounded in experience at sea. However, the US Navy ensured sea experience by creating a wide range of sea-going intelligence billets in key locations, such as Fleet flagships and major units. However, whatever the pros and cons of the two systems, all five navies cooperated above and beyond, fortified by the special navy-related operations at NSA, GCHQ, and the equivalent facilities in Canada, Australia, and New Zealand.

Both UK and US naval intelligence organizations faced similar challenges with the creation of centralized defense intelligence agencies, the Defense Intelligence Agency (DIA) in the US and the Defence Intelligence Staff (DIS) in the UK. The Office of Naval Intelligence (ONI) and the US Navy Director of Naval Intelligence (the DNI) survived integration and remained a separate entity, reporting to the Secretary of the Navy and the Chief of Naval Operations. However, in the case of the Royal Navy the British Director of Naval Intelligence and his staff were subsumed under the DIS who had its own organizational hierarchy and chain of command to a Deputy Chief of the Defence Staff for Intelligence (DCDS (I)) under the Central Defence Staff controlled by the Chief of the Defence Staff (CDS). This was a significant change in the UK that naval intelligence in the US never experienced. Much to the chagrin of many in the UK, the position of Director of Naval Intelligence was replaced by a lower grade post of Commodore (Intelligence)—a one-star position.

During World War II Vice Admiral John Godfrey, DNI, was a three-star officer with immediate access to Winston Churchill, the Prime Minister. As a result of these centralization changes that occurred in parallel with the overall defense organization changes described earlier, the Royal Navy's intelligence arm found itself as part of a highly bureaucratized central staff with civil servants occupying many of the key posts. The one value of this was that the civilian staffs did maintain continuity while the officer corps turned over. The Canadians, Australians, and New Zealanders tended to follow the British model, with integration and jointness hallmarks.

US Overhead Intelligence and the National Reconnaissance Office (NRO)

The US National Reconnaissance Office (NRO), became responsible for space-based intelligence systems, with other US departments and agencies participating, including the US military departments and the CIA. Since September 6, 1961 and until September 18, 1992 the NRO was truly the only classified US intelligence agency whose identity, role, and location were highly secret. The NRO shares its information with the other Five Eyes on unilateral bases, with citizens of each of the other countries being deeply vetted before being given access to US satellite "overhead" data. Space based intelligence encompasses many of the "INTs," including SIGINT, ELINT, IMINT, MASINT, and other geospatial data, much of which is processed and analyzed for distribution by the US National Geospatial Agency (NGA). The quality of NRO/NGA data is prodigious. Several NRO facilities are based in Five Eyes countries, and this has been a significant factor in the overhead data sharing regime between the US and the other four nations. Personnel exchanges have been significant in the bonding process for overhead derived intelligence.

Geographic location has been an important element in the Five Eyes community, with each member state contributing unique geographic advantages in terms of collection means and opportunities. Colonial and post-colonial UK was particularly important, and still is, because of the location of various sites around the world that were suitable technically for signals collection. Overseas bases provide the means not just for collection systems, but also for basing and operating surveillance and reconnaissance aircraft, and today unmanned aerial vehicles and drones. For example, the British island of Diego Garcia in the Indian Ocean provides a location for a variety of intelligence-based operations, as well as logistics support. The legacies of British de-colonization brought geographic benefits to the Five Eyes as a whole.

The Five Eyes as a unified body recognized that they could each listen and look at threats based on their geographic locations. This involved not just direct intercept, but the more sophisticated task of listening to those listening to others, exploitation at levels not comprehended in Blinker Hall's day. If for example the Soviet Union had successfully penetrated the communications of other states, then there were multiple benefits derived from listening to just one nation's communications. Nowhere has this been more vital than the Middle East and South-West Asia.

The Five Eyes took on the Soviet Union and the Warsaw Pact and, in effect, won the intelligence battle. There were exceptions, mainly in regard to classical espionage, and more recently to issues associated with disclosures by US traitors such as Aldrich Ames and penetration of worldwide email and social media networks. Defense against cyberattacks has entered the signals intelligence lexicon, rather than just "attack." In the domain of grand strategy, and the critical domain of nuclear deterrence based on mutual assured destruction the vigilance of the Five Eyes proved unbeatable in terms of monitoring nuclear programs and deployments, their associated surveillance, communications, and launch systems. The hotline between Washington and Moscow was underpinned by first class signals intelligence, with indicators and warnings (I&W) becoming an intelligence art and science.

CHAPTER 2

Challenges from the Soviet Union, 1974–78

Johnny Frost and the Legacy of Operations *Biting* and *Market Garden*

It is always important when looking at the investment nations make in their intelligence services to ask one simple question: What is the true added value, whether to national security, to national economic or political self-interests, or to the maintenance of the international order? In the long run, does intelligence make a difference?

In 1978 I was privileged to provide a Royal Navy honor guard from the Royal Navy's Ordnance Engineering School for a special ceremony in Southampton to mark the anniversary of the commando/special forces raid of February 27–28, 1942 on the French coast at Bruneval to capture key components of a vital Nazi radar station. Operation *Biting* was stood up by the newly formed Directorate of Combined Operations, led by then Rear Admiral Louis Mountbatten. Knowledge of the Wurzburg radar's capabilities at Bruneval was regarded by the British technical intelligence community, led in this matter by the legendary R. V. Jones, Prime Minister Winston Churchill's special programs lead, as absolutely vital. This radar was thought to be used by the Nazis for detecting and tracking Royal Air Force Bomber Command's raids into Germany and also for assisting the Luftwaffe in its attacks on the UK. In 1942 the RAF was suffering heavy losses in its nighttime raids over Germany, and before the US Eighth Air Force had arrived in numbers in the UK to begin daylight raids with B17 aircraft. There was urgency in defeating German detection capabilities of RAF bombers ingressing Germany. Combined Operations determined that the optimal way to capture the key radar components and bring them to the UK was a nighttime parachute drop into the Bruneval area, followed by an attack on the radar site, and then a naval evacuation from the beach. This was a daring raid and was 100 per cent successful. In addition to bringing back the key radar components the raiding force also captured a key German radar technician. British radar specialists were then able to design countermeasures against this and similar German radars.

The raiding force was led by Major John Frost's C Company of the Second Battalion, the Parachute Regiment, and a part of the British First Airborne Division. Major Frost was to follow his exploits at Bruneval with yet more courageous acts. In the fall of 1944, now Lieutenant Colonel Johnny Frost was in command of the Second Battalion, Parachute Regiment, and led his battalion after being dropped into the Low Countries to the famous Arnhem Bridge as a key part of the ill-fated Operation *Market Garden*. This was conceived as a daring thrust to capture the key Rhine bridges. This would be a precursor to invading Germany by a northerly route that would take General Sir Bernard Montgomery's army to Berlin by the fastest possible route before the Soviet Red Army could occupy key parts of East Germany and Berlin itself. The strategic concept was bold and imaginative but was fatally flawed. Frost's battalion held the Arnhem Bridge, waiting for the arrival of 9,000 men from the British XXX Corps that never arrived. On September 17, 1944, Frost's men, 745 in total, very lightly armed with no armored support whatsoever, faced the wrath of a full German SS Panzer corps, a quite extraordinary feat of arms and heroism. Frost's men fought to the bitter end, a four-day battle that left only 100 of his men facing a complete panzer corps. In 1978 the Arnhem Bridge was named the John Frost Bridge. In the movie, *A Bridge too Far*, the British actor Anthony Hopkins plays Lieutenant Colonel Frost.

In 1978, after Lord Mountbatten and Major General Frost had inspected the guard, and warmly complimented the Officer of the Guard, Royal Navy Special Duties Lieutenant Derek Rowland, on the fine turnout and performance of his men, I had the privilege of meeting the attending distinguished dignitaries at the reception following the parade. After pleasantries and a discussion on the modern Royal Navy, General Frost and I entered into a detailed discussion on the intelligence successes of Bruneval and the total failure of intelligence in support of Operation *Market Garden*. What did General Frost think?

General Frost expounded. All source intelligence went into the planning of the Bruneval Raid—from SIGINT collection, ENIGMA data, aerial photography and work by MI6's agents in France together with reports from the French Resistance. Timing and the weather were everything, and the role of the meteorologist was paramount for the drop into the Bruneval area and for the Royal Navy's evacuation from the beach—wind, tide, wave height, moon status, and beach profile. The Royal Navy needed precise data on the whereabouts of opposing German naval forces and Frost and his men needed not just estimates but precise knowledge of the opposition that they would meet—force composition and locations down to the most detailed unit level—weapons, training status, combat experience, and likely state of readiness. Surprise and security were crucial. Intelligence never failed them, and the mission was a huge success and a great morale booster for the British public in the dark days of 1942. He stressed one critical, overwhelmingly important factor, the need for reliable, secure, and redundant communications that would hold up in any weather conditions and locations. Radio numbers counted. It was no use having insufficient numbers when one radio failed, was damaged or the operator became a casualty or was captured. Multiple systems were required to ensure survivable communications. What General Frost described to me was what today we call situational awareness—the ability to know in or near real time the overall picture regarding the enemy. In 1942 British intelligence gave Frost and his men the best situational awareness for the time and the best communications available. Simple techniques work well: just one codeword can summarize a total situation; many codewords can cover a whole range of contingencies and events so that reporting is kept to a minimum and limits interception and decryption. By contrast, Operation *Market Garden* was, to quote General Frost, an unmitigated disaster caused largely, but not wholly, by, extremely poor intelligence planning and execution, and the failure of the high command to accept the intelligence provided as ground truth. He said that underscoring this failure to appreciate the intelligence provided was a mindset that was so fixated on the strategic plan that the tactical level detail and execution were assumed to automatically follow as a matter of fact like day follows night. He was emphatic about the detail of failure. The key failure lay in the assessment of the location, movement, and strength of potentially opposing German units, and in particular German heavy armor, tanks. These tanks proved to be the nemesis of the Second Battalion, the Parachute Regiment, at the Arnhem Bridge. Key telltale signs of the location, movements, and strengths of one key German panzer division were overlooked to the point of incompetence. Frost stated that insufficient thought and planning had gone into examining and creating a Plan B should the original operational plan begin to fall apart. There was no back up and nowhere to go for Frost's brave men. There was no relief on the way because the British Corps that was supposed to drive hard and fast to the key bridges soon found itself faced with innumerable threats and sheer terrain problems that had not been properly thought through, and certainly not anticipated. Communications became non-existent because of radio failures. What he stressed was that in the two-plus years since Bruneval, the knowledge and operational templates developed by Combined Operations had not become doctrine and had certainly not reached the mindset of Operation *Market Garden* planners. Most of all, vital intelligence was ignored.

One of the important lessons learned from this conversation was simple but vital. As the years pass technology tends to produce better solutions, and operational experience can be built into the doctrine, tactics, techniques, and procedures of fighting forces. However, if there is no organizational and cultural willingness to make changes and implement lessons learned, the same mistakes can be made time and time again in new and often different operational settings. Intelligence aims to mitigate failure by providing the very best total situational awareness with the best timely information flow that communications permit. The Five Eyes have shared their collective experience, knowledge base, and technology via a wide range of formal

The John Frost Bridge at Arnhem, Holland. (Wikimedia Commons)

exchange agreements and cooperation in field operations, whether military in nature or across the spectrum of intelligence collection operations. A powerful cultural element has been ingrained within the Five Eyes community. The fundamental check lists that started in 1942 continue today, with the tragic lessons of Arnhem sad examples of what goes wrong if the check lists are not meticulously followed.

The Five Eyes check lists are all about why and what needs to be known for strategic and tactical intelligence planning and execution at all levels. Five Eyes checks address likely threats, force levels and composition, deployments, basing and logistics, together with tactical development, Research and Development (R&D), acquisition, and most of all the intelligence that frames the choices, options, and decisions associated with the foregoing domains. The amalgam of the collective body of Five Eyes distilled and carefully analyzed intelligence is simply, in one word, prodigious.

The Beginning of New "Special Relationships"

I recognized the immense significance of the Royal Navy's relationship with the US Navy and the critical value of the intelligence relationships between the two navies, and the Five Eyes as a whole. I began to assess where I might fit into this changing seascape with the career implications that may transpire. I considered that I could contribute most in due course by working between the US and the UK, because in this relationship lay not just real strength but also meaningful and productive work where my experience and skill set could be best employed. In 1974 I was unsure how the practicalities of this would work, if at all. The influence of Bryan Ranft at Greenwich and Harry Hinsley in Cambridge had given me the knowledge, insight, and encouragement to think beyond the present to a longer-term view of how I could best contribute to national security.

My time at Greenwich came to an end early in 1974 and I departed London for a series of what the Royal Navy called "Long Courses." These were major career-enhancing professional courses, at the School of Maritime Operations, HMS *Dryad*, the Communications School, HMS *Mercury*, the gunnery and parade training school, HMS *Excellent*, the Nuclear, Biological, and Damage Control School, and various management courses. I spent a good amount of time at sea in HMS *Eastbourne* doing advanced navigation qualifications in the North Sea, operating out of Rosyth, on the Firth of Forth, in Scotland. I left all things intelligence behind me, at least in a formal sense, since I was not being appointed after these "Long Courses" to any intelligence-related jobs. I would spend the next few years at sea, based initially out of Plymouth in Devon in south-west England and then later out of Portsmouth in Hampshire. In HMS *Fearless* and HMS *Intrepid* I would sail tens of thousands of miles, in the Mediterranean, the North Sea, the Norwegian Sea and Arctic, the Baltic, and several Atlantic crossings to the West Indies, South America, and the United States, multiple times to all these locations, with short duration deployments to places such as Morocco, Madeira, the Azores, and the Scottish islands.

My ships were involved in all the major Cold War NATO exercises in the eastern Atlantic, the North and Norwegian Seas, the Baltic, and the Mediterranean, and joint training operations with just the US Navy off the eastern US coast and places such as Roosevelt Roads in Puerto Rico. Our operations were virtually all related to deterrence by exercises, forward-persistent presence, and a consistent show of Allied naval power to signal the Soviet Union and its Warsaw Pact allies that a war at sea would be counterproductive. We were often trailed by various Soviet warships and their AGIs, or "Auxiliaries General Intelligence," the NATO acronym for their intelligence gatherers, ostensibly noncombatant vessels but sprouting with eaves dropping antennas. We received regular and highly valuable intelligence updates and we continuously were aware of our own transmission modes and possible intercept. Our communications specialists used their skills to minimize intercept even of administrative traffic, with high-grade traffic fully encrypted. We participated in multiple NATO exercises such as "Northern Wedding" in the Norwegian Sea, deterring the Soviet Northern Fleet, called the Red Banner Northern Fleet until 1991. We were constantly watching and receiving intelligence on movements from their main bases in Severomorsk, Murmansk Oblast, Arkhangelsk Oblast, and the Kola Inlet.

We conducted major carrier-based air operations and major assaults, together with anti-surface and anti-submarine operations. Similarly we conducted air and amphibious operations against simulated Soviet targets in the eastern Mediterranean in places such as Saros Bay in Turkish Thrace, an inlet in the northern Aegean Sea located north of the Gallipoli Peninsula in north Western Turkey, the strategic objective being to deter Soviet incursion into the region in the event of a crisis. These exercises included major amphibious units of the Royal Marines and the United States Marine Corps. The types of amphibious landings that we supported turned out, in retrospect, to be extraordinarily good training for the retaking of the Falkland Islands in 1982. We were continuously updated and briefed by our senior flag leadership on strategy, tactics, and the current operational intelligence that underpinned our operations. For several weeks at a time we would be on a simulated war footing, enduring the same routines and hardships while at battle stations that our forebears endured for years during World War II. We were very much "All of One Company" and the close proximity and camaraderie with our NATO allies made life at sea during these lengthy exercises all very bearable. I witnessed 24/7 the incredible value of current intelligence and my previous two appointments had given me experience and knowledge of how this was derived, analyzed, and transmitted to the front-line user.

While I was at sea, I was notified that I was being "positively vetted" by the British Security Service and the Naval Security organization. This was known colloquially as being P-V-ed. I was naturally keen to know what this was about, particularly as multiple friends, neighbors and professional contacts had let me know that they had been interviewed. The reason became apparent when I was next back in port in Portsmouth, Hampshire. I visited my appointer in London and he informed me that my next appointment would be in Washington DC, based for administrative purposes in the British Embassy, but working with and for the US intelligence community and the United States Navy.

In 1976 the Cold War was at its height. The Central Front in Europe was relatively stable in terms of both the deterrent effects posed by the large US presence and of course the MAD (Mutual Assured Destruction) doctrine that influenced any major aggressive acts against Western Europe by the Soviet Union and its Warsaw Pact allies. The relative stability in central Europe was very simply not true in the maritime sphere. The Soviet Union had figured out that the sea was a means to an end, the latter being the expansion of Soviet presence and influence in those areas where it considered political-military-commercial exploitation achievable. The oceans of the world were the means by which Soviet influence could spread, uninhibited by territorial boundaries, a factor that the Chinese have also learned and are exploiting currently through their "Belt and Road" strategy discussed later. At the same time the Soviets also calculated that the use of localized countervailing sea-based power could both challenge and neutralize US and NATO influence around the globe. Admiral of the Fleet Sergey Gorshkov's (1910–1988) Soviet Navy was therefore being used as an instrument of strategic influence and diplomacy that was impossible for the Red Army and Air Force. Navies require access, port visits, and logistics support while conducting forward based naval operations and diplomacy. By 1976 the Soviet Navy was challenging the West.

I joined a specialist group of Soviet and Warsaw Pact experts who were tasked to examine in fine detail where the Soviets had come from and where they were headed in the future and by implication, what were the projected needs of the United States to counter growing Soviet naval power and influence. This task was non-trivial and it required analyzing a vast amount of intelligence source material and operational data not usually found in intelligence sources and methods. The skill sets, knowledge, and experience of this team were prodigious. One of these was none other than James McConnell who I had worked with at Greenwich. He was typical of the high quality of this fine American team. I was the only non-American and had access to the most sensitive material through a US SCIF (Sensitive Compartmented Information Facility).

My specific tasking was to examine all aspects of Soviet operations in the Mediterranean and to pay specific attention to and fully report on the June War of 1967. My part was just one of many looking at the global activities of the Soviet Navy and its surrogates.[1] What this total work provided the US Naval leadership, the Department of Defense, the Congress, and the intelligence community with, was a detailed overview of how the Soviet Union was using sea power in the widest sense (not just the Soviet Navy but its merchant fleet, those of its Warsaw Pact allies, and third parties) to pursue both its vital national interests and expand Soviet influence around the globe. My work involved intensive and all source research and analysis into every aspect of the 1967 June War, and also the highly controversial attack by Israel on the US intelligence ship USS *Liberty* on June 8, 1967.[2] After my return to the United States in 1983 I was invited to join the board of the USS Liberty Alliance by its chairman, Admiral Thomas Moorer, retired Chairman of the US Joint Chiefs of Staff and Chief of Naval Operations. There were many distinguished members on this board, including US Marine Corps General and Medal of Honor winner, Ray Davis, and a former Chief Judge Advocate of the US Navy, Rear Admiral Merlin Staring, who as a captain on the staff of Commander-in-Chief US Naval Forces, Europe (CINCUSNAVEUR) in London had been dispatched by Admiral John McCain (father of the late Senator John McCain) to begin the preliminary investigation into the attack after USS *Liberty* had been towed into Malta. In due course I became the third chairman of the board of the USS Liberty Alliance, almost by default, with the sad passing of Admiral Moorer and the second chairman, Rear Admiral Clarence "Mark" Hill, a distinguished US naval aviator and battlegroup commander. I spent much time several years later working closely with Admiral Staring, now retired, on the board of the USS Liberty Alliance.

My intelligence collection work took me regularly to several key agencies. The facility from which we operated was conveniently located about halfway between the Pentagon and the CIA Headquarters. The Soviet involvement in the June War was to some extent the less difficult aspect of my June War task. It was not easy but less demanding that all the circumstances leading up to Israel's attack on Syria, the taking of the Golan Heights, and the attack on *Liberty*, all within a very short time frame of just days in June 1967. The highlight for me of this work was meeting with and interviewing several key players on the US side in the June War. The most significant of these was the Secretary of State at the time, Dean Rusk. He was open and frank in our several discussions. He was aware that we both had full knowledge of all the most sensitive intelligence. He is on the record as stating that the Israeli attack on the USS *Liberty* was deliberate. He shared with me what he saw as the worst crisis since the Cuban Missile Crisis of 1962 when Moshe Dayan's Israeli force looked as if it would go beyond the Golan Heights and march on Damascus, the capital of Syria, a massive political disaster that could bring Syria's patron, the Soviet Union, into the war against Israel. We knew from excellent intelligence what the Soviet retaliatory plans entailed. Rapid hair-raising communications took place between Washington and Moscow and the hotline was used.[3] Much of this highly sensitive SIGINT may not be released for many years, even though the June War is now 53 years old at the time of writing.

The Foundational Institution of the Five Eyes Navies

The intelligence relationship of the Five Eyes navies is probably the single most outstanding aspect of the history of intelligence evolution and the special UK–US relationship. The great British naval historian of the Royal Navy in World War II, Captain Stephen Roskill, once told me that without the intelligence that the United States, the UK and its Commonwealth allies Canada, Australia, and New Zealand possessed throughout World War II, the outcome of that war may have been entirely different. Plans, policies, and operations were critical, he said, but intelligence was simply golden.

This assessment was reinforced by my personal mentor, Professor Sir Harry Hinsley, the official historian of British intelligence in World War II, written in five quite outstanding volumes and published by the British government by Her Majesty's Stationery Office. Hinsley had worked at Bletchley Park during World War II. At the time of his passing in 1998 he was regarded as one of the fathers of British intelligence. Readers will recall that I had worked with him in the late 1960s in the basement of a British government facility adjacent to the Foreign Office near Parliament Square in London. My eyes were opened to the wealth of all source highly classified intelligence material from the 1930s through World War II and its aftermath.

The pressures of the Cold War demanded a constant evaluation not just of Soviet force levels, dispositions, capabilities, and operational patterns that showed their tactics, techniques and procedures, versus the NATO and other allies, but an ever

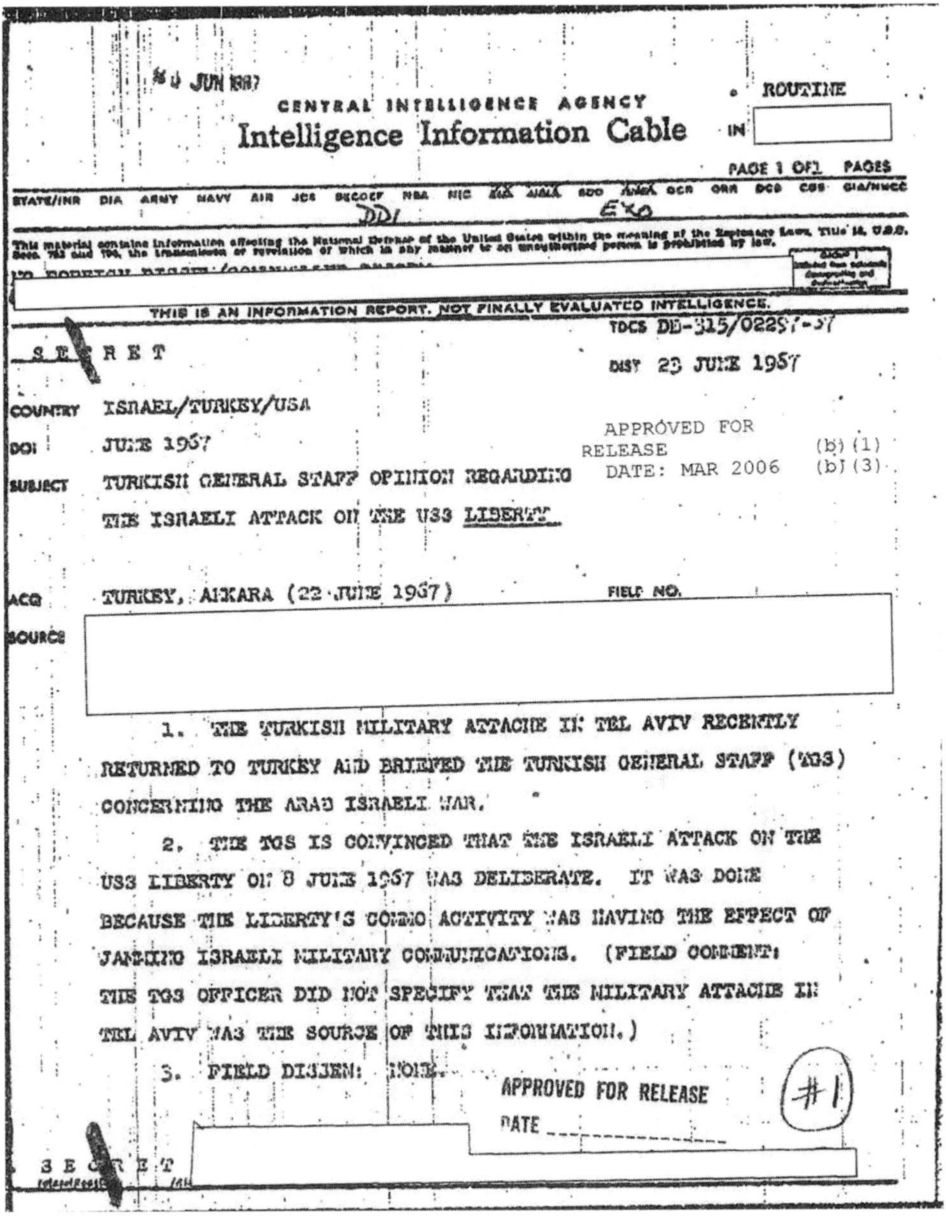

8 JUN 1967

CENTRAL INTELLIGENCE AGENCY

ROUTINE

Intelligence Information Cable

IN

PAGE 1 OF 1 PAGES

STATE/INR DIA ARMY NAVY AIR JCS SECDEF NSA NIC XXX XXXX ODO XXXX OCR ORR DCS CGS CIA/NMCC

DDI EXO

This material contains information affecting the National Defense of the United States within the meaning of the Espionage Laws, Title 18, U.S.C. Secs. 793 and 794, the transmission or revelation of which in any manner to an unauthorized person is prohibited by law.

THIS IS AN INFORMATION REPORT, NOT FINALLY EVALUATED INTELLIGENCE.

SECRET

TDCS DB-315/02297-67

DIST 23 JUNE 1967

COUNTRY ISRAEL/TURKEY/USA

DOI JUNE 1967

SUBJECT TURKISH GENERAL STAFF OPINION REGARDING THE ISRAELI ATTACK ON THE USS LIBERTY

APPROVED FOR RELEASE DATE: MAR 2006 (b)(1) (b)(3)

ACQ TURKEY, ANKARA (22 JUNE 1967)

FIELD NO.

SOURCE

1. THE TURKISH MILITARY ATTACHE IN TEL AVIV RECENTLY RETURNED TO TURKEY AND BRIEFED THE TURKISH GENERAL STAFF (TGS) CONCERNING THE ARAB ISRAELI WAR.

2. THE TGS IS CONVINCED THAT THE ISRAELI ATTACK ON THE USS LIBERTY ON 8 JUNE 1967 WAS DELIBERATE. IT WAS DONE BECAUSE THE LIBERTY'S COMMO ACTIVITY WAS HAVING THE EFFECT OF JAMMING ISRAELI MILITARY COMMUNICATIONS. (FIELD COMMENT: THE TGS OFFICER DID NOT SPECIFY THAT THE MILITARY ATTACHE IN TEL AVIV WAS THE SOURCE OF THIS INFORMATION.)

3. FIELD DISSEM: NONE.

APPROVED FOR RELEASE

DATE

#1

SECRET

Three redacted classified CIA HUMINT reports regarding the attack on USS *Liberty*, June 8, 1967. (USS Liberty Document Center, Library of Congress, Washington DC, 2017, usslibertydocumentcenter.org) *(Continued on the next two pages)*

CONTROLLED DISSEM | C-O-N-F-I-D-E-N-T-I-A-L

COUNTRY Israel

REPORT NO. [redacted] 3403-67

SUBJECT Prospects for Political Ambitions of Moshe Dayan/Attack on USS Libary Ordered by Dayan

DATE DISTR. 9 Nov 67

NO. PAGES 1

REFERENCES. [redacted] 16835-46

DATE OF INFO. Oct 67

PLACE & DATE ACQ. Tel Aviv -- 1967

THIS IS UNEVALUATED INFORMATION

SOURCE [redacted] /Source is normally available should this report generate requirements./

1. [redacted] discussions included the future political role of Moshe Dayan. [redacted] said that the longer Israel waits for elections, the less chance Dayan has of becoming Prime Minister. They recognize that Dayan's appointment as Minister of Defense provided impetus to the Israel war effort. Since the war, responsible Israelis have given and continue to give less credit to Dayan and more credit to General Rabin. [redacted] also are emphatic in saying that there will never be a negotiated peace with the Arabs so long as Dayan is Defense Minister.

2. [redacted] commented on the sinking of the US communications ship, Liberty. They said that Dayan personally ordered the attack on the ship and that one of his generals adamantly opposed the action and said, "This is pure murder." One of the admirals who was present also disapproved the action, and it was he who ordered it stopped and not Dayan. [redacted] believe that the attack against the US vessel is also detrimental to any political ambition Dayan may have.

-end-

INFORMATION REPORT INFORMATION REPORT

1 AUG 1967 CENTRAL INTELLIGENCE AGENCY

This material contains information affecting the National Defense of the United States within the meaning of the Espionage Laws, Title 18, U.S.C. Secs. 793 and 794, the transmission or revelation of which in any manner to an unauthorized person is prohibited by law.

CONTROLLED DISSEM C-O-N-F-I-D-E-N-T-I-A-L

COUNTRY Israel

REPORT NO 20396-67

SUBJECT Comment on Known Identity of USS LIBERTY/ Resumption of Oil Production of Red Sea Wells by Israel

DATE DISTR 27 Jul 67

NO PAGES 1

REFERENCES

DATE OF INFO. Early Jun 67

PLACE & DATE ACQ. Tel Aviv -- Early Jun 67

THIS IS UNEVALUATED INFORMATION

SOURCE

1.

2. brought up the attack on the USS LIBERTY by Israeli airplanes and torpedo boats. He said that "you've got to remember that in this campaign there is neither time nor room for mistakes," which was intended as an obtuse reference that Israel's forces knew what flag the LIBERTY was flying and exactly what the vessel was doing off the coast. implied that the ship's identity was known at least six hours before the attack but that Israeli headquarters was not sure as to how many people might have access to the information the LIBERTY was intercepting. He also implied that there was no certainty of control as to where the intercepted information was going and again reiterated that Israeli forces did not make mistakes in their campaign. He was emphatic in stating to me that they knew what kind of a ship the USS LIBERTY was and what it was doing offshore.

3. inquired as to resumption of production facilities. He talked about two fields near the Gulf of Suez on the Sinai Peninsula which had been set afire by the Arabs. Israeli forces extinguished the fires the same day that the fields were captured and were then (10-11 Jun 67) starting to pump oil. Both Egyptian fields were said to have been developed by foreign companies and Israel intends to continue pro-rata payments.

- end -

APPROVED FOR RELEASE DATE: 02-24-2009

FULL TEXT COPY DO NOT RELEASE

INFORMATION REPORT INFORMATION REPORT

U YES C-O-N-F-I-D-E-N-T-I-A-L S YES

The dissemination of this document is limited to civilian employees and active duty military personnel within the intelligence components of the USIB member agencies, and to those senior officials of the member agencies who must act upon the information. However, unless specifically controlled in accordance with paragraph 8 of DCID 1/7, it may be released to those components of the departments and agencies of the U. S. Government directly participating in the production of National Intelligence. IT SHALL NOT BE DISSEMINATED TO CONTRACTORS. It shall not be disseminated to organizations or personnel, including consultants, under a contractual relationship to the U. S. Government without the written permission of the originator.

increasing need to stay ahead of the Soviet Union technologically. The latter required not just better knowledge of the Soviet industrial base, and the R&D that was a precursor to innovation and keeping an edge, but also preventing the opposition from stealing Five Eyes secrets by espionage and other means. It was a constant never-ending process of measure, countermeasure, and counter-countermeasure, an incessant demand on both governments to commit the right resources to sustain the lead that would ensure naval superiority in the very worst scenarios. At another level this arms race was also a symptom of each of the Five Eyes nations to uphold the values of the Western democratic and capitalist system and way of life. As a result, each nation shared its best technologies and intelligence products with the others.

The Five Eyes navies created a series of well-established and developing programs that meant that whatever organizational changes occurred, the highly secret world of these navy-to-navy programs endured in their own right, and under their own impetus with special security and safeguards that prevented access by the new bureaucratic machinery that may have inhibited other parts of both defense intelligence and the other Five Eyes national intelligence agencies. Access was severely limited and need-to-know criteria rigorously applied. The programs had a deeply buried life of their own. The need to stay well ahead of the Soviet Union in the special Five Eyes relationship reached its climax in the 1980s, before the beginning of the end of the Soviet Union and the Warsaw Pact. This was the era in the US of the 600-ship navy, challenging the Soviet Navy and its allies head on in forward-deployed[4] operations that took, for example, the US Second Fleet within the Atlantic Fleet, to the doorstep of the Soviet Northern Fleet in northern waters, ably assisted by the Royal Navy and the Royal Canadian Navy in major NATO exercises such as Northern Wedding. In Pacific waters the Royal Australian Navy and the Royal New Zealand Navy operated similarly with the United States Pacific Fleet. Sound, joint, shared intelligence drove these operations.

British, Canadian, Australian, and New Zealand intelligence benefited enormously from their interwoven imperial past, predicated on geography. The residual relationships and facilities that endured after decolonization meant that there still existed locations from which each of the four nations, plus the United States as a partner Five Eyes beneficiary, could continue to both operate and, in many cases, retain special clandestine and covert facilities. This applied to not just the SIGINT and ELINT domains, but also to the HUMINT world. While the US developed and expanded its space intelligence systems and capabilities, the other four nations quietly and unobtrusively expanded in areas in which they were uniquely suited. There was mutual benefit all round, for US space-based derived intelligence for the other four nations and, in return, quite extensive benefits from the UK–Canada–Australia–New Zealand worldwide special communications networks and HUMINT products from myriad clandestine sources and methods, many of which were and still are uniquely CANUKAUSNZ, and which the US, and particularly the CIA, have never been quite able to replicate. The UK, for example, was able to place at the disposal of the US various key sites around the globe and also at home inside the UK. There are generations of Americans that look back to the Cold War and remember being posted to very sensitive facilities inside the UK that were highly secret in terms of missions, and often where the local communities were not privy to the sensitive activities that were ongoing behind secure fences. The same was true of Australia, with generations of Americans becoming part of communities down under.

The Five Eyes navies always aimed to be technically and operationally superior to the Soviet Navy and its Warsaw Pact allies in those scenarios that war planners envisaged, never to be outclassed in any crucial domain and always to have the numerical strength so that numbers alone could not drive superiority.

The Threat of the Soviet Submarine Navy

The Soviet Union rapidly realized in the 1960s that a maritime war, and certainly one on a global scale, could be won or lost as a result of submarine warfare. The nuclear-powered attack submarine, armed with highly capable torpedoes and anti-ship (and much later land attack variants such as those fired by the US Navy in the First Gulf War in 1991) cruise missiles with its endurance, range, speed, stealth, covertness, and persistent presence, had the capability to destroy not just vital commercial fleets, the merchant traffic of the world, but also high-value surface targets. These included aircraft carriers, cruisers, destroyers, frigates, and a wide range of amphibious and supply ships. In other words, the ability to destroy fleets when disposed in sufficiently large numbers. Once the Soviet Union embarked on the course to build a large, capable submarine, Five Eyes intelligence knew that the balance of effort and resources had to shift dramatically in that direction. What were the key requirements and the driving parameters?

It was not just about knowing where the threat was most of the time, being able to locate, track and observe the Soviet Navy close up and collect operational and technical intelligence. There was a constant and urgent need to know exactly what the base line design and technical capabilities were of the Soviets' new classes of submarines. Their surface navy was much easier to observe, collect against and then analyze key technical parameters and capabilities. The Soviet submarine navy was a far more difficult problem. The Five Eyes needed to know on a 24/7 basis where Soviet submarine forces were located, but they also had to know well in advance, in fact several years in advance, what the Soviet design bureaus were planning and what their shipyards would produce and when, and in what numbers, and for what fleet dispositions. Breaking into this hugely complex Soviet R&D, design, build, and production organization was a daunting proposition. At the heart of the initial challenge was one critical aspect, acoustic intelligence, or ACINT. Four of the five countries within the Five Eyes had the submarine capabilities to do this, with New Zealand being the exception as a non-submarine operating nation.

Submarine quieting technologies predicate the noise levels of a submarine class and individual submarines. Noise reduction or quieting is a quintessential design and production requirement. A noisy submarine will be detected, and then tracked and, in the worst scenario, destroyed by a very quiet well-handled opposing submarine. Noise is produced by machinery, the propulsor or propeller(s), and by various types of flow noise associated with the submarine's movement through the water as a direct result of the submarine's hull design and shaping, including the very nature of the hull surface. Even the most minor piece of badly designed and housed equipment may be a fatal give-away. A small pump or generator that is not housed on the right type of sound suppressing mounting, or with internal design features that generate acoustic tonals at certain key frequencies, may in due course at sea be the nemesis of a submarine that has good weapons and a well-trained crew, but has fatal acoustic flaws. In short, knowing the noise profile of a Soviet submarine class, and each individual submarine within that class, was like knowing the submarine's DNA and most of all, its critical vulnerabilities, those acoustic emissions from multifarious sources that would give away its presence and location. The need to baseline each Soviet submarine class and to predict the next generation Soviet submarine class design and noise levels was not only essential, it was indeed critical in the worst-case scenario, for success or failure at sea for the Western alliance. This challenge was compounded by the fact that the Soviets began to design and build multiple submarine classes in parallel, including nuclear and non-nuclear-powered boats. This daunting proposition was further exacerbated by the large numbers of Soviet research institutes where key R&D was performed, the many design bureaus associated with different types and classes of submarines and the complexity of what in the West is termed the acquisition process. Furthermore, the submarine building yards were diverse and in several locations, and the Soviets quickly reacted to US overhead capabilities by building large fully covered submarine construction halls that hid their new construction. The ability to image a new Soviet first of class submarine when it emerged initially from say the Admiralty Yard in Leningrad (St. Petersburg) was far too late. Such a first of class could exhibit major technical changes that could potentially present serious operational challenges. The US Navy and the Royal Navy needed to know years in advance what the Soviets were designing and the likely capabilities. At the heart of this complex intelligence requirement was matching base line data with continuing Soviet research, design efforts, capabilities, and production schedules. To access the latter would need every capability in combined Five Eyes intelligence inventories—IMINT, SIGINT, ELINT, HUMINT, MASINT, ACINT, and a range of highly specialized technical intelligence collection and analysis tools. Just having the very best US satellites over facilities that were generally inaccessible to Western eyes was indeed critical, but it would take a lot more to stay ahead. Satellite data was good, but never completely good enough.

The Five Eyes navies had a head start over the Soviet navy submarine force. They were able to baseline their acoustic signatures by extremely capable ACINT collection. In the early years that collection was executed almost solely by US and British submarines on special missions. They were later augmented by the Canadian and Australian *Oberon*-class diesel electric submarines, followed post-Cold War by the six *Collins*-class in Australia and the four *Upholder/ Victoria*-class (type 2400) class in Canada. Those missions were critical, whether in the North Atlantic, in the far north of the Norwegian Sea, or in the enclosed waters of the Baltic and Mediterranean Seas, and in the Pacific Ocean. Locating, tracking, and collecting ACINT against Soviet submarines is one of the great achievements of the Cold War. It kept the West ahead. Planning such operations required detailed a priori knowledge from all source intelligence, with special technical fit that would enhance intelligence collection and special "sea riders" for such missions. Five Eyes submarines had to be handled with the utmost care to maintain their own stealth and acoustic advantage in close-quarters collection operations. The data from these operations provided the bedrock on which everything else was built. The logic is as follows. When the signature of a Soviet submarine was collected and stored it meant that the West knew how to characterize their opponent, to hear him, locate him, and track him in either deep recesses of the ocean, in the littorals or indeed in close proximity to his bases when egressing on deployment. When that location capability was acquired the Soviets were naked underwater. When that ACINT was obtained all other collection operations could be conducted in a confident manner with extremely well-planned foreknowledge. For example, if other intelligence indicated that the Soviets would deploy for instance from Severomorsk, the main Soviet Northern Fleet base, area for a new underwater missile test sequence (particularly if this involved a submarine-launched ballistic missile test to, say, the Kamchatka Peninsula in Asiatic Russia) than having the ability to not just locate an egressing Soviet submarine but to individually characterize it was incredibly powerful. The platform could be located and tracked to the test area, and the whole test sequence observed, and critical SIGINT, ELINT and vital missile telemetry obtained. None of this would have been possible without superior ACINT.

"Sea War 1985": Planning to Wage and Win a War against the Soviet Union

My next major assignment was to work side-by-side with a fine US Navy captain and naval aviator, John Underwood, in what would become known as "Sea War 1985." As the title implies, this project involved an extensive group of wide-ranging and multi-talented specialists from several parts of the defense and intelligence community, examining and then defining how best the United States and its allies could fight a war at sea against the Soviet Union in the 1985 time frame and win, without escalation to nuclear warfare, a demanding and important assignment. The output from this would have impacts on future systems and acquisitions, as well as Fleet dispositions and operations, and the overarching strategy driving these. The detailed devolution from grand strategy down to the detail of tactics, techniques, and procedures was a key part of the output. It was a task that must have the very best intelligence as a starting point to ensure that the premises were reliable and the operations analysts who war gamed the multifarious scenarios and dissected the fine detail of Soviet capabilities and operations were well served. John Underwood and I set about this task with dedication and energy, supported by an incredibly able staff and access to all source intelligence.

Critical to Sea War 1985 was excellent all-source Five Eyes intelligence that would frame our thinking and permit the large number of operational analysts and war gamers involved to play out this projected war at sea. In 1977 the 600-ship navy was not even a twinkle in the eye of anyone in the US Navy, let alone a smile on the face of anyone in the White House. However, what Sea War 1985 and other work within the Five Eyes intelligence contributed was to set the stage for political change, the recognition of the critical need for maritime superiority and how it would contribute vitally to keeping the Soviet Union in check. When Captain Underwood and I and the very large team that constituted Sea War 1985 went to work in 1977, none of us could ever have foreseen the demise of the Soviet Union, but one thing was certain: that those powerful and well-led Five Eyes navies could and would counteract any aggressive moves from the Soviet Union. In order to stay ahead various key elements had to be known, understood, and acted upon.

What becomes clear with the benefit of hindsight decades later is that a major project such as this would have been working in the dark, almost a guessing game, blind without the light shed on the extraordinary amount of detailed information on every aspect of Soviet grand strategy down to the minute detail of their capabilities, operations, training, personnel, and the complexities of the Soviet political-military infrastructure and the communications systems that connected all the various moving parts. Within the latter lay intrinsic weaknesses.

The very centralization of the Soviet Communist Party and the political-military infrastructure that underscored all their military and intelligence organizations and operations was their weakest link. This was very exploitable, and from a planning and operational viewpoint permitted a measure of reassurance that the Soviets would behave in predictable ways, with limited initiative shown outside the strict hierarchical structure of their command, control, and communications protocols. From a psychological perspective the leadership of the Soviet Union, devolving down through the command structure of the Soviet Navy, Air Force, and Red Army, was definable and like their military plans and operations, very structured and falling within understandable parameters for Western intelligence analysts. We could make reliable assumptions how the Soviets would behave in various scenarios, from the highest levels of the Politburo of the Communist Party of the Soviet Union down to, at the detailed operational level, how a Soviet submarine commander was likely to conduct tactical operations. Within that structure lay, in my opinion, the intrinsic weakness not just of the Soviet Union per se, but the whole communist edifice during the Cold War. The demise of the Soviet Union I firmly believe, lay within its own institutional weaknesses and the personality cult of its leadership, unable to escape the straitjacket of its intrinsic sterility. Sea War 1985 concluded after I left Washington, but its effects were resounding, culminating in the 1980s with the era of the 600-ship navy under President Reagan and his hard-charging Secretary of the Navy, John Lehman. The 1980s became, in retrospect, a golden age of maritime strategy that helped drive the Soviet Union into decline and disintegration.

The Five Eyes Impose their Superiority

The Five Eyes had superior signal processing capabilities over the Soviet Union for the duration of the Cold War. These resided in passive sonars of many types, fixed domed arrays, lateral flank arrays along the hull, and towed arrays reeled in and out astern of the submarine. The hydrophone technology and processing became more and more capable, and with the advent of powerful onboard computers and advanced mathematical algorithms, together with the development of generations of sonar experts onboard, the Soviets were up against an implacable foe in the shape of US and British nuclear-powered attack submarines, and quiet, extremely well-handled Canadian and Australian diesel boats. In the airborne domain the US Navy and the Royal Navy (with the support of the Royal Air Force) acquired very capable passive sonar buoys that would detect Soviet submarines and permit attacks by very capable air-dropped anti-submarine torpedoes.

This was the crucial base line. The other parts of the intelligence process were equally complex. How do you ascertain what is going on inside, for example, the Soviet Institute of Hydromechanics, one of their key design bureaus, their acquisition organization in Moscow, and the production scheduling in their yards, let alone the very detail of their next design and likely capability improvements?

Espionage is not easy under any circumstances. At the heart of any compromise of a foreign citizen to betray his or her country's national secrets is the handler or trained agent, British or American, or their non-national surrogates. During the Cold War the counterintelligence of the Soviet Union and the countries of its Warsaw Pact, worked at a premium. Internal watchdog security agencies in all the Warsaw Pact countries created controls and pressures that made it very difficult for even the most diehard would-be spy for the West, who hated the Soviet regime, to make sustained successful and regular contact with Five Eyes handlers or their surrogates. The Soviets could establish without too much difficulty who of the various Five Eyes Embassy staffs was likely to be holding diplomatic cover for espionage operations. The ability of the Soviets to monitor and track Five Eyes diplomats and their associated staffs was prodigious. Even the most inept counterintelligence service could quickly figure out who, for example, was the US CIA Chief of Station and who composed his or her staffs, whatever the official diplomatic list may state. The nature of people's movements, their contacts, their travel requests, and their round-the-clock surveillance made life very tough during the Cold War for regular full-time members of the clandestine services who operated under official diplomatic cover. The one significant benefit of course for the latter was that if compromised and, worst case, arrested they could use diplomatic privilege to counter the possibility of trial, imprisonment or execution. However, once cover was blown, that person would be expelled and in essence could never operate globally again because the KGB would simply be looking out for that person's next overseas assignment.

Five Eyes naval attachés had a higher probability of seeing and hearing about Soviet naval developments and activities than the so-called conventional Five Eyes agents. They could travel normally where requested, albeit often under intense surveillance, but at least they could openly travel to Leningrad and do their best to see what was developing inside, for example, the Admiralty yard. They could openly meet Soviet naval officials, collect open data, and where possible take photographs unless officially restricted in advance of a visit. Of course, the latter did not prevent clandestine photographic collection by attachés or collecting randomly whatever came their way. A classic example of this was the priceless piece of titanium weld that one attaché literally gathered up from the floor after it fell from a truck near a crucial Soviet yard. That one piece of metal told US and British technical intelligence how the Soviets were managing to perform extraordinarily capable titanium welds on the new titanium-hulled nuclear-attack submarines, the *Acula*-class, very lightweight, extremely strong that, together with a new advanced liquid metal reactor, enabled the *Acula*-class to achieve high underwater speeds. The likelihood of successful attraction, conversion or corruption of a Soviet citizen for espionage was very low if conventional embassy or consular-based clandestine operations were used. In fact, the highest likelihood came from walk-ins or via diplomatic encounters at embassy cocktail parties or other professional diplomatic gatherings where a Soviet citizen could make an advance, the first indication of a willingness to commit espionage for one of the Five Eyes nations. These were very few and far between.

The higher probability of successful classical espionage came via other means, surrogates, commercial and industrial connections, academic contacts, travelers and tourists, and well-trained long-term plants that were either inserted or maintained via contacts in other countries of the Warsaw Pact. Surrogates included citizens of other countries, often with neutral or benign relations with the Soviet Union who had greater access, could travel more freely and had good cover, professional, commercial, and sometimes diplomatic status such as with one of the United Nation's agencies. Non-Five Eyes business and commercial travelers and particularly those doing serious business with the Soviet defense sector made ideal agents, together with neutral scientists, academics and visitors attending conferences and trade gatherings. Tradecraft and discreet technology play great roles in these operations to collect against a Soviet target. The risks were high. If compromised there was likely to be serious consequences, from long term imprisonment to execution after a secret trial. The reward was significant financial benefits for high-end risk taking. The British have tended to be very capable in this and the secret for success is self-evident: to ensure that there is zero information available to counterintelligence agencies that could connect with a British intelligence operation. A well-trained surrogate agent must not, under any circumstances, do anything that compromises his or her status. This is not the stuff of novels or the few well-known classical Five Eyes espionage cases where either money, sex, or ideology (or some combination of all three) were one or more of the reasons for the compromise of UK citizens spying for the Soviet Union during the high points of the early Cold War, such as Philby, Burgess, and McLean. The real work and value added came from surrogates.

However, what were the real benefits? What were the intelligence products and how good were they? Very good material was produced when integrated with other sources and methods to both illuminate the overall Soviet naval capability picture and also direct other sources and methods to high-value targets and locations that may not have been spotted in say the satellite data. For example, a non-Five Eyes citizen with very well-established credentials from another country and with regular legitimate business in the Soviet Union made for an ideal agent if trained and handled with care. The ability to have direct connect with Soviet Navy personnel, research facilities, or the higher echelons in Moscow, and to listen to, observe, and visit directly places banned to Five Eyes personnel, and later record this for Five Eyes intelligence, was indeed valuable. The same applied to non-Russian Warsaw Pact citizens that had to travel to key parts of the Soviet Union where there was critical naval activity, and particularly in cases where they had relatives in the West or other parts of the Warsaw Pact. West German, Czech or Hungarian citizens who had families in Russia and had the necessary permits to visit them in Russia, could act as information couriers for individuals that were so disaffected with the Soviet regime that they would risk spying for one of the Five Eyes nations. Such agents had to be handled with the utmost care by either surrogates or undercover handlers with well-developed long-term deep cover that could not be penetrated. The British in particular were masters of these particular brands of tradecraft with decades of experience that started before World War II. No such British handler would ever have been seen by Soviet watchers in the UK ever entering or leaving one of the UK intelligence facilities monitored by the Soviets. The culture, the modus operandi and the trade craft were intensely buried in layers of cover—the only way to succeed and to stay alive in the Cold War espionage business.

The Five Eyes, together with NATO as a whole, never wanted to be caught short or surprised by a major technological advance by the Soviet Union in the key area of underwater warfare, and in particular submarine construction and order of battle. NATO simply could not afford to lose maritime supremacy. NATO had to be able to reinforce Europe and the Central Front from the US and keep the US and Western economy alive and well in the worst-case scenarios. Soviet submarines challenged these key strategic assumptions. By comparison, today there is a similar strategic imperative that the US Seventh Fleet and its formal Asian allies, particularly the three non-US Five Eyes Pacific nations, and associated friendly countries, will be able to counter the growing significance of the Chinese submarine threat. That threat may challenge the East Asian sea lines of communication, the critical resources in the South and East China Seas, and the valuable islands that are in dispute.

The life cycle of either a nuclear or non-nuclear submarine starts with R&D in laboratories, research institutes, and in the industrial base that actually constructs submarines. Almost all the major Soviet centers for the latter were well known during the Cold War and afterwards. However, finding out what was transpiring inside these far-flung centers, separated in many cases by thousands of miles, was

A Soviet *Sierra*-class nuclear-powered submarine. (Wikimedia Commons, US Navy)

a huge challenge. Second, and very important, was the Design Bureaus and Soviet Acquisition Authorities that integrated R&D, executed the detailed submarine design work across all the key areas (the hull, propulsion, quieting, combat system, weapons and their load out, communications and sensors, all the many and varied mechanical and electrical systems, and crew habitability or hotel functions as they are termed in the US) and then managed the construction programs with the many and varied yards across the Soviet Union. This complexity was furthered heightened by the Soviets beginning to plan, design and then build multiple submarine classes in parallel; an extraordinarily ambitious goal that they achieved, which gave US and British intelligence decades of concern. As new Soviet classes were being constructed, not only was there already a modernization program on the drawing boards for that class, but a whole new separate class would be in the design stage. The US never tried to emulate the Soviet model. UK and US submarine classes were developed and built in a well-conceived sequence as single classes, with the exception of the British diesel electric propulsion design and build running in parallel with the nuclear submarine program. This was a very rare exception and occurred in the cases of the British *Porpoise*- and *Oberon*-classes of diesel electric submarines and, later, towards the end of the British employment of non-nuclear submarines, the *Upholder*-class submarines that were eventually transferred to the Royal Canadian Navy.

This complex Soviet process had to be penetrated, understood and key intelligence garnered fed back into the key user communities. Intelligence is of zero value if it does not provide actionable information—data of whatever kind that enables strategic planners, operators, designers, scientists, engineers, and budgetary authorities in each of the five governments to understand and then make the right decisions to counter the Soviet threat. The political leadership of the five nations had to be briefed and given the very best data that existed in order to authorize and fund programs to counter the Soviet Union. The same applies today with the emergent Russian threat, cyber, the Chinese threat, and Islamic Fundamentalism.

The sea is where key intelligence data is initially obtained. From 1960 until today the Five Eyes jointly amassed and shared almost without exception operational intelligence derived from at sea-based collection operations. Simply put, it takes a very capable submarine to locate, track, identify, and then collect intelligence on another submarine. Without this major baseline advantage, the Five Eyes navies would have been in a different situation. The history of the Cold War may indeed have been very different. What the Five Eyes built was a very well informed and fully documented data base on each and every Soviet submarine class, and indeed each hull within each class.

Early on in the Cold War the constant round-the-clock forward-deployed locating and tracking of Soviet submarines enabled several critical tasks to be achieved. Forward-deployed operational intelligence collection operations varied from locating a Soviet submarine in either egress from or ingress to its home base, a foreign port, or sometimes an anchorage such as the much frequented Soviet anchorages in the Mediterranean, when in company with other Soviet surface assets, and at critical geographic choke points through which the Soviets had no choice but to transit. The latter included the Greenland–Iceland–United Kingdom gap, the Danish straits (the Kattegat and Skagerrak), the straits of Gibraltar, and the key straits in the Indonesian archipelago—the Sunda and Malacca straits. There were many other choke point locations or operationally well-used transits where the Soviets could be detected, and then tracked.

Over time the Five Eyes developed a profile of each Soviet submarine, in particular its noise levels or acoustic signature across a range of frequencies that characterized that specific submarine. ACINT or acoustic intelligence is arguably a far more valuable intelligence source than many of the better known HUMINT or human-derived intelligence sources, classical espionage, in other words. Speed, depth, operating characteristics and crew performance could all be observed and recorded and, very significantly, Soviet sensor data could be collected, including active and passive sonar. In addition critical communications could be monitored and recorded, including modes and frequencies, and any discreet hitherto unknown techniques. In addition to collection operations against Soviet submarines the Five Eyes collected against Soviet airborne naval strike and anti-submarine assets. These included the Soviet NATO designated BEAR D and F aircraft flying from well-known and well-monitored Soviet air bases in the Kola Peninsula in northern Russia. Most of all, the tactical procedures that were ingrained in Soviet submariners were analyzed by Five Eyes submariners and played back in their submarine schools. In particular the US and the UK acquired first-hand experience of the different training and operational culture of Soviet submariners, and their dependence upon a centralized command and control, and communications system. This created vulnerabilities for them, as well as preventing their submarine command teams from developing independence, self-confidence, quick thinking, and innovative tactics. Deviation from strict tactical procedures by Soviet submariners was almost unknown. As a result, the UK and US became able to predict Soviet maneuvers and anticipate their every move, and share this information.

New Soviet submarine weapons were high on the collection list. The acoustic advantage of superior, quiet, and well-handled stealthy UK and US nuclear submarines permitted the penetration of the most discreet and dangerous areas for observing and recording Soviet weapons trials. It was essential that NATO had the best and latest intelligence of new Soviet weapons as they went on sea trials. Collecting such vital intelligence in the recesses of the Barents Sea was a high risk and dangerous task, but it was accomplished for decades and the product was first class. The operating characteristics, ranges, and key sensor frequencies of new Soviet weaponry could then be distributed to the NATO community under secure umbrellas that never revealed the sources and methods of collection. Classical SIGINT and

ELINT played heavily in all these collection operations during the Cold War. This entailed passive listening and interception of Soviet communications by multiple means from special collection suites. Translation was an essential part of this process, and back in the UK and US a small body of highly trained translators would make sense of all the technical and verbal intercepts. These translators were the natural successors to the Bletchley Park and US MAGIC cryptanalysis teams of World War II fame. In many cases technical translators were deployed for certain special missions where real-time onboard intelligence was necessary to fully understand on the spot what the Soviets were executing. These "Sea-Riders," as they were called, would often spend weeks at sea in precarious operational scenarios, enabling NATO to stay ahead of the game by knowing exactly what the Soviets were either testing in a prototype system or weapon, or putting though an operational test and evaluation phase a more developed capability that was close to initial operational capability (IOC as NATO termed this process).

The next critical stage in this complex process, running concurrently with operational intelligence collection, analysis and distribution, was to penetrate the program base itself inside the Soviet Union, the centers in Moscow where Soviet R&D and design bureau work came together in their acquisition authorities. Penetration of these centers by classical espionage was extraordinarily difficult.

Penetrating Soviet Intelligence

The likelihood of key Soviet officials betraying their country's secrets was very low. This was borne out by the small number of Soviet defectors and agents. Little reliance was placed on acquiring regular and reliable HUMINT. US overhead sources, although critical during this whole period, and still today, have limitations in addition to their great values. Satellites cannot see inside buildings in Moscow and Leningrad or inside the building halls at the Soviet submarine shipyards. Satellites can listen as well as watch and considerable intelligence can be obtained from space in the SIGINT, ELINT, and related fields. However, in a pre-digital communications era before cell phone communications, microwave towers, and the international transfer of massive amounts of digital communications, the US and the UK relied on classical communications technologies, frequencies and procedures associated with the radio frequency (RF) spectrum. The latter permitted intercept by a multitude of different methods, platforms, and geographic locations. In addition to RF transmissions the Soviets, the Warsaw Pact in general, and NATO used landlines extensively, many of which were secure and separate from regular landlines operated by the various user governments and corporate communications suppliers.

The same applies to transoceanic communications cables and satellite communications that became more and more available and used during the post-Cold War period. The US and the UK had to follow classical communications intercept technologies and procedures that dated from the World War II era, combined with more advanced technologies, to deal with RF transmissions while working and staying ahead in the satellite communications and later the digital communications era. The Soviets naturally had highly secure communications procedures to avoid penetration and decoding of classified encoded messages. The weakness of the centralized Soviet system in military acquisition management was like many other aspects of the Soviet Union's military and intelligence machinery—its very centralization made it vulnerable because its very organization could be identified and understood.

Success in breaking into the communications of the central Soviet acquisition process, together with the hugely valuable operational intelligence that defined the base lines discussed earlier, enabled the Five Eyes to make very informed assessments of what was likely to emerge from the many Soviet building yards and the likely capabilities of the next generation submarine classes.

This picture was not always rosy. US intelligence in the 1970s tended to underestimate future Soviet capabilities. The US-based assessments to a large extent, though not completely, relied on the Soviets' failure to master advanced computer-based digital signal processing, particularly in the discreet domains of low-frequency narrow-band signal processing. The US argued that this key weakness prevented them from resolving the critical issue of submarine quieting and the concomitant noise levels in their hull designs. The US assessed that the Soviet active acoustic sonar programs and significant extensive investment in a wide range of non-acoustic anti-submarine systems and technologies were all due to their failure to both understand and then acquire the technologies to execute highly capable passive sonar detections of quiet well-handled UK and US submarines.

By contrast the UK showed, in very detailed intelligence reports, that the next generation of Soviet submarines that were likely to appear from the building halls from 1980 onwards would be significantly more capable in all regards, and in particular in noise quieting and the type of weapons that they would embark. In the event, the launch of the Soviet cruise-missile-firing submarine class *Oscar* and the ballistic-missile submarine class *Typhoon* (both NATO designated names) proved that the UK had very accurate assessments, and operational intelligence quickly proved them to be correct. The UK assessments had been made on the basis of all-source collection and concentration on relating data on the Soviet R&D base, the highly sensitive Soviet procurement system, very important open-source data that was clearly not Soviet deception, and all the baseline databases. The UK saw that by 1980 the Soviets would demonstrate a step change in capability, and that their non-acoustic ASW programs were indeed running in parallel with new, advanced passive acoustic signal-processing programs. All this added up, from a British perspective, to significantly new Soviet capabilities for the 1990s.

The *Victor III*- and *Acula*-class Soviet nuclear-powered attack submarines joined the ranks of the *Oscar*- and *Typhoon*-class submarines as being step changes from their predecessors' classes. A highly sensitive British "Harmonized Threat Paper" that I published with a British colleague in 1982 made accurate assessments of the new Soviet submarine classes' capabilities, with one notably minor technical exception that the Soviets corrected after initial sea trials. The discrepancies in this time frame, late 1970s to the early 1980s, between the US and the UK was most likely caused by the diverse and varied capabilities of the US intelligence agencies who could often not agree on final assessments. The British enjoyed the benefits of being smaller and well integrated, with extremely close working relations between the intelligence collectors and the analysts, and the way in which final assessments could be harmonized within a much tighter knit community than the massive intelligence organizations of the US, where cooperation was not always the hallmark.

Once the new baselines had been established, the US and the UK could get back to amicable business-as-usual modes, but to say there was not friction would be to gloss over a critical transition phase in Soviet capabilities that took place from the late 1970s into the 1980s.

As the 1990s progressed this would become patently clear.

On the operational intelligence side, both collection and analysis, extraordinary fine work continued between the US Navy and the Royal Navy. The use of US Sound Surveillance System (SOSUS) is illustrative. The location of critical SOSUS monitoring stations in the UK that could track the deployment (both egress and ingress) of Soviet submarines from the Kola Peninsula in the Soviet Arctic through the Greenland–Iceland–United Kingdom Gap (GIUK Gap as it was known in UK–US naval parlance) was not just vital—their location was critical for directing scarce UK–US ASW forces to then search, locate and track Soviet submarines in the vastness of the Norwegian Sea, the North Sea, and the north east Atlantic. The UK–US coordination of airborne ASW assets (US P-3 aircraft and UK Shackleton and later Nimrod ASW aircraft) with surface and subsurface assets was highly organized through the UK maritime headquarters at Northwood, England and the outlying lower command echelons, such as the Flag Officer Scotland and Northern Island, and other NATO centers, such as the Royal Norwegian Navy and Air Force and their key operations from the Lofoten Islands in northern Norway. The US base at Keflavik in Iceland was another key link in this chain. The British Royal Air Force bases at RAF Kinloss on the Moray Forth east of Inverness in northern Scotland and at St. Mawgan in Cornwall in south-western England were key airborne centers and locations where US aircraft could land for refueling and rest for crews. The Royal Navy's air station at Lossiemouth, which lay to the east of RAF Kinloss, was the Royal Navy's shore-based center in northern Scotland for interdicting Soviet air force reconnaissance and bomber aircraft. In addition, the US maintained hugely discreet SIGINT stations in various UK locations. One such location that was legendary, and is now closed, was on the far north-east coast of Scotland near to a small village, Edsell, where the locals kept the secrets for several generations of the activities of the US Naval Security Group.

UK–US Intercept Stations and their Intelligence Yield

This US intercept station, together with other GCHQ UK-based stations, provided invaluable real-time SIGINT intercepts. These stations covered the communications activities of the Soviet spy ships, the AGIs, together with Soviet and non-Soviet Warsaw Pact merchant ships that were echelons of the Soviet Ocean Surveillance System (SOSS), and that provided key intelligence to the motherland on UK and US naval and other Allied operations. However, such vessels had to communicate, and even when communicating in highly encrypted modes, GCHQ, and their opposite numbers in the US at the National Security Agency and the naval cryptologic centers were able to unravel these discreet messages. This coordinated cluster of sources and methods resulted in the US Navy and Royal Navy keeping round-the-clock surveillance and tracking of the Soviet Navy as a whole in the Soviets' main Fleet area, the Northern Fleet, and in particular the location and movements of its most formidable assets, the Soviet submarines. The Canadian, Australian, and New Zealand Five Eyes members performed equally highly classified roles from locations that are still sensitive. Their product was invaluable.

However, this positive picture of successful monitoring of every stage of Soviet core naval capabilities and operations was being challenged in two key domains. One was the extraordinary damaging consequences of the US spy ring led by John

Soviet *Oscar*-class nuclear-powered cruise missile submarine. (Wikimedia Commons, US Navy)

Anthony Walker (1937–2014). The other was by the internal efforts of the Soviet Navy research and development community to challenge the UK–US acoustic advantage by other means. At the same time the Soviets began programs that sought to challenge the UK and US strategic deterrent postures. These were different from the well-established pattern of Soviet AGIs standing off UK and US bases and attempting to provide the SOSS with up-to-date operational intelligence. Such intelligence traditionally helped vector Soviet SSNs, such as the new *Victor III*-class, to locate and engage by tracking egressing UK and US SSBNs, the very heart of the Western nuclear deterrent posture. The Soviet aim that underpinned these was destabilization of and offsetting the West's technical advantages. The Soviets made a major strategic decision to go under the northern ice cap while at the same time developing alternative technologies to active and passive acoustic signal processing in parallel with improving submarine quieting. The Walker spy ring in the US provided intelligence that played significantly in the Soviets initiating these major changes.

The UK had not been bereft of Soviet spies in the naval sphere. The Portland spy ring from a generation earlier had made significant inroads into UK naval programs at the Admiralty Underwater Research Establishment at Portland in Dorset on the south coast of England, but their activities were nothing like as devastating as the work of the British Philby, Burgess, and McLean spy ring who had infiltrated the highest echelons of the British Secret Intelligence Service (SIS), and betrayed countless invaluable British HUMINT secrets and agents to their Soviet masters. The devastating effects of what Philby in particular caused to MI6 were very much comparable with the disastrous consequences for the US Navy and its associated intelligence agencies of the Walker spy ring.

In the contemporary world, the recent betrayals by Edward Snowden highlight the effects of the betrayal of critical intelligence sources and methods, and content. With this comes serious damage to public perception of the UK and US, and their NSA–GCHQ operations. The one positive aspect is that Snowden, who had woefully never been detected by counterintelligence, clearance investigators, or immediate fellow employees, still does not know what he does not know. This is a huge credit to the highly secure, tightly knit community in key parts of Five Eyes intelligence, to which he did not have access. The Five Eyes navies' intelligence collection programs were successfully protected during the Cold War. Some of the product of those programs were compromised by the Walker spy ring, but the key critical operational aspects were never compromised because the Five Eyes reduced the number of need-to-know personnel to an absolute minimum, while critically not sharing information with other agencies inside which were potential weak links such as Edward Snowden. It is to the lasting tribute of the Five Eyes navies that since the 1950s the very secure inner workings of Five Eyes navy collection programs remain sacrosanct.

The value of Five Eyes intelligence was immeasurable at one level. However, at another, it is clearly very much subject to well-defined metrics based on scientific and technical intelligence criteria, supported by political-military-economic intelligence. The Five Eyes were collectively far superior at this business than any other nation, or their allies, such as the Warsaw Pact. This overwhelming advantage cannot be undermined or underfunded, only at the peril not just of the national security interests of each of the Five Eyes nations, but the interconnected world of the global economy, where any major destabilization may precipitously put the world economy into a tail spin.

CHAPTER 3

Political and Structural Changes, 1978–83

Returning to the UK in late 1977 after such a challenging and exciting tour working with and for the Americans was tough. Leave was spent adjusting psychologically, visiting family, and working on yet another move from our London house to the Portsmouth, Hampshire area. I was to be the second-in-command of the Royal Navy's Ordnance Engineering School (OE School for short), where all the Royal Navy's weapons engineering specialists, both officers and enlisted, were trained in accordance with their specialties, rank, and next sea-going appointment. The OE School had over 700 personnel that included trainees and staff. During my time running the day-to-day operations of the OE School, we were directed by the Commander-in-Chief Portsmouth to transform the OE School into a new structure that must reflect the rapidly changing nature of naval weapons systems and the training required to operate and maintain them. In retrospect it is clear that our higher leadership in Her Majesty's Naval Base Portsmouth and the team that I led were at the forefront of what became the digital and information revolution.

The new creation was the Royal Navy's Electro-Technology School, ET School for short. We restructured training and brought in several highly capable weapons engineering (WE) graduate-level officer instructors with recent sea experience on the latest systems, and those involved in the development and acquisition of systems coming into service shortly, to lead in the day-to-day training; a mixture of classroom instruction and hands-on practical training with the systems themselves. We were training officers and enlisted personnel up to and including the lieutenant commander level, the latter being those officers appointed to be weapons engineering department heads on Royal Navy frigates and destroyers. Unlike the US Navy, the Royal Navy has specialist graduate weapons engineering, marine engineering, and air engineering career "General List" officers, with the same career opportunities to reach a four-star rank as those officers in the US Navy. Categorized as Unrestricted Line Officers, with the exception that Royal Navy General List engineers may not hold sea commands but may hold major shore commands and other senior flag positions as co-equals with General List seaman specialists (the ship drivers). It was an exciting time, and I was surrounded by a training and administrative staff that was simply first class. The OE/ET School also excelled at sports and events such as the Portsmouth Field Gun Competition. We passed our flag-level inspections with flying colors.

While still in London and on leave, I was directed to make calls on the top naval and intelligence leadership to hold discussions regarding my tour in Washington. These meetings were invaluable and took place over several days and were fully supported by the Washington Embassy staff. I held a unique position in Washington and the naval and intelligence leadership wished that my position be continued. I had in essence been a "one off" event. I had no predecessor and no successor. The position had been tailor-made for me. The senior leadership set in motion the necessary actions to search for and find a successor, and to liaise with the Americans on my replacement. In due course I was informed that the right person had been found after some considerable search. He would be sent to Washington by the end of 1978, or early 1979.

My family and I moved to a modern house in a small Hampshire village, Clanfield, near to Petersfield, just north of Portsmouth, that has a rail station with fast trains to London Waterloo station. During and since my time at Greenwich I had become interested in the law of the sea and the wider aspects of international law. I had been admitted to Lincoln's Inn in July,1975. I had steadily progressed under my own steam with Royal Navy support and funding to read for the Bar. The location of the Clanfield home enabled me to attend the necessary dinners in Lincoln's Inn in London as part of fulfilling the requirements to be admitted to the English Bar. I could be home in time in the late evening from London to rise and be in the OE School by 0700. I was called to the Bar by Lincoln's Inn in November 1980. I had been greatly influenced to study international law while at Greenwich as a result of the major 1973 Law of the Sea Conference to celebrate the 100th anniversary of Greenwich as the senior Naval College. During the conference I had been responsible for hosting Professor Daniel O'Connell, the Chichele Professor of International Law at Oxford, and regarded as the premier expert on the law of the sea. He had a lasting impact on my thinking and motivation to be professionally qualified.

During this period of being back at the front end with 700-plus naval personnel of all ranks and ratings, I wondered if all my prior experience in Washington and earlier would be a stepping stone up the career ladder, and if the service had other things in store for me. The Royal Navy and the intelligence community did indeed have a plan. I just did not know it until early in 1979 when I was summoned to the Old Admiralty Building in Whitehall to be informed that I was to leave the OE/ET School appointment. I was to be appointed to a Special Program Office whose oversight came directly from the Cabinet Office in Whitehall. My "appointer" knew none of the details. He informed me that he was "not cleared." I subsequently received the official notification without any mention of the nature or location of the appointment, just the date. I was naturally concerned about promotion prospects and these worries were allayed when I was selected for promotion. I was wined and dined royally by my terrific ET School colleagues and I went on leave knowing that I would be living in an apartment in London until my wife and I could sell the home in Clanfield and relocate to a house within easy distance of central London. I was soon to find the nature of what would be a series of different assignments working across and with each of the four UK intelligence agencies, and each of the major intelligence agencies that I had worked with in Washington DC.

The Cultural Underpinnings of the Five Eyes

Where the World War II special relationship endured most, after the centralization processes had been put in place and the new hierarchies established, was in the very closely held, highly secretive operations conducted by and under the umbrella of each of the five countries' navies and their naval intelligence organizations. Because of the very nature of these operations all five navies were able to preserve their unique separation from the new central organizations, with special access and routes to the political leadership that no other service or intelligence agency enjoyed. Furthermore, each navy was entwined in these operations. Such operations often required special highly classified Presidential Executive Orders, or signed orders by the Prime Minister in the case of the UK. Everything and everyone in between was out of this loop. One key element drove this requirement. Each of the five navies was forward deployed globally. They were present where no other assets or intelligence entity could go. Even after space-based systems became significant only naval assets could perform certain key real-time intelligence functions based on persistent presence. There continues to this day a major requirement for forward-deployed naval intelligence assets. Security and need-to-know are the guardian angels of these Five Eyes operations.

The Western democracies have based their national security policies on what are clearly identifiable values and strategic considerations. Primary has been the need to protect their citizens from invasion and threats that challenge the core geographic and political integrity and identity of the individual nation state: the right to live in both peace and harmony; the right to determine via cherished democratic institutions national self-determination; and the right to exist as an independent nation, free from oppression or threat from any source. Deep-rooted historical, cultural, ethnic, linguistic and economic factors bond each of the Five Eyes nations. The strategic requirements for each and every nation to maintain their national identity and right to self-determination varies across time and geographic space. These factors have determined for example the national reactions by each of the Five Eyes countries to a changing balance of power, where the status quo of free, well-established independent states is threatened.

A key lesson of the first half of the 20th century may be summarized as the need to anticipate and prepare for defense when the gathering clouds of imminent threats indicate that the world is changing in ways that cause deep concern for future security. The clear and best example of this is the rise of the Nazi Party and the German elections of 1933 leading to Germany's ever-increasing belligerent challenges from 1936 to the outbreak of World War II in September 1939. Unpreparedness may lead to a perception of actual weakness and the ability of an aggressor to challenge the status quo. The latter in today's environment may not necessarily be classical territorial violations, with worst-case invasion scenarios, but economic, including resources such as water and oil, pandemic challenges, the acquisition of monopolistic trade in key raw materials, and the exploitation of cyberspace, At the extreme of this primary strategic requirement is national survival.

Secondly, nations such as the Five Eyes have formed alliances to protect their security and vital national interests. Conversely, those nations with belligerent and often expansionist intent have allied with nations where they perceived apparent gain. The Nazi–Soviet Pact, the Nazi–Japanese–Italian Axis, and the later denouncement of the Nazi–Soviet Pact by Germany are good 20th-century examples of *realpolitik* played out by adversary nations who perceived apparent gain from making and breaking alliances.

Thirdly, the key lead 20th-century democratic powers, the US and the UK, allied to Canada, Australia, and New Zealand, have led in exalting self-determination and, in the case of the UK, decolonization and the right of self-government. President Woodrow Wilson was the father of the post-World War I League of Nations, and the Five Eyes nations were at the heart of the founding of the United Nations Organization (UNO), and in the North Atlantic Treaty Organization (NATO), the US, UK, and Canada. The former was conceived in peace to foster international cooperation and allay future wars, and the latter was conceived to preserve peace in ways that built on the lessons learned from the failure of the League of Nations to maintain international order. NATO's strength lay in its military cohesion, organization and military capabilities that aimed to deter, not threaten.

The cultural underpinnings of the Five Eyes, and the need to show strength by clear military capability, national resolve, and cooperation in well-organized alliance structures point to one very clearly definable thread that runs through their strategic thinking—that preparedness for a changing threat environment is paramount. The Five Eyes have found that the tools of international security diplomacy, or the use of power in the pursuit of peaceful outcomes, is comprised of a very mixed bag. The latter includes diplomatic pressure and multi-national pressure point applications of economic sanctions, isolation, restrictions on the flow of goods, materials and capital. Where the above have failed the use of force has tended to be the tool of last resort, whether in the shape of blockade, mining, increasing the level of war preparedness status, or, worst case, open and declared commitment to war.

In certain cases the Five Eyes, particularly the UK–US–Canada, have been in positions where the use of the above tools was constrained because the overall strategic situation and balance of power was not in their favor. The Soviet invasion of Hungary, Czechoslovakia, and Afghanistan showed how a combination of circumstances rendered the US, Canada, and the UK, and their allies impotent—an unhealthy state of affairs. The sphere of influence of the Soviet Union in all three cases was such that NATO could not react in any meaningful way other than protest. There is a deep and abiding lesson in those three scenarios, not least that military power as an instrument of foreign policy and overall national security policy, has limits. Understanding those limits is crucial and the issue of centralization and the impact on the Five Eyes.

World War II was undoubtedly the greatest conflict fought in human history. What is quite astounding about World War II is that neither the US nor the UK, or their Commonwealth allies, fundamentally changed their key defense organizations during the conflict. There was tighter control and necessarily enforced cooperation, but none of the latter was opposed or certainly resisted by any of the military services. Given the complexity of World War II at every level—particularly the quite amazing ability to build in short order the massive industrial base war machine and to innovate technologically in extraordinarily short timelines—one thing is very clear: the system worked. Nothing is perfect, but the UK and US World War II defense organizations worked brilliantly well. Changes were made on the fly—bureaucratic inertia went out the window and those in the way of change or direct orders were soon removed. Any form of incompetence or inability to perform was rectified.

The question therefore arises, why change? Furthermore, why did change, from individual service centricity to centralization, take place? None of the Five Eyes military services during and after World War II can be accused of not being team players, worst case playing selfish service politics in pursuit of some self-serving goal—nothing was further from the truth. The political leadership and the service chiefs and their staffs agreed grand strategy and then allocated service resources to execute. Inter-service rivalry was not about any deeply fought issue over deciding the resource pie—but more about the highly valued rivalry to perform, to excel, indeed, to show worthiness in all regards—a hugely healthy state of affairs. The Five Eyes were never in bitter contentious battles with the other services over resources and who would do what to execute the grand strategy. During the Battle of the Bulge, Patton's Army was never so pleased to see the US Army Air Force appear to provide air-to-ground support once the weather improved, and on countless occasions surface naval forces heralded an overhead Liberator or Short Sunderland to attack a surfaced U-boat. Inter-service rivalry was about combined mutual effectiveness, not internecine service rivalries.

World War II proved three traits that are axiomatic about defense organizations—they have to be relevant, efficient, and effective. What emerged from World

War II was a desire to have greater integration and top-level control because control of each of the independent service organizations through the apparent benefits of centralization would lead to greater efficiency versus a concept of perceived service rivalry and inefficiency. What happened in reality was a massive bureaucracy with significant political overlay placed on top of the existing structure. In the US and the UK defense infrastructures grew. Once the basic political changes took place, underpinned by legislative action, the Office of the Secretary of Defense and the Chiefs of Staff structure in the US and later the Ministry of Defence and the Central Defence Staff in the UK grew exponentially. These changes took valuable resources to execute and incurred massive costs. But was it all worth it if what both countries had during World War II, plus or minus some lessons learned, worked well?

Change and the Mountbatten Factor

Several prominent post-World War II figures were centralists. In the UK the greatest advocate was perhaps surprisingly Admiral of the Fleet the Lord Louis Mountbatten, who personally oversaw the creation of the Central Defence Staff. How could this be? Admiral Mountbatten genuinely believed that greater efficiency could be achieved by centralization. He believed firmly in inter-service cooperation, not rivalry. He had been Chief of Combined Operations 1941–1943 as his first major flag officer appointment, where he was an advocate of joint service operations. In the Far East he saw the great value of inter-service cooperation as Supreme Allied Commander South East Asia 1943–1946. In this role he commanded forces that would become after World War II the emergent Five Eyes.

Lord Louis Mountbatten (June 25, 1900–August 27, 1979) was unique in all regards—a second cousin once removed to Queen Elizabeth II and an uncle of Prince Philip, Duke of Edinburgh, husband of Queen Elizabeth II. His family pedigree was impeccable: the youngest child and second son of Prince Louis of Battenberg and Princess Victoria of Hesse. He entered the Royal Naval College at Osborne in May 1913. In 1914 his father became First Sea Lord and Chief of Naval Staff. A very sad blight on the Battenberg family (the name was changed to Mountbatten because of the deep German family relationships) was the removal of his father from office because of anti-German feelings in the UK. The young Mountbatten overcame this heritage to achieve the highest military offices as First Sea Lord and Chief of Naval Staff from April 1955–July 1959, and as the first Chief of the Defence Staff from 1959–1965, making him the longest ever serving Chief of the Defence Staff. He and his father made Royal Navy history by both being First Sea Lord and Chief of Naval Staff.

Lord Mountbatten therefore had enormous influence. The 1950s witnessed the Korean War, intensification of the Cold War, the invasion of Hungary by the Soviet Union, and the growth of nuclear rivalry after the detonation of the first Soviet

Admiral of the Fleet Lord Louis Mountbatten of Burma when Supreme Commander Allied Eastern Forces. (Wikimedia Commons)

weapon in August 1949. Mountbatten clearly and unequivocally believed that the British services needed to be one in not just name but actual organization. He began systematically working with the governments of Harold Macmillan (January 1957–October 1963), Alec Douglas Home (October 1963–October 1964), and Harold Wilson (October 1964–June 1970) to transform the organization of British defense. In effect he dismantled the historic organization of the Royal Navy in terms of its political-military structure. The representation of the Royal Navy as a single service directly in parliament by the First Lord of the Admiralty, who was also a member of the Cabinet, was now gone. This single fact had dramatic and long-term consequences to which Lord Mountbatten was either oblivious or did not consider important because he assessed that change was necessary.

The Royal Navy no longer had separate and independent representation in parliament and direct access at the Cabinet level. The Admiralty as an organization of state was subsumed by the Ministry of Defence. The Naval Staff, headed by the First Sea and Chief of Naval Staff, still existed in its prior form. The key directorates of Naval Plans, Operational Requirements, and Operations and Trade remained intact. These key Naval Staff directorates, along with the Controller of the Navy's staff that headed acquisitions and procurement, and the Chief of Naval Personnel, were always lean organizations that were renowned for their hard work and efficiency and were never bureaucratic or over manned. The Directorate of Naval Intelligence had also been similarly manned. With the loss of direct political access and influence the Naval Staff now had to work through a Central Defence Staff structure. This structure had new and what many perceived as duplicative coordination staff functions that in prior decades had worked through the Chiefs of Staff Committee, a similarly lean organization that was now expanded under the Chief of the Defence Staff's organization. The latter replicated at the joint staff level the individual staff functions that in the case of the Royal Navy were embodied in the highly effective Naval Staff. The latter had a historic record of high performance through two world wars in the 20th century.

The four-star leaders in the Navy now found that they were bereft of direct political access and a reporting chain to a Central Defence Staff in a unified Ministry of Defence, and a Chief of the Defence Staff hierarchy and Deputy and Deputy Assistant Chiefs of the Defence Staff for all the main defense functions—policy, plans, operations, intelligence, personnel, and acquisition (including research and development). There was therefore an enormous layer of added staff function and the attendant manpower and bureaucracy placed on top of the former Admiralty structure that had functioned well not just for decades and both world wars, but indeed centuries. The culture shock was not inconsiderable. In addition, the Royal Navy suddenly found itself not just working with and through these new defense hierarchies but also with a growing and, after time, an entrenched civil service bureaucracy that added process and cost to the business of running the Royal Navy. The possible long-term organizational impact of these changes was not fully analyzed or understood in 1964 and in the years leading up to the formal changes. Centralization and jointness were considered good for their own sake in the names of greater service cooperation, integration, and planning to meet the security challenges posed by the Cold War.

The Royal Navy had found itself competing in this new environment and no longer had direct political representation for a maritime strategy. This was transformational because since Nelson's time the Royal Navy regarded itself as the self-evident and a nationally accepted embodiment of British grand strategy through sea power, typified most of all by maritime expeditionary warfare.

In the 1960s, following Prime Minster Harold Macmillan's famous "Winds of Change" speech, the UK began systematic and wholesale decolonization, particularly in Africa, Asia, and the West Indies. The Labor government of Harold Wilson and the Minister of Defence, Denis Healey, saw the independence movement from the last vestiges of empire that began with Indian independence (and the creation of the separate states of India and Pakistan, and later Bangladesh vice East Pakistan) as reason to draw back to Europe. "Withdrawal" became an operative word in

UK defense parlance, particularly with regard to the Far East, and the British Far East Fleet based in Singapore and Hong Kong. Defence Minister Healey saw no need for the size of the fleet that the UK had maintained through the 1950s into the early 1960s. He did not articulate a maritime policy or indeed a strategy that melded the Royal Navy into the new global maritime Cold War environment other than to become North Atlantic focused. The historic domain of the Mediterranean was withdrawn from systematically, with the ending of the Commander-in-Chief Mediterranean Fleet to a Flag Officer Malta status, to an eventual closure of the Malta naval base and the final ending of the continuous presence of the Royal Navy in the Mediterranean. This pattern followed with the rundown of the Far East bases to support facilities and the eventual lowering for the last time of the Commander Far East Fleet's flag in Singapore. The process by which this happened was not just driven by budgetary and foreign policy considerations as the UK's territorial possessions diminished, but also by the structural changes in defense organization.

The new defense organization had created a different political-military environment in which key decision making occurred. The new Ministry of Defence had many conflicting priorities to meet at a time of colonial retrenchment and withdrawal. Not least of these was the balance of conventional forces against the need for strategic nuclear defense, and the perceived need to support NATO in Europe with ground forces through the British Army of the Rhine (BAOR), as UK forces in West Germany were termed. Within these often-conflicting issues for resources lay other underlying problems. Not least was the growing rivalry between the Royal Navy and the Royal Air Force.

After the historic meeting between Prime Minister Macmillan and President Kennedy in Bermuda in December 1961, the US agreed to share its nuclear submarine and strategic nuclear ballistic missile technology with the UK. The Royal Navy would build both nuclear-powered attack submarines (SSNs) and nuclear-powered ballistic missile submarines (SSBNs)—the latter becoming the core, and today the mainstay of UK national strategic defense through nuclear deterrence. The Royal Air Force competed for resources to maintain its nuclear capable V-bomber force of Vulcan, Victor and Valiant aircraft carrying nuclear bombs similar to the capabilities of the US Air Force B-52 aircraft of Strategic Air Command. These were resource intensive requirements and capabilities. Denis Healey associated withdrawal from the former disposition of UK territories as akin to withdrawal from maritime presence and forward deployment. This fact confronted a navy that had been globally disposed. Healey saw in this withdrawal major cost savings, downsizing of the Royal Navy, and concentration on European defense via the deployment of the British Army and Air Force to Europe, and the concentration of the Royal Navy in north European waters to contribute to the NATO challenge to the burgeoning Soviet Northern Fleet. The latter sought increasing access through the Greenland–Iceland–UK gap

(GIUK gap) to the Atlantic and the oceans beyond. The overall strategy was driven by available resources, rather than deep analysis of the UK's primary strategic goals other than the need for a national independent strategic nuclear deterrent based on US support and technology. The Royal Air Force wanted to maintain roles for the air defense of the UK in addition to RAF Germany's role in Europe, plus maintenance of the role of maritime patrol that transitioned from RAF Coastal Command to 18 Group Royal Air Force, initially with squadrons of Shackleton and then Nimrod maritime patrol aircraft.

The Royal Navy found itself in an unenviable position when the decision to replace the major Fleet aircraft carriers came across Denis Healey's desk. The Naval Staff now had to compete not just with the Royal Air Force but in a Central Staff environment that was focused not only on strategy but also cost saving. The least factor considered was the vital UK national strategic interests other than nuclear deterrence. The core concept of maritime expeditionary warfare was not addressed in a global context as an alternate to a European focus.

Denis Healey and Change

Secretary of State for Defence Denis Healey was an intellectual and one of the key thinkers in the post-war Labour Party (see Appendix). He had declared views on aircraft carriers. He thought them far too vulnerable to torpedo attack from the new nuclear-powered attack submarines and he characterized them as floating slums that sailors had to inhabit. His analyses went no further and did not explore how the new hunter-killer submarines would protect in the future the aircraft carrier battle groups. He chose to not recognize that the Royal Navy's surface force was being configured around anti-submarine warfare to protect the carriers and amphibious assault ships as well as merchant shipping, together with new air-defense missile systems to protect these capital units from air attack. The strategic value of mobile fixed-wing strikes from the sea was not in Secretary of Defence Healey's strategic lexicon. The scene was set therefore for a major challenge to British naval aviation, the likes of which the Royal Navy had ever witnessed hitherto. The new political–military structure that was instituted with the major changes in 1964 would not help the Royal Navy in the debate about the replacement carrier program because the Service had lost its political clout with the demise of the First Lord of the Admiralty Cabinet level position and the creation of a Central Defence Staff in a centralized Ministry of Defence.

The fixed-wing aircraft carriers HMS *Victorious, Hermes, Eagle* and *Ark Royal* had well-understood service lives, with two of the light carriers, HMS *Albion* and *Bulwark* having been converted to helicopter-carrying commando carriers for the Royal Marines. The Royal Navy lost the battle for a replacement fixed-wing carrier program that would culminate in the end of Royal Navy major fixed-wing aviation

Denis Healy. (Wikimedia Commons)

until approximately 2020, when the first of the two *Queen Elizabeth*-class carriers will enter service with the Lockheed-Martin F-34 as their aircraft of choice. HMS *Ark Royal* was the last major carrier to leave service in 1979, her service stretched as far as possible by the Naval Staff. Her squadrons of F-4s, Buccaneers and Gannets were either transferred to the Royal Air Force or scrapped. The Naval Staff set about planning a short-term recovery operation from what many naval and independent strategic experts regarded as a monumental error of judgment by the Ministry of Defence and the Central Defence Staff. It took 50 years to correct this major decision with the commissioning of the largest ships ever acquired by the Royal Navy, the aircraft carriers HMS *Queen Elizabeth* in December 2017, and HMS *Prince of Wales* in December 2019.

The process by which this decision occurred was very typical of the way the Royal Navy now had to operate at the Whitehall level. Without direct representation at the Cabinet and parliamentary levels the Navy lost access to political influence and debate in ways that had been traditional. The new Central Staff and Ministry functions placed the Naval Staff out of the mainstream other than to perform its own immediate service functions. The First Sea Lord was now no longer the primary

HMS *Ark Royal* alongside USS *Nimitz* in Norfolk, Virginia, April 1976. (Wikimedia Commons)

player in a historic Admiralty, but a service chief who was increasingly required to both champion his cause and also be a team player in a Chief of Defence Staff structure. The First Sea Lord had to recognize that his voice was not just one of four at the table (the three service chiefs plus the Chief of the Defence Staff) but also that his naval staff had to contend not only with a heavy duty civil service secretariat that was powerful but also with a Central Defence Staff, some of whom were Navy, but at best only one third, often on a rotational basis between the three services. All of the above was not conducive to formulating, articulating and convincing government of the need for a maritime strategy as the primary strategy based on the well-founded historic role of the Royal Navy as the guardian of the UK's security. The Royal Navy's ability to compete for the primary place was diminished.

The new Central Defence Staff became characterized as a process-driven organization in which intense highly bureaucratic committee work, balancing conflicting interests, and constantly attempting to meet each service's requirements and funding requests by compromise became the order of business. In this process the core and vitally important function of debating, deciding, and agreeing grand strategy based on the key vital national security interests of the UK were often lost in the noise of service compromise. The UK Strategic Defence and Security Reviews (SDSRs) of the recent past decades have been described as such.

US Political System Staves off the Negative Effects of Change

The United States Navy was most fortunate in one critical regard when compared with the Royal Navy. The very nature of the political system and Constitution of the United States helped maintain the enduring influence of the US Navy after the organizational changes described earlier. Two factors were paramount. First, the legislative and the executive in the US are separate, and secondly the position and role of the Secretary of the United States Navy remained intact and unchallenged, even though the Secretary of the Navy lost a seat in the Cabinet in 1949 and the new Secretary of Defense was all powerful in a hierarchical sense. Secretaries Franke, Connally, Korth, Fay, Nitze, Ignatius, and Chafee from 1960–1972 still enjoyed autonomy to act in the best interests of the US Navy via well-established constitutional channels. The Chiefs of Naval Operations during this period—Admirals Burke, Anderson, McDonald, Moorer, and Zumwalt from 1960–1974 never faced the dilemmas confronting the First Sea Lords and their staffs during the same period. Both the naval political and uniform leadership had well-defined and legally correct means to access the Congress at several levels and by multiple means. They had ways to represent not just their programmatic and funding interests but also core strategic issues that drive the annual defense budgets. The open forum of public unclassified hearings spoke well for US Navy interests. The personal strengths of successive Chiefs of Naval Operations shone through in open questioning in the House Committee on Armed Services (HASC) and the Senate Committee on Armed Services (SASC), and in the closed-door classified hearings to which the public and press were not admitted. Key strategic issues were aired in public—hotly debated, often with rigor, candor and good humor, but sometime also with aggressive and well-placed direct questioning by members and senators who had been well briefed by extremely competent and knowledgeable committee and personal staffs. The chairman and ranking members of these committees were hugely powerful. The US Navy therefore had constant opportunities to state its case for resources, based on thoroughly staffed congressional presentations. The staff of the Chief of Naval Operations has its own Congressional Liaison Staff that can legitimately interface with congressional committees and influence the defense debate and the case for programs, manpower, ships, submarines, aircraft, weapons, and key operations and maintenance (O&M) funding.

Another element in this process is the industrial–naval relationship—the contractors who seek naval business at every level of production and service. These contractors, their lobbyists, and the very congressmen and senators in whose districts and states they reside and run their businesses, have a close interwoven relationship to pursue those programs in which there are crucial employment and other interests. The corresponding Appropriations Committees of record on both sides of the Congress control the purse strings for naval funding—the HASC and the SASC may authorize but only the Defense Appropriations Sub Committee of the House and Senate Appropriations Committees can legally appropriate funding. These committees are all powerful, sounding at one level the bell of success for a program or conversely ringing the death knell of a failed program by ending appropriations. The ability of the US Navy to constitutionally influence this process is well defined, well understood, and practiced with great expertise. Senior flag officer success in part rests on the ability to perform on Capitol Hill. Three- and four-star officers have their days on the Hill, often with the Secretary of the Navy sitting there between the Chief of Naval Operations and the Commandant of the Marine Corps. The Royal Navy has no such privileged constitutional process to make its case in parliament and seek funding by direct influence.

Culture and relationships run deep, and often silently, as factors in US Navy and congressional relationships. Many members of Congress have served in the US Navy, several with great distinction, notably the late John McCain, who represented Arizona, and Senator John Warner of Virginia were distinguished Navy veterans. There are countless others. Many members of Congress have served on both sides of the Potomac, in the Pentagon and on the Hill. As a result they not only understand the process, they had predisposed loyalties and views on what is what and how things should be done. Their personal loyalties to the US Navy were ingrained and they understood the Navy's strategic arguments. Their staffs would fill in any gaps in technical knowledge and work with the uniformed Navy to obtain briefings and documentation from the staff of the Chief of Naval Operations. There has always been in the post-World War II era a healthy, dynamic and ever changing political–military dialogue between the executive and legislative branches of government. The system in the UK is very different indeed and does not serve the interests of the Royal Navy well in an era of defense cuts.

Nothing is perhaps more representative of the above fundamental political–military differences between the environments in which the Royal Navy and the US Navy have to do business than in the very nature of their top political leadership and their constitutional positions. In the United States several presidents have prior experience in the Congress—they have seen the other side of government from a different perspective. President Roosevelt had been an Assistant Secretary of the US Navy earlier in his career, just as Prime Minister Churchill had twice been First Lord of the Admiralty. Several post-World War II presidents have been US Navy veterans. Presidents Kennedy, Johnson, Nixon, Ford, Carter, and G. H. W. Bush were all distinguished US Navy veterans. Several were highly decorated with extraordinarily commendable war records. They all understood the Navy: how it works, what the Navy does and why, and the strategic significance of sea power. By contrast, only one British Prime Minister since World War II has served in the Royal Navy: Prime Minister James Callaghan (1976–1979) who served in World War II from 1942 to the war's end. His father had been a Royal Navy Chief Petty Officer. Prime Minister Callaghan joined the Royal Naval Volunteer Reserve (RNVR) as an able seaman, completing the war as a lieutenant, RNVR, with very creditable service. However, the UK top leadership has enjoyed nothing like the deep personal knowledge and experience of these US presidents, several of whom experienced intense combat operations. This factor makes a significant difference when the US Commander-in-Chief faces difficult decisions and choices—that they know the face of battle and the consequences of their decisions. Moreover, regarding the equally critical aspect of budgetary allocations and priorities, a Navy President was likely to understand and respect what and why the Navy was asking for in the annual budget cycle. In the spring of 1982 Admirals Lewin and Leech had to provide Prime Minister Thatcher with a naval primer overnight, following the Argentinean invasion of the Falkland Islands. She had zero prior knowledge, but most fortunately she was a very quick study and under the most expert guidance of these two fine World War II veterans grasped the plans they laid before her. Twenty years earlier, in 1962, at the time of the Cuban Missile Crisis President John Kennedy needed no such instruction in the use of naval power to thwart Soviet intentions and operations.

The Strategic Impact of Change

The changes in the US and UK were quite monumental compared to the status quo of World War II. The US Navy came out of the major changes of 1947 with a consistent and enduring ability to make its case directly to the Congress and argue for the resources required. The Royal Navy, by contrast, became politically constrained and placed in the position of a second cousin, once removed—a member of the family, but with no real direct standing with, or access to, the family leadership. One key observation needs to be made: inimical to and ingrained in the US system in which the US Navy operates is the fundamental backbone of the US Constitution and the very culture and modus operandi of government that enables the US Navy to work through bureaucratic and organizational change. The Royal Navy enjoyed no such bounteous privileges in the UK. Change in the UK, along the lines described above, stymied a service that was used to being not just the senior service but operating in an environment and ways where its case could be both constantly heard and understood. Centralization, jointness, and political concentration of power in a highly civilianized bureaucracy and process-oriented Ministry of Defence and Central Defence Staff, rung the death knell of a tradition-bound Royal Navy that had enjoyed centuries of political access.

The Five Eyes faced the strategic challenges together. In 1962 the US faced its greatest challenge since World War II and the Korean War, the Cuban Missile

Crisis. This was followed in 1963 with the assassination of President Kennedy and the escalation of the Vietnam War during the presidency of his successor, Lyndon Johnson. As a huge backdrop to these events the Cold War intensified and US–Soviet rivalries played out across the globe, not least in the oceans of the world, where the US Navy and the Royal Navy faced the Soviet and Warsaw Pact navies on a daily basis. Allies and client states of both the US and the Soviet Union became part of this great game until the collapse of the USSR. The June War of 1967 between Israel and the Arab nations of Egypt, Syria and Jordan saw a crisis erupt that the Secretary of State at the time, Dean Rusk, regarded as more threatening than the Cuban Missile Crisis. By the end of the decade the European situation deteriorated—the Central Front that separated Western Europe from the Warsaw Pact and NATO's FEBA (Forward Edge of the Battle Area) was an area of heavy military presence, constant exercises, and readiness events. Within the NATO military structure, the Supreme Allied Commander Europe (SACEUR) was always an American four-star general who was the guardian of retaliatory plans that relied on an underlying nuclear deterrence posture of Mutual Assured Destruction (MAD). The latter environment created a military balance on both sides of the Iron Curtain that made no sense in terms of a conventional invasion of Western Europe because of the avowed policy of NATO to have to respond with nuclear weapons if the FEBA collapsed and the Red Army made inroads into Western Europe. The MAD doctrine was, therefore, well named. When the Soviets occupied Czechoslovakia in 1968 after an intense period of protests by the Czech leader, Dubcek, it was transparently clear that NATO could offer no support to the tragic situation in Prague, given the military balance and overwhelming threat of escalation.

The one domain where the Soviet Union and the West could play out the intense competition for global influence and the strength of either communism or democracy was at sea, and in those regions where maritime access provided a way into countries that were ripe for economic and ideological penetration. With regard to the Soviet Union, this process of influence by the growing Soviet Navy became characterized as Soviet Naval Diplomacy. It was on the great oceans of the world that the Cold War was truly fought.

NATO responded with the creation of a significant naval command structure, centered on the Headquarters of the Supreme Allied Commander Atlantic (SACLANT), in Norfolk, Virginia, with a US Navy four-star Admiral always in the lead position. Within this structure the strength and power of the US Navy was critical, embodied in the numbered fleets—the US Second Fleet in the Atlantic and the US Sixth Fleet in the Mediterranean. The US Third and Seventh Fleets in the Pacific were important as countervailing forces to Soviet naval power in the Pacific, but geography and other geopolitical factors played against the growth of the Soviet Navy in the Pacific comparable to developments with the Soviet Northern Fleet based on the Kola Peninsula, and the Soviet Fifth Escadra based in the Black Sea. The growth and operational activities of the Soviet Northern Fleet and its associated Warsaw Pact allies, together with the roles and missions of the Soviet Baltic Fleet based in Leningrad (St. Petersburg today) challenged NATO in a sea war that was as real as any conflict could be short of exchanging fire in open hostilities. The strategic underpinnings of this maritime conflict that endured for the life of the Soviet Union are undoubtedly, with the benefit of hindsight and analysis, far more significant than the land situation in central Europe because the Soviets had real opportunities outside a nuclear umbrella strategy to expand, influence and undermine the West. It was the task of the US Navy and its allies to prevent this from happening. The strategy to achieve all this was complex, challenging, evolving, and highly technical.

***

The UK experienced a decade long identity crisis in the 1960s as decolonization reached a peak and then subsided with a withdrawal from what was termed an "East of Suez" policy. The military strategy that supported this policy was based primarily on a naval strategy of forward-deployed presence and basing that aimed to support the UK's allies and British economic interests east of Suez by naval forces—surface, air, subsurface and amphibious. The UK's confrontation with Indonesia in the 1960s in support of its former colony, Malaya (now Malaysia), was hugely significant—it demonstrated that naval and marine forces, together with special operations forces (the Special Air Service and the Royal Marines' Special Boat Service) could contain in the jungles and rivers of Borneo (East Malaysia) inroads by Indonesian regular and paramilitary forces. The Royal Navy and the Royal Marines worked together in fighting a war reminiscent of operations of the British Fourteenth Army in the jungle war against Japan and the post-World War II operations against communist insurgency in Malaya. The Borneo campaign was in retrospect an example of how to conduct a jungle war against insurgent forces. British textbooks on such campaigns have been written with first-hand experience in Kenya with the Mau, Cyprus with EOKA and in the Middle East in the region today that composes the United Arab Emirates, the Yemen and Aden, Muscat and Oman.

The planned withdrawal of the British Far East Fleet, the reduction and later closure of the major facilities at the Singapore and Hong Kong naval bases signaled not just the demise of empire but a shift in strategic thinking. The latter was no longer maritime and global. The policies of the Wilson government and Defence Secretary Healey were Europe focused and equated to a "maritime withdrawal" without a broad and deep analysis of the implication of no longer being a global maritime power. The UK was, in fairness, resource driven and after several economic crises and devaluations of the pound the UK was not in an economic position to support three services in global deployments. Foreign policy based on decolonization indicated a withdrawal to Europe and a concentration on the Central Front, the

North Atlantic sea lines of communication and the creation and maintenance of an independent nuclear deterrent.

The political–military reorganization analyzed earlier played to a highly bureaucratized process driven view of running defense in the UK. Words that were significantly absent in the 1960s in the Ministry of Defence were "Grand Strategy." The case for a maritime strategy based on understood and extraordinarily well-documented and analyzed concepts of maritime power were lost in a turmoil of NATO-driven and nuclear jargon that became a huge bureaucratic compromise. The latter was no more evident in the annual defense budget exercise where the pie was cut to satisfy the needs of the three services within an environment that was driven by a European-centric view, not a global maritime view. The psychology of this issue is as important perhaps as the economic realities that faced the UK in the 1960s. In retrospect what happened was the balancing of an over simplified equation: Withdrawal from empire equaled withdrawal from a global maritime presence. Within this equation lay the seeds of strategic discontinuity in the UK for decades. The UK in essence forgot its heritage as a maritime power, not based on colonization, but on one very simple fact—trade. The UK has always been a maritime trading nation since the time of the first explorations. In order to survive the UK must not just trade, it has to use the sea to do business. The daily prayer in many British schools for, "Those who go down to the sea in ships and do their business in Great Waters," was not a patriotic curiosity. It was a real and abiding reflection on one very simple economic fact that Britain depended on the sea to survive, first as an agricultural and later as an industrial nation. Furthermore, the Royal Navy had not just been the protector of these trading, and indeed survival interests, it had been the main military instrument for British foreign policy by forward-deployed presence and operations to support political-economic interests.

The UK's involvement in major land campaigns had historically been with "Citizen Armies," not large, regular, and permanently maintained armies. The latter was true of Henry the Fifth's Army at Agincourt, with John Churchill, later Duke of Marlborough, at the battle of Blenheim, with Sir Arthur Wellesley, later Duke of Wellington, in the Peninsular War during the Napoleonic era, just as it was true of General Bernard Montgomery's Eighth Army at El Alamein or General William Slim's Fourteenth Army at Kohima—these were citizen armies recruited and trained for the duration of conflict by a much smaller cadre of peacetime professionals. The Royal Navy was different—it was a large and permanent body of highly trained and experienced professional officers and men—sailors in the widest sense. When Denis Healey made the monumental decision not to replace the Royal Navy carrier fleet he was, in essence, disavowing centuries of well-conceived and executed British maritime strategy. It was indeed ironic that in the 1960s while distinguished academics like Professor Bryan Ranft were teaching maritime strategy and naval history at the

Royal Naval College Greenwich in the War and Staff Colleges, the Central Staffs of the Ministry of Defence were systematically disestablishing centuries of successful maritime strategy.

By contrast, the US Navy went in a diametrically opposed direction compared with the UK in the 1960s, in spite of the political–military organizational changes. The Cuban Missile Crisis in 1962 showed how a US President, who had served in the Navy during World War II, could use naval power to avert a national crisis. The blockade of Soviet naval incursions into Cuba conveying a panoply of nuclear missile capabilities was stopped short by diplomacy underscored by heavy duty naval power—the power and strength of the US Navy to stop Soviet operations at sea in their tracks. Without the perception and physical reality of that power, backed by the avowed intent of the US President to use that power if need be, the outcome would undoubtedly have been very different. Furthermore, President Kennedy was able to offset the somewhat frightening countervailing arguments of his military staff, such as General Curtis Lemay of the United States Air Force, by the use of naval power. As a naval man he kept his hands firmly on the tiller and without the power of the US Fleet he may never have been able to bring Premier Khrushchev to the negotiating table and keep at bay the extreme hawks within his own military establishment. The use of nuclear weapons in 1962 by the US may seem in retrospect not just outrageous, but somewhat unbelievable, but the fact is, it was an option, and there were advocates given certain circumstances moving out of control against US interests. President Kennedy remained cool, calm, and collected, in spite of intense pressures, and used his Navy with great skill.

The Cuban Missile Crisis underscores the way ahead for the use of US Naval strategy in the 1960s. Resources were never a serious issue. The Navy received what it wanted for its well-documented requirements in support of a well-articulated maritime strategy. In addition to actual operations, and certainly US Navy combat operations in the Vietnam War and the Royal Navy in East Malaysia, there were some aspects that were not given analytical prominence at the time and now have significance for contemporary events and certainly future naval operations.

The Significance of Overseas Bases

Underpinning British naval strategy over the centuries was the need to provide overseas basing facilities. The Royal Navy historically had a chain of naval bases and other related facilities such as wireless stations, and in the days of steam, coaling stations. Their names reel off the tongue without effort—Hong Kong, Singapore, Gan in the Maldives, Trincomalee in Ceylon (Sri Lanka), Masirah near the entrance to the Persian Gulf, Aden, Bahrain, Diego Garcia, Mombasa, Mauritius, Simonstown, Gibraltar, Malta, Bermuda, bases on Canada's eastern seaboard, a whole group of West Indies facilities, and the Falkland Islands (Port Stanley) in the South Atlantic.

This was an impressive logistics chain that spanned the globe and included reciprocity with Australia and New Zealand for port access. Without fixed bases and the availability of refueling, victualing, and maintenance facilities a navy faces serious problems unless it uses nuclear power and it has a large fleet replenishment at sea capability that can be sustained in a trans-oceanic environment without recourse to land bases. Crews need rest and recreation and port visits have always played a major role in diplomatic and trade relations. Access to port facilities on a guaranteed and regular basis is a must for a global navy. Such facilities, or lack thereof, will dramatically affect transit time, time on station, rearming, and crew morale. These are critical non-trivial factors. Even a nuclear-powered attack submarine transiting from Pearl Harbor to the South China Sea has to spend a long time in transit and although its nuclear reactor will provide non-stop fuel, electricity, and fresh air and water, the crew's stamina is a major factor as are factors such as rearming in the event of hostilities, and the need to conduct routine and emergency maintenance on electronic and mechanical systems.

The Cuban Missile Crisis. (United States. Department of Defense. Department of Defense Cuban Missile Crisis Briefing Materials. John F. Kennedy Presidential Library and Museum, Boston)

When the UK withdrew primarily to the North Atlantic with occasional forays to other parts it sadly disengaged from its historic bases without due diligence to what the future may hold. Decolonization and independence for those countries where these bases existed did not preclude future usage—however, once the knots were cut it would become increasingly difficult to re-engage and equally important for a major ally such as the United States to engage in lieu. However, time and international realignments have favored the US. Outside the NATO theater the US Navy has established good relations in places such as Singapore and Bahrain, taking up the slack from the Royal Navy. The UK wisely granted base rights to the US in Diego Garcia, a pivotal Indian Ocean location. While Naples in Italy and Rota in Spain remain active the British closure of Malta has not affected US operations in the Mediterranean, though there were early fears that potential belligerents may seek access, none of which has amounted to date to anything significant. Base relations become really important in forging navy alliances based on a strategy of mutual cooperation—this was never so more true than during the Cold War with North European and Mediterranean port visits and in 2020 the burgeoning relations in Asia between the US Navy and the Royal Malaysian Navy, Singapore Navy, Indonesian Navy, the Philippines, Vietnam, Thailand, South Korea, and Japan all speak to one end—that underpinning joint operations and exercises are port visits and the facilities that go with port visits. The latter are the cement in the building blocks of naval cooperation in Asia today.

Rearming, refueling, and victualing at sea are major seamanship skills—they are acquired by practice and having the best technology to meet the needs of challenging and dangerous environmental conditions. The US Navy and Royal Navy are past masters of these skills. Both navies developed substantial fleet replenishment capabilities: indeed, a navy within a navy without which the fighting navies would not have been able to function. Even nuclear-powered aircraft carriers need to refuel for aviation gas, rearm with munitions, and resupply. Without the "Fleet Train" as the British dubbed the Royal Fleet Auxiliary (the replenishment ships) the navies could not have successfully executed the Cold War in its entirety. Conversely the Soviet Union was at an enormous disadvantage because of its slowness in developing and mastering the skills and technology associated with at sea replenishment. The great work of the American Marvin Miller (1923–2009) at the US Naval Station, Port Hueneme, California in leading the development of advanced underway replenishment systems and technologies was never equaled by the Soviet Navy.

Strategic technology exchange and intelligence cooperation and sharing between the Five Eyes navies became third and fourth critical dimensions in the 1960s. Suffice to say here that the impact of both factors in the 1960s did, at the most critically important levels of daily operations and long term acquisitions, save the Royal Navy in particular from sliding down a slippery slope of retrenchment after the policy of withdrawal started to hit.

The UK–US Nuclear Submarine Agreement

The Nassau Agreement was a treaty negotiated by President Kennedy and Prime Minister Macmillan, signed December 22, 1962. This agreement provided the UK with the Polaris ballistic missile capability, with British warheads, and the US Navy with a long-term lease arrangement for a US submarine base at Holy Loch in Scotland. The meeting in the Bahamas also meant the end of the US AGM-48 Skybolt nuclear missile program that the Royal Air Force planned to acquire as a result of an earlier agreement between Prime Minister Macmillan and President Eisenhower. The Royal Air Force maintained a tactical nuclear capability with their V-bomber force and later with the Tornado aircraft. However, the Royal Navy was now the lead service for maintaining an independent deterrent. This was in spite of earlier misgivings by senior Americans such as Robert McNamara and Dean Acheson. They had questioned the wisdom of the US enabling the UK to have a viable deterrent, after the failures of the UK Blue Steel standoff missile system, and UK Blue Streak intermediate-range ballistic missile, and technical difficulties experienced with the US AGM-48 Skybolt system that the UK planned to purchase.

As the Cold War heated up the two navies became closer and closer in collecting, analyzing, and sharing intelligence and providing information for not just operational use but for the equally critical task of staying ahead of the technological curve and ensuring that the acquisition process included the very latest high-level threat inputs. The intelligence staffs of both navies created in the 1960s a bedrock of highly classified cooperation at all levels of the intelligence space. Nowhere was this more evident than in the underwater domain.

Five Eyes intelligence sharing went hand-in-glove with technology exchange. The Royal Navy was the recipient of enormous largesse by the US government and especially the nuclear navy created by Admiral Hyman B. Rickover—the acquisition of nuclear submarine technology, which augured the beginning of the longest UK–US industrial relationship, between the Electric Boat Division of General Dynamics at Groton, Connecticut and Vickers Shipbuilding and Engineering at Barrow-in-Furness, UK (later acquired by British Aerospace). Underscoring this exchange between the US to the UK was the extremely sensitive exchange of acoustic intelligence (ACINT) and other Special Intelligence (SI) collected and exchanged between all Five Eyes navies.

***

In spite of all the changes in the UK and US defense organizations and all the turmoil of the UK withdrawal from east of Suez the US Navy and the Royal Navy remained tightly bound between themselves and the other three nations' navies. This was a unique institutional relationship, within five separate institutions, indeed a state within five states, built not just on agreements and high-level security arrangements, but equally on personal relationships, trust, and the abiding connectivity brought by at sea operations, and facing a common threat on a daily basis. Such a unique relationship between the Five Eyes navies has never been enjoyed by other institutions, nor within the much wider context of the North Atlantic Treaty Organization and the other major international agreements, treaties, and alignments that each of the Five Eyes nations have.

It becomes clear why the Five Eyes remained a unique club. The nature of their intelligence collection and exchange defines the key reasons. But it still goes beyond these, to the essence of mobile, forward-deployed intelligence collection assets, with persistent presence, covert and clandestine. Only these five nations through their major gatherings, and continuous daily cooperation and personnel exchanges know the true extent of their involvement with one another. The various legal agreements and more formal diplomatic intelligence exchanges are the outward manifestations of formal relationships, but the heart and soul of the Five Eyes resides in the historic abiding personnel relationships developed over the past 79 years since Winston Churchill and Franklin Roosevelt shook hands on board HMS *Prince of Wales* in August 1941. The changes and indeed upheavals described have been surmounted by the individuals from each member nation who have kept the relationship not just alive but thriving. This is where I fitted into this great legacy, and my involvement across each of the UK intelligence agencies and those of the other Five Eyes nations at the height of the Cold War until my permanent return to the United States in December 1983.

Action against the Soviet Union, its Allies and Surrogates

During the period up to late 1983 I worked across multiple domains and programs of British and US intelligence and the UK's special relations with Canada, Australia, and New Zealand. A very real insidious threat was posed by the Soviet Union to the very heart of the UK's security and overall wellbeing. I joined initially a group that had two related missions, both interconnected organizationally but separate in terms of leadership and reporting chains. However, the latter were conjoined ultimately in the Joint Intelligence Committee (JIC) in the UK's Cabinet Office. There was natural synergism between the threats posed by the Soviet Union, its Warsaw Pact allies, and their surrogates. One involved the non-commercial use of Soviet and Warsaw Pact merchant ships and those of other flags of convenience and surrogates that the two Soviet intelligence agencies, the KGB and the GRU, used to mask their activities.

The other was the threat posed by the deeply buried KGB agents and highly trained "Spetsnaz" (Special Purpose Forces or Units) that were controlled by the main military intelligence service, the GRU. Both entities infiltrated personnel into the UK, and other NATO countries, not with the avowed intent of executing classical espionage (subverting British citizens in key sensitive positions to spy for the Soviet Union and collecting technical and scientific intelligence against UK targets) but the much more insidious role of preparing for the worst-case scenario of a major war between the Soviet Union and the Warsaw Pact and the UK and NATO. These deeply buried personnel were trained to be British lookalikes. They had already mastered the language, had studied the culture and the location from which they would live and operate as apparent British citizens. In the pre-digital encryption era such people could successfully use fake passports and other identification without what today would be most likely instant detection of false documents. They were funded clandestinely and could be quickly extracted if things went wrong. Their missions were directed at the heart of the UK's security and survival in the cataclysmic event of a major war, including: the assassination of key political and military leaders; the disruption and destruction of key communications facilities; the sabotage of military installations, and also the penetration and destruction of the UK's national deterrent communications system. The latter was particularly crucial in terms of the maintenance of the UK's deterrent and the infrastructure that supported the UK SSBN force of four submarines.

Readers will appreciate the sensitivity of this task, to detect, locate, disrupt, apprehend, and or deceive and manage this most worrisome threat. Our team was small and directly linked to a Task Force within the Special Branch of Scotland Yard, that as a law enforcement authority had the legal powers to apprehend those persons whom we assessed as particularly worthy of arrest rather that permitting them to go on conducting surveillance and intelligence collection at great cost to UK national security. During my two years plus working both operationally in the field and doing data analytics on the threat I became concerned with the absence of imaginative strategies and tactics to both contain and, most important from my perspective, subvert this vicious threat. I had been trained by the best of the best from World War II who created and managed the "Double Cross" system against Adolf Hitler and his whole Nazi apparatus. My recommendation was to reinvent this in a new and innovative guise, using many of the extremely clever and covert means at our disposal. I worked side-by-side in the field with an extremely capable and highly intelligent Detective Chief Superintendent from Scotland Yard. We shared many issues and how to address them in the best interests of national security. He and his very small team liked my approach. However, our civilian bureaucratic leadership was risk averse. The reason my immediate working colleagues and I agreed this was not in fact real technical and operational risk, that Sir John Masterman and his great people knew all about that in World War II, but more protection of their own upwardly mobile career prospects in case something may go wrong for which they may be accountable. I found this very sad and somewhat disenchanting.

I recall a late night in the London facility from which I operated, asking my civil service boss for authority to proceed early next day on a critically timed operation against the threat. His response was simply bureaucratic, wanting to pass responsibility most likely to the minister in question. I naturally concurred, but privately realized that no such approval would be sought. The Soviet Union continued unabated to collect most sensitive intelligence against certain UK targets. Over coffee my Scotland Yard counterpart and I mused, what if the Prime Minister Margaret Thatcher was fully briefed on the fact that she was a major target for assassination in the event of conflict, would she not want clever, covert, and extremely well-managed and executed clandestine action to undermine, control, and manage the threat? We both concurred, but neither of us had access at the right level without blundering into a solid bureaucratic brick wall, reminiscent of that old saying, "What happens when an unstoppable force meets an unmovable object?" As a result, the Soviets got away with a lot. There is a significant lesson to be learned from this in the contemporary world. Vladimir Putin, the current Russian leader, will use all means to continue to undermine the great Western democracies, just as did the Soviet Union did when I was doing my part to counter their operations. Nothing has changed. The one exception is the digital revolution, the internet, and the new means of penetration inside the World Wide Web beside the classical methods referenced above. Good counterintelligence and new and innovative tools and operations are required. However, the old ways are still most relevant and equally valuable operationally. We have to teach the new generation the old tricks, lost in the understandable generation change and institutional memory loss.

***

As discussed earlier, the Soviets employed merchant ships in various guises for both insertion and retrieval of covert personnel, all under the guise of merchant ship personnel. Controlling arrivals and departures, and checking on personnel, was not an easy task in a non-digital database era. Many ships' crew members were of non-Soviet nationality, another confusing factor, and ideal for covert insertion using false data and passports. Are the same persons that go ashore in say Tilbury or Hull the same people who return on board before sailing? Added to the personnel issue was the technical intelligence collection threat. Soviet, Warsaw Pact, flags of convenience, and surrogate merchant ships entering the UK 12-mile limit and ports, or transiting exercising the internationally accepted right of innocent passage, were a most serious threat. These ships were often equipped with special communications intercept capabilities as well as ELINT collection devices, plus an assortment of other equipment that we associated with underwater operations. They were particularly threatening when their positioning was coordinated with UK and allied naval ship and submarine movements, particularly in the egress or departure stage when, for example, submarines would be on the surface for navigation, safety, and water depth reasons. Such vessels were often berthed in ports, ostensibly unloading and loading cargo, closely juxtaposed to naval facilities and naval vessels.

We knew that these Soviet clandestine assets were part of the Soviet Ocean Surveillance System, collecting technical intelligence while also providing real-time operational intelligence on ship and submarine movements. To counter such operations was a key role for the group and me. Our worst concern was that such vessels could provide intelligence that could be fed to Soviet submarines deployed off shore and along the likely tracks of deploying UK and US ships and submarines that had to stay within the confines of restricted depths and channels, usually on the surface, before reaching safe diving positions. We were concerned that trailing operations would then ensue. To offset these contingencies, we worked up several ways to counter these threats. We likely learned as much, if not a lot more, about them as they could garner about us. EMCON (emission control) is always a safe tactic to avoid communications and ELINT intercepts and of course we rapidly learned who were the rogue ships and could adapt accordingly to their required notice of arrival and departure. Like many operations that the KGB and the GRU executed during the Cold War they were cleverly conceived, but they were never quite good enough and of course allowing them to believe that they were getting away with penetrating UK waters and ports by clandestine means was itself a valuable ploy.

In a much wider context than the violation of UK sovereignty by clandestine means we were able to learn a tremendous amount about how the non-commercial use of their merchant fleets played globally, their dispositions, movements, technical capabilities, and covert insertion efforts. All this intelligence was invaluable in the worst-case scenarios of knowing which assets would need to be removed from the scene in the event of hostilities. Fortunately, with the benefit of hindsight we know reliably that we countered these diverse threats by good intelligence collection and operations, while staying under the countersurveillance of both the KGB and the GRU.

Today Vladimir Putin's FSB (the KGB successor organization) and the GRU still contrive to take reprisals on Russian defectors and those who have spied for the West. Inserting assassination personnel into the UK has occurred, and there are well-recorded media events of a particularly insidious nature, including the use of chemical and biological agents. There is still therefore an urgent extant requirement to keep track of all Russian and their surrogates' entries into the UK and allied nations by both covert and open means. A Russian citizen stepping off a flight from Moscow with a legitimate passport and right of entry may be just as much a threat as a covert entry via a visiting Russian or surrogate merchant ship to a British port. Databases, video screening, biometrics, discreet fingerprinting, and the use of CCTV and other TTL devices (tagging, tracking, and locating) make life more difficult for the clandestine insertion of assassins, classical espionage agents, or other nefarious personnel that want cover and deception while on UK soil and the territory of UK allies and friendly nations with whom there is intelligence reciprocity. Terrorist and other clandestine atrocities have tended to pale in recent years compared with internal threats from, for example, ultra-right wing groups and individuals, together with misguided and often psychopathic killers executing mass shootings, often as part of revenge killings of religious groups and minorities. Hate crimes have become as prevalent, if not more so, than classical covert operations by foreign intelligence services and their surrogates.

I returned to the United States in late 1983, as the United States became increasingly aware under President Ronald Reagan's leadership of the diverse threats posed by the Soviet Union and the need to have plans and operations to counter them. Before this happened, I transferred from front-line field work to leading several special program areas of a very different nature and over the next three years I became immersed in both collection and analysis of Soviet strategic threats.

Margaret Thatcher's Largest Investment and Intelligence Inputs

In addition to day-to-day collection and analysis of Soviet naval capabilities, operations, building plans, and research and development programs, one aspect dominated the scene when I joined, in the late 1970s, a special scientific and technical intelligence group under the leadership of one of the UK's top government scientists, Nigel Hughes, who had been immersed for many years in the intelligence process and knew the Whitehall scene and its politics better than most. I was designated Head of Special Programs.

In 1979 Margaret Thatcher had been elected Prime Minister and one of her first tasks in national security was to determine the future of the national deterrent, in the shape of the four Royal Navy ballistic missile firing submarines (SSBNs). It was time critical that the plans and finances for the current boats be laid if it was determined that this was the best way for the UK to proceed, to replace the aging Resolution Class SSBNs (HMS *Resolution, Repulse, Renown*, and *Revenge*, built between 1964 and 1968, armed with Polaris A-3 missiles) with what would be designated the *Vanguard*-class (introduced to the Fleet first in 1994 with the Trident missile system—HMS *Vanguard, Victorious, Vigilant*, and *Vengeance*, and built between 1986 and 1999 at Barrow-in-Furness by Vickers Shipbuilding and Engineering, subsequently owned by BAe Systems). The plan was to decommission the Royal Air Force's nuclear capability, leaving the four *Vanguard*-class submarines the sole platforms for the UK's nuclear deterrent. This occurred in 1998 when the Royal Air Force decommissioned its WE.177 free-fall thermonuclear weapons. The UK is planning currently to replace the *Vanguard*-class in parallel with the United States replacement of its *Ohio*-class SSBN with the *Columbia*-class. Both these building programs will run into the early 2030s, providing both nations with outstanding submarines. Returning to 1979, Prime Minister Thatcher wanted to be one hundred per cent sure of making the right decision. This devolved naturally to the intelligence community and specifically to the Scientific and Technical Intelligence specialists. My earlier deep background in Soviet capabilities made me a good candidate to be in the group that would provide the intelligence leadership.

At the forefront of everyone's mind were not just current Soviet capabilities but where they may go in the future and during the life of the UK's largest single defense and security investment ever. The key question was survivability. Could these submarines over the 30-plus years from fleet introduction remain invulnerable when on patrol? The UK has at least one boat permanently on patrol with at least one boat egressing to replace an on station boat (for non-submariners, submarines are called "boats," not ships), so that a force of four boats can maintain a permanent deterrent capability, allowing for repairs and maintenance.

Accurate projection of Soviet capabilities was therefore essential to ensure that these four highly expensive platforms could never be detected, trailed, and potentially disabled or worst case destroyed while on a war footing patrol. Peacetime compromise of their non detectability would therefore jeopardize their deterrent value. The sources and methods discussed earlier were the sum total of the assets available to us, and collectively they were prodigious. The bottom line was that the UK was in general overall agreement with US intelligence—we agreed that the Soviets were behind the curve in noise-quieting, narrow-band signal processing, and in the rarefied domains of acoustic intelligence and passive sonar—but there were exceptions—such as on projections of Soviet capabilities—and these were non trivial.

The Impact of the US Walker Spy Ring

What the US did not know was that the Walker spy ring was operating for the Soviet Union from 1968 to 1985. After 1985 the US realized the magnitude of what had been given to the Soviet Union and led to reassessment of earlier National Intelligence Estimates (NIEs). The Walkers gave away valuable intelligence and I believe led key parts of US intelligence into complacency during the 1970s. In meetings with my opposite numbers in Washington during the 1970s and early 1980s it was difficult to convince them otherwise, notwithstanding the content one of our significant British intelligence reports that I led that was very limited in distribution because of its sensitivity, with more codewords that even to this day I cannot fully recollect. While working with our opposite numbers in the United States we followed some unwritten but very important guidelines regarding what the British perceived as organizational problems arising from the often-competing rivalries between the many US agencies. For example, there was a very clear dysfunctional relationship at times, not always, between the CIA and US Naval Intelligence. The latter did not share its highly classified and often extremely sensitively collected data, with the Agency.

I was often put in the embarrassing position by people at CIA Headquarters of being asked about data that they knew from sources was only shared between

US Naval Intelligence and the type of organization for which I was responsible in London. One was constantly having to be diplomatically tactful while both honoring the special clearances and data and at the same time working positively with those echelons of the CIA that were not only extremely competent and dependable but also came up with very high quality analysis. It was difficult, but surmountable, particularly as the Agency did have a significant uniformed military presence. The US Navy was quite rightly very conscious to minimize the risk of compromise of invaluable intelligence collection operations and its output. From the UK's perspective we also found that the US National Intelligence Estimates (NIEs) were inaccurate because of their generalization to satisfy the disparate and sometimes conflicting assessments of the different US intelligence agencies. To some of us back in London the NIEs seemed like compromises, not reliable and definitive statements of Soviet capabilities, intentions, plans, and operations.

These aspects came to the fore when I briefed both the US Navy and the CIA on our concerns about alternative technologies that the Soviets were developing in order to narrow the gap in submarine capabilities, particularly strategic detection and tracking. For some time, the US Navy took a less than positive approach to the concerns that I and others from the UK presented in Washington. This was particularly true in the area of alternative anti-submarine warfare (ASW) detection technologies over and beyond traditional passive sonar detection, that the West dominated and had outstanding capabilities. Non-acoustic ASW became a critical issue. I led the UK in this domain and did my utmost to alert key authorities in the US of the growing investment and detailed programs that the Soviets were pursuing.

There was reluctance and for a while a certain amount of intransigence that did not sit well with key people in the CIA. What I understood after many visits and briefings in Washington DC was that the US Navy, and the dominance of the submarine force in particular, insisted on dealing directly with such issues very much under the cover of both deep security, keeping exposure to an absolute minimum. We in the UK greatly respected this position, and I can safely say that no UK intelligence person ever violated this US Navy mandate. The rivalry between the US Navy and the US Air Force over strategic capabilities (the B-52 and ground based missile capabilities of the US Air Force and the highly covert and undetectable capabilities of the US Navy's nuclear-powered ballistic missile force) was very much understood back in the UK. We never once strayed from our total unwavering loyalty to both the US Navy as a whole and the submarine force in particular. We stayed well clear of US politics in these matters.

However, we had to face facts. The Soviets were threatening us with programs that were not just the efforts of a power that could not meet the traditional passive sonar capabilities of the US and the UK, but were in fact, as far as my team was concerned in London, actually doing both. The Soviets were not only catching up in those domains that my American opposite numbers insisted were many years behind catching up, but in parallel they were pursuing new and innovative systems and technologies to steal potentially a very serious lead over the US and the UK. It was tough making this case in Washington in the highly secure vaults of the very tight and small community of people that mattered, and this was not the CIA, not the Defense Intelligence Agency, or the then still highly secret National Reconnaissance Office.

Back in the UK there was a moment in time when things changed dramatically with a special visit of key US personnel. I was in charge of the visit. Rather than hold the meeting in central London I arranged for a facility at the Royal Aircraft Establishment (RAE) at Farnborough in Hampshire where we could be secluded and unimpeded by day-to-day activities. I was very much involved as the Special Programs lead in my directorate in day-to-day Soviet and Warsaw Pact operations and the collection and analysis of the vital scientific and technical components, and I needed to be free of the daily intelligence process to spend a day listening to our American visitors. The US visitors were in agreement with our own assessments of where the Soviets were headed. This was a group from the National Security Agency at Fort Meade in Maryland. The key technical personal was not a Federal employee but a highly qualified PhD in physics from Princeton, Dr. Denis Holliday, with considerable experience in both the intelligence and science behind Soviet programs. He worked for a distinguished and relatively small company, by US defense and intelligence comparisons, called R&D Associates (RDA), that was headed by a well-known nuclear physicist, Dr. Albert Latter, headquartered in Marina del Rey in Los Angeles, California, with offices in Arlington, Virginia. RDA was composed of multiple US scientists that were highly connected to the US defense and intelligence establishment, such as Albert Wohlstetter (1913–1997), husband of Roberta Wohlstetter (1912–2007), who wrote the seminal work on the attack on Pearl Harbor, December 7, 1941, "Pearl Harbor: Warning and Decision." On November 7, 1985 both received the Presidential Medal of Freedom from President Reagan. RDA senior personnel sat on the PFIAB, the President's Foreign Intelligence Advisory Board, and were conversant with the latest and highly classified US intelligence. What came out of this crucial meeting was total concurrence on the significance of Soviet programs and the potential threat to UK–US national security, and in particular the maintenance of the inviolability of both countries' primary deterrent. We agreed a course of cooperation and technical exchange. However, there were sensitive political issues that we addressed, not least relating to US Naval Intelligence, with whom my group were joined not just at the hip, but were the lineal successors of the World War II special relationship forged by President Roosevelt and Prime Minister Winston Churchill. I was conscious that we, the British intelligence group, could not and would not step on the toes of our friends and colleagues in the US Office of Naval Intelligence. Diplomacy became the order of the day and as the months and years passed on this crucial subject, we steered a delicate course between total professionalism by sharing all our assessments with ONI while continuing to maintain discrete and critical connections with the NSA group. This was at a time in the late 1970s and early 1980s when the British assessments of the newly emerging submarine classes had proven correct. At the same time, in parallel to the highly sensitive technical intelligence work, I maintained close contact with James McConnell and his group who were making ground-breaking assessments of Soviet plans and intentions.

The upshot of this work that became deeply classified was a series of UK–US initiatives and programs. Then came not just a game changer for me at a personal and professional level but an invitation that was to change my whole life and my family, and why I wrote this book 37 years after emigrating to the United States. The work that we were doing was perceived as critical. The United States was initiating various programs and I received the invitation to leave the Royal Navy and my career and take my family to Washington to work on at least one program under the auspices of RDA. I discussed this with my leadership, and in particular Nigel Hughes, the Director of UK Scientific and Technical Intelligence, and the Director General of Intelligence, Vice Admiral Sir Roy Halliday. They blessed the invitation with enthusiasm and full support, including the transfer of my clearances to the embassy in Washington and to help in the transition from my Royal Navy career to a civilian role in the United States. All saw this as an opportunity to both enhance UK–US relations in several domains and for me to help forge special program relations with the US.

I retired from the Royal Navy after an exhaustive process on most favorable terms. With the full support of my mentors, superiors, and working friends and colleagues in the intelligence community and Royal Navy, my wife, three children and I boarded a British Airways flight to Washington DC shortly before Christmas 1983 and this was the beginning of a whole new chapter and life.

CHAPTER 4

The Special Relationship at its Best, 1983–2001

The next seven years from 1983 to 1990 were extraordinarily challenging, hectic, and demanding, with intense international travel. By the time the Berlin Wall came down and the Soviet Union imploded I had witnessed from my new vantage point in Washington DC a whole new world unbeknown to almost every British citizen that I knew. The latter included those diplomats in the British Embassy whose mission was to understand and report on American politics and maintain the special relationship. I was based in Wilson Boulevard, in Arlington, Virginia, conveniently situated on the south side of the Potomac River near to the Pentagon and a short distance up the George Washington Memorial Parkway to the CIA Headquarters in Langley, Virginia. I was so proud to be sworn in as an American citizen in the US District Court in Alexandria, Virginia, supported by the staff of Senator John Warner of Virginia, the legendary Chairman of the Senate Armed Services Committee.

In 1984, President Reagan was pursuing an aggressive posture regarding the Soviet Union and his Navy Secretary, John Lehman, was hard charging to create a 600-ship navy, that would challenge the Soviets in every corner of the globe. These were heady times, and the race was on in Washington to constrict, control, and undermine Soviet influence and expansionism. Within weeks of joining RDA I was on Capitol Hill meeting and briefing key members of the HASC (House Armed Services Committee), the HPSCI (House Permanent Select Committee on Intelligence) and their equivalent in the US Senate. This came about because of the urgent need to counter the Soviet Union. RDA was simply extraordinarily well placed and connected through the Pentagon and the national intelligence community to render the very best technical support to the Committees and their key staff. This was not lobbying in any shape or form but representing various Department of Defense and intelligence entities who wanted their own professionals supported by people such as my colleagues and I at RDA. It worked well, and I soon became immersed in the political–military–intelligence process using, until I became a US citizen, my Five Eyes and British Top Secret SCI (Special Compartmented Information) Clearances that were acceptable and were held by the British Embassy.

Success came when the UK and US governments took actions to combine their best and brightest in a new initiative. This endured until after the Cold War ended and the joint program enjoyed attention at the very highest levels of government. The details are still classified but suffice to say the UK–US team, of which I was one, produced exceptional results that both clarified the threats posed by the Soviet Union while taking actions to counter them. New and exciting science and modifications to established principles emerged from these years. What it also demonstrated to me was the World War II cultural aspects, where you did not need an army of people, or a plethora of contractors in the 1980s environment working key issues when a few very exceptional people, men and women, could solve problems that even the best of us could not address by conventional means and scientific approaches. This work took up a good part of my time well into the 1990s. However, I ran additional programs as a result of work and connections that I had from my time in the UK before I emigrated to the US.

I had very strong professional and personal contacts in South East and East Asia. My key contacts were in Malaysia. I brought those connections to the United States and under a US State Department Technical Assistance Agreement I became the "Technical Advisor" to the Sixth Chief Minister of Sabah in East Malaysia on the island of Borneo. In effect it was much more than this. I worked personally and directly with the legendary former Minister for Home Affairs (1973–1981) and then latterly the Foreign Minister of Malaysia (1981–1984), Tan Sri (Lord) Ghazali Shafie (1922–2010), an incredible man of great courage and distinction, and a member of the United Malays National Organization (UMNO). During World War II he was a key member of the clandestine resistance to the Japanese occupation. He once showed me where he personally executed, at the end of the war, a senior Japanese officer who had ordered the execution of all the adult males in a village for having harbored resistance fighters who had attacked Japanese units. They were all beheaded. He showed me the bridge where their heads were planted, and it was by that bridge that the Japanese war criminal met his maker. Tan Sri, as I always addressed him even when in very private settings, was a national hero, endearingly called "King Ghaz." We worked closely with Tan Sri Datuk (Sir) Seri Panglima Harris bin Mohd Salleh (born November 1930), the Sabah Chief Minister (1976–1985). As Chief Minister Datuk Harris, as he was commonly known and called, he ceded the island of Labuan off the coast of Sabah to the Federal government in Kuala Lumpur, making Labuan the second Federal territory in Malaysia. Datuk Harris was the President of the Sabah Berjaya Party.

That island became important for one key project, situated strategically in the South China Sea, with an excellent harbor, and shipbuilding and repair facilities. It had, for example, the very latest 7,000-tonne capacity syncrolift system in Victoria Harbor. We initiated a program in the mid-1980s to build submarines for the Royal Malaysian Navy. On the US side I had the assistance of an outstanding retired US

Navy Vice Admiral, Jerome King (1919–2008), a Yale graduate and World War II veteran, serving in the light cruisers USS *Trenton* and USS *Mobile*, and who had been the Commander of US Naval Forces in Vietnam, retiring in 1974 having been latterly the Deputy Chief of Naval Operations Surface Warfare and the J-3 (Operations) on the Joint Staff in the Pentagon. Jerry, as I always called him, was key in liaising with the US Navy while I worked with Tan Sri and the Federal government in Kuala Lumpur, where we had many meetings with Dr. Mahathir bin Mohamad (born July 1925), the Prime Minister from 1981–2003, and who returned to office in 2018. Dr. Mahathir is a highly capable man, having originally trained as a doctor (1946–1952) at what was the King Edward VII College of Medicine, now part of the National University of Singapore. The project saw completion in 2002 when Malaysia signed contracts for two French Scorpène-class submarines. It was a lengthy process, but success came in due course.

In parallel to this project I was involved in multiple other initiatives with Tan Sri in Indonesia, the Philippines, Thailand, Pakistan, Brunei, and in China. I traveled extensively and virtually all of the work that we covered is still either highly classified or sensitive. It was a magic time for me. I really understood Asia, Islam, and the geopolitics of the region that has become the economic powerhouse of the world. My multiple visits to Pakistan and the connections that I developed, enabled me to become both a special source in unraveling various key issues that faced the US President and the intelligence community.

While working in Asia the work that I had helped initiate in the United States in advanced strategic ASW technology sprang into life. The latter years of the Soviet Union brought more concerns and I was involved in the detailed work of starting a joint UK–US program. This became a major focus for a number of years, working directly for the Office of the Secretary of Defense and the Defense Advanced Research Projects Agency (DARPA), and key parts of the national intelligence community. I traveled extensively during this period and took pride in helping make UK–US relations harmonious, as the best and the brightest UK and US brains sought and found solutions to otherwise extractible physics and operational issues.

I had two short hiatuses after the Berlin Wall came down. I had an enriching time, both professionally and financially as the Director of Navy Marketing for Kaman Aerospace and then as a partner on Capitol Hill with retired US Congressman William L. Dickinson, who had been the Ranking Member of the House of Representatives Committee on Armed Services. We had a superb office on First Street close to the House and Senate office buildings and we worked hard to advise key companies on how they should invest resources in the best interests of US national security. We were not lobbyists and refused to do so for ethical and legal reasons. We rendered outstanding advice. Congressman Dickinson knew in detail the "Black Program" world, having been instrumental in initiating with the Department of Defense, and I had become knowledgeable both during my time in Washington in the 1970s and then throughout the 1980s. Our two key staff members had been active committee staff during the worst and height of the Cold War. Collectively we knew the threat and where all the programs were located, and what the future should hold in the best interests of the United States and allies, and particularly the United Kingdom.

After the demise of the Soviet Union and the end of the Cold War, between November 9, 1989, when the East Berlin Communist Party announced that as of midnight that day citizens of the German Democratic Republic (GDR) were free to cross East Germany's borders, and September 11, 2001, there were almost 12 years of relative international calm compared with the period since Hitler made his first aggressive moves in central Europe in the 1930s. German reunification took place on October 3, 1990. This was momentous in terms of the history of European conflict and the impact on and ramifications for the rest of the world. In the period leading up to the rise of Islamic extremism the US intelligence community and its allies in the Five Eyes continued business as usual.

The Importance of British and American Naval Intelligence in the Five Eyes

The two longest existing and persistent intelligence organizations of the Five Eyes community are the British Naval Intelligence Department (NID) formed in 1887 from the Foreign Intelligence Committee established in 1882, and the United States Office of Naval Intelligence (ONI), formed in 1882. Given the history of British and US naval intelligence from 1882 until post-World War II, it is clear that they were not just the dominant force in intelligence generally, they were, very clearly, the lead organizations. When MI6 was formed in the UK in 1909 its first head was Commander Mansfield Cumming (later Captain Sir Mansfield Cumming), Royal Navy, who ran MI6 until his death in 1923. He became known as "C" because he signed documents personally with just a simple "C," in green ink. This custom was followed by later directors of MI6, though some claim that "C" now stands for Chief. Ian Fleming in his James Bond novels called the head of MI6 "M," taking a leaf from Cumming's customary signature.

In the UK NID was formed in 1887, MI6 and MI5 were formed in 1909 and 1916 respectively, the Government Code and Cipher School was formed in 1919, which led to Bletchley Park at the beginning of World War II, followed by the creation of the Government Communications Headquarters (GCHQ) in June 1946. The British Special Operations Executive (SOE) was created in July 1940 and closed in January 1946. The British government created a centralized Joint Intelligence Committee (JIC) within the Cabinet Office in 1946, and in 1964 with the formation of the Ministry of Defence and the Central Defence Staff, the various service intelligence departments were integrated in the Defence Intelligence

Staff (DIS). In 2009 the latter was designated Defence Intelligence (DI). The UK government created a National Security Council (NSC) as a Cabinet Committee on May 12, 2010, overseeing all issue related to national security, intelligence coordination, and defense strategy. Included in the UK NSC's terms of reference were foreign policy, defense, cybersecurity, resilience, energy, and resource security. The Prime Minister chairs the British NSC.

In the United States the ONI (founded in 1882) has been subsumed into a US Navy N2/N6 organization, within the Office of the Chief of Naval Operations, and remains the oldest intelligence organization in the Unites States, with a three-star admiral commanding the organization. US Coast Guard Intelligence was formed in 1915, making this the second oldest intelligence organization in the United States, and again emphasizes the maritime aspects of US intelligence. US naval intelligence dominated communications intercept and code breaking until post World War II. The other entities' histories are modest in comparison.

The President of the United States is head of the US intelligence community, established by an Executive Order of President Ronald Reagan on December 4, 1981.[1] Under the President, the Office of the Director of National Intelligence (ODNI) directly oversees the Intelligence Community (IC). In addition to the naval intelligence component, this comprises: US Air Force Intelligence, created in 1948 and managed by the 25th Air Force; the US Army Intelligence and Security Command, created in 1977; the Central Intelligence Agency (CIA), created in 1947; the Defense Intelligence Agency, created in 1961; and the Department of Energy (DOE) Office of Intelligence and Counterintelligence, formed in 1977. The DOE is responsible for US nuclear weapons programs and manages the key US national laboratories and facilities such as Oak Ridge, Tennessee, responsible for nuclear weapon development and production.

The Department of Homeland Security Office of Intelligence and Analysis was created in 2007. However, the US Department of State Bureau of Intelligence and Research was formed in 1945, predating the CIA. Following the 9/11 attacks, in 2004 the US treasury created the Office of Terrorism and Financial Intelligence. The Drug Enforcement Agency (DEA) has an Office of National Security Intelligence, formed in 2006 within the US Department of Justice. The Federal Bureau of Investigation has historically not been involved in classical intelligence collection and operations, as a primary investigative law enforcement organization. However post 9/11, the Department of Justice formed an FBI Intelligence Branch in 2005 that recognized the changed world post 9/11 and the need for closer working relations with other US intelligence agencies such as the CIA and the National Security Agency. The creation of the National Counter Terrorism Center (NCTC) in 2003 grew from the urgent need to coordinate foreign and domestic intelligence in light of terrorist and other threats to the internal security of the United States. The US Marine Corps, as part of the Department of the Navy within the Department of

Defense created a separate Marine Corps Intelligence Activity in 1978. On the highly technical and scientific side of US intelligence three key agencies predominate and have made an extraordinary contribution to UK–US intelligence and the Five Eyes overall, and across multiple intelligence collection and analysis domains. These are the National Security Agency (NSA), a US Department of Defense entity created in 1952 and the sister agency to GCHQ in the UK, the National Reconnaissance Office (NRO), formed in 1961, providing space-based multisource intelligence, and the National Geospatial Agency (NGA), formed in 1996, that complements the NRO and indeed all other key US agencies, with highly specialized and quite brilliant geospatial intelligence from space-based and other products. In all, the US currently has 16 intelligence agencies and departments, a quite remarkable situation compared not just with the other four members of the Five Eyes, but with any other nation's intelligence organizations.

The Strength of the Five Eyes: Canada, Australia and New Zealand

The three other non UK–US member nations of the Five Eyes have tended to follow, certainly in their early years, the British model, given their historic connections to the United Kingdom as colonies, later dominions, and then independent states within the British Commonwealth of Nations.

In Canada the Royal Canadian Mounted Police (RCMP) provided national intelligence through an intelligence division created in 1920. Canada followed the GCHQ model with the creation of the Communications Security Establishment (CSE). There were controversies in Canada with the ways in which the RCMP may have handled various perceived internal threats, particularly those associated with the Quebec separatist movement. In 1984 the Canadian government disbanded the RCMP Security Service and created in its place a new entity, the Canadian Security Intelligence Service, separate from the RCMP. The Canadian military services followed the British model of the post 1964 period with the Canadian Forces Intelligence Branch, enjoying across the board liaison with all the key Five Eyes intelligence organizations relevant for the roles and missions of the Canadian Armed Forces. The Royal Canadian Navy, for example, during and after World War II worked naturally in close collaboration with British Naval Intelligence.

In Australia the government created the Australian Security and Intelligence Organization (ASIO) and the Australian Secret Intelligence Service (ASIS), akin to the British Secret Intelligence Service (SIS) or MI6. On the military side of Australian intelligence, the Australian Department of Defence has a Signals Directorate (ASD) and a Defence Intelligence Organization (DIO), very much akin to the British DIS/DI. In addition, Australia has a Defence Imagery and Geospatial Organization (DIGO). At the center is an Office of National Assessment (ONA), again somewhat akin to the British JIC. It is no longer a secret that the US and Australia enjoy a very special relationship as a result of the extensive facility at Pine Gap, at Alice Springs, where a significant number of Australians and Americans work side by side 24/7 in the interests of Five Eyes intelligence.

New Zealand, despite being the smallest country in terms of population, contributes significantly to the Five Eyes. New Zealand has a Government Communications Security Bureau (GCSB), with several hundred highly talented staff, a mini GCHQ in the south Pacific, and a New Zealand Security Intelligence Service (NZSIS), a mini SIS/MI6. Although the staff of the latter may appear small it is a very professional organization. Like the UK and Australia, the New Zealand government has a JIC equivalent, the National Assessment Bureau (NAB). On the defense side New Zealand has a Directorate of Defence Intelligence and Security, together with police, customs service, and immigration service intelligence components. For its size New Zealand more than pulls its weight. For example, on the GCSB side of things there are two key stations in New Zealand that provide invaluable intelligence within the Five Eyes community.

When we examine the detail of who does what within the Five Eyes it is very important to compare two inter-related factors, the population size of each member state and their gross domestic product (GDP). These factors very much drive intelligence investment strategies and what each nation can reasonably afford within their annual budgets. Because of the nature of Five Eyes intelligence operations their budgets are classified and are passed separately behind closed doors or are covertly subsumed in other budget elements. As part of the total budgetary process of each of the Five Eyes countries, each hides funds associated with covert and clandestine operations.

When the population size and GDP of each of the Five Eyes are compared, one can begin to appreciate the significance of each country's invaluable contribution to not just Five Eyes, but global security.

	Population (millions)	**Gross Domestic Product (US$ trillions)**
United States	325.7	18.57
United Kingdom	65.64	2.619
Canada	36.29	1.53
Australia	24.13	1.205
New Zealand	4.693	0.185
Total	456.453	24.109

The numbers for China and Russia compare as follows:

	Population (millions)	**Gross Domestic Product (US$ trillions)**
China	1.379 (billion)	11.2
Russia	144.3	1.283[2]

What these numbers reflect are the considerable wealth of the Five Eyes and the huge disparity in average incomes per head of population with China and Russia. The combined GDP of China and Russia is about one half of the Five Eyes. The gross domestic product of the state of California is US$2.448 trillion, twice the GDP of Russia. Where does this effectively place Russia in the world economic league table? Less than Canada, and only slightly more than Australia, where the population is 24.13 million, versus 144.3 million in Russia. The differentiating factor in Russia's case in terms of the international balance of power, other than Russia being a permanent member of the United Nations Security Council with an historic veto power, is the key fact that Russia has a significant nuclear arsenal, and a nuclear-powered submarine force.

The Five Eyes are therefore an intelligence powerhouse by any reckoning, sustained by formidable economies. Their combined ability to sustain and indeed increase their individual and collective intelligence capabilities is considerable. The other key factor is the aggregation of the individual parts that make up the whole. The combined strength is a multiple of the individual agencies' products, sustained by collective assessments. The big issue for the Five Eyes in the coming decades is not funding, or commitment, but rather the much more difficult decisions about investment in new and relevant sources and methods given both the nature of the changing threats, but critically the rapidly changing technological environment, where Moore's Law, for example, may be seen as a bygone relic of a long past computer age.

Gordon Moore, the co-founder of Fairchild Semiconductor and Intel, hypothesized in 1965 that the number of transistors in a dense integrated circuit doubles in about every two years, an observation and projection, not a physical or natural law. The information and digital revolution is moving at such a pace that predictions may be difficult if not impossible. What to invest in and why are increasingly more important than how much. If we go back to the Zimmermann Telegram era of 1917 and then onwards to the great triumphs of the UK's Bletchley Park and the US Office of Naval Intelligence during World War II it is indeed a bygone technological age where high-frequency encoded communications were cleverly intercepted and decoded, leading for example to the demise of villains like the Japanese admiral Isoroku Yamamoto. Yamamoto was chief of the Japanese Combined Fleet during World War II and shot down on April 18, 1943 in Buin, New Guinea, when US code breakers intercepted his flight plans. Vint Hill Farms was the key station west of Washington DC in the Virginia countryside that led this work. The station was closed in 1997, and now houses, in part, Federal Aviation Administration air traffic control facilities. The station was built in 1942 and was pivotal during World War II for eavesdropping on enemy communications. For example, Vint Hill in 1943 intercepted a key message from the Japanese ambassador in Berlin to his leadership in Tokyo, and later the detailed description of Nazi fortifications along the French coast. The Supreme Allied Commander, General Dwight David Eisenhower, stated that the Vint Hill data made a significant contribution to the success of the D-Day landings at Normandy. Vint Hill conducted similar operations against the Soviet Union during the Cold War. There were many other sites, too numerous to detail here, spread across the Five Eyes community, that contributed to both the Allied victory in World War II and to the successful conclusion of the Cold War. Vint Hill is just one illustration of past glories that have faded with the march of technology. High-frequency communications are largely, but not completely, a thing of the past. Technology has changed and intelligence targets have changed.

The Impact of the Demise of the Soviet Union

The demise of the Soviet Union and its aftermath in the 1990s created not so much lethargy in the Five Eyes but rather a need to focus direction elsewhere. This necessitated calibrating threats that were already appearing to many people in the community that had not yet received media attention. The 1990s witnessed defense downsizing and a sense of "all is well with the world" before the realities of the Middle East manifested themselves.

Middle East tensions existed before, during, and after the 1967 June War. The effects of that war continue to embroil not just the Middle East countries involved, but the United States, the European nations and, from an intelligence perspective, the Five Eyes, ever vigilant to collect and analyze not just Middle East intelligence but all the relevant intelligence connecting the other players to center stage. These together include Russia, Iran, Syria, Iraq, Jordan, Israel, Saudi Arabia, Egypt, the Gulf States, Oman, the Yemen, the Lebanon plus Hezbollah, and Turkey. Other surrogates and third-party arms suppliers play in this mix, complicating the collection process. If we add the role of the United Nations, then quickly most of the active and responsible member states have a voice and an opinion.

Within the crucible of the post-June War years and into the 1990s there grew and festered a deep hatred by various Arab minority groups with both wealth and influence, for the role the United States played in the Israeli-Arab controversies over the lost Arab territories. At the same time the historic theocratic and cultural divides between the Sunni and Shiite nations, and the subgroups within each of the Arab nations was a disaster waiting to happen if ignited by an outside source. Intelligence provides informed, actionable information to decision makers. Intelligence never ever makes policy or should try to influence policy. Its key role is to provide unvarnished hard-core reliable data to those who make and execute policy. At times it may appear axiomatic that certain outcomes will pertain and maybe there are only so many choices to be made, but nonetheless intelligence is not a decision-making function or authority. Many observers over the decades since World War II, and I am one of them, have stated that the quality of a nation's intelligence and those who are entrusted with its execution, is one of the defining qualities of a nation.

Technical and scientific excellence, professional commitment and loyalty, integrity regarding security and safeguarding sensitive information, and most of all the professionalism associated with independent thinking and analysis, unperturbed by political pressures and prejudices, are all critical for an operator. Coupled to this are the physical demands for field operatives of courage, and the ability to stay the course in often the most challenging circumstances.

The publicly unseen slow rise of Islamic extremism, until it was staring the media and the man in the street in the face, went in parallel with a dramatic communications revolution. The two coincided and at one level, in terms of the intelligence collection and analysis process, collided. The United States is the father of the internet as a result of the ARPANET, a pioneering communications network developed at the US Department's DARPA. The first demonstration was as long ago as 1968 when the first router was developed by BBN Technologies. In short, the information revolution followed. Then along came a brilliant Oxford-trained physicist and computer scientist, now Sir Timothy John Berners-Lee (born June 8, 1955), who first proposed what became the World Wide Web in March 1989.

The combination of the internet and the web revolutionized global communications at all levels of connectivity, whether individual, corporate, or government. In parallel came a digital communications revolution sustained by US investment and brilliant foresight by people such as Bill Gates at Microsoft and Steve Jobs (February 24, 1955–October 5, 2011, died aged 56) and his colleagues such as Steve Wozniak and Ronald Wayne at Apple, literally started in the garage of Jobs' home in Los Altos, California, on Crist Drive. By the time the tragedy of 9/11 occurred Islamic extremists were communicating via satellite phones. The Five Eyes not only had to keep abreast of these developments, they had to attempt to stay ahead of them. There was the inevitable time lag. The internet sprouted commercially and exponentially well outside the reach of the US Department of Defense and its DARPA forebears.

In addition, a political–theocratic Islamist revolution occurred fired by intense hated of the United States and its allies, coupled to a communications revolution that rapidly became global in nature. No one, with a very few exceptions, in the Five Eye near the center of real power and influence saw this all coalescing and predicting the likely effects on not just Middle East stability, but global stability. Jessica Stern in her book, *Terror in the Name of God,* and in several other equally distinguished analyses that are openly available, was at the center in the US National Security Council when the activities of Osama Bin Laden and his associates became known in the mid to late 1990s, and his movements were being tracked. His location in the Sudan and his agenda, with the most likely goal to attack United States' interests, became known and made him a clear and present danger. The US National Security Council, as the key entry point to White House policy and thinking, either could not or would not change the course of history by recommending the disposal of Bin Laden and his family, plus his entourage while in the Sudan, before they fled to the Afghanistan mountain retreat. There were many missteps in the intelligence process prior to and after the attacks on the East African embassies on August 7, 1998, in which over 200 people were killed in nearly simultaneous truck bomb explosions in two East African cities, one at the US Embassy in Dar es Salaam, Tanzania, and the other at the United States Embassy in Nairobi, Kenya. At the end of the day decisions such as this rest with one person ultimately, the President of the United States.

The warnings and indicators were there, but only political decisiveness will prevent the worst calamity. None of the terrorist leaders were political leaders or state recognized. Their removal did not fall under the US law forbidding the assassination of political leaders. The analogue with the 1930s and the removal of Adolf Hitler and his coterie of Nazi leaders is only germane insofar as his assassination may have saved the world and tens of millions from death and suffering. He was a state leader, and no nation was prepared to take the momentous step to organize a clandestine attack on the Nazi leadership. There are few if any parallels with the prelude to the 1998 Embassy attacks and then the lead up to the 9/11 attacks. Bin Laden was a modestly funded terrorist with a small loyal following masterminding an asymmetric attack. The Five Eyes had good data, but actionable intelligence is only valuable if it is acted upon.

The US East Africa US Embassies after the 1998 bombings. (Central Intelligence Agency)

Who Will Use Actionable Intelligence to Prevent Catastrophe?

The signs were already there, very clearly, after the First Gulf War concluded and before the World Trade Center bombing in New York City on February 26, 1993. On that day a 1,336-pound urea nitrate-hydrogen trick bomb device was detonated below the North Tower (Tower 1) of the World Trade Center. The terrorists' goal was to send the North Tower crashing into the South Tower, bringing both towers down, and killing potentially tens of thousands of people. Fortunately, this objective was not achieved, with six people losing their lives, five Port Authority employees and a businessman whose was in the parking garage. 1,042 people received injuries, most from the evacuation that followed the blast. The terrorist group was led by Ramzi Yousef, with his uncle, Khaled Sheikh Mohammed, providing the financing (a US$660 wire transfer). In March 1994 and November 1997, the United States achieved six convictions of the perpetrators. Yousef was a Kuwaiti by birth and was trained at an Al-Qaeda camp in Afghanistan. Yousef's trial transcript shows that his motivation was revenge on the United States for support of Israel against Palestine. The trial transcript revealed an FBI informant, a former Egyptian army officer, Emad Salem, who provided significant information. He claims to have provided warnings of an attack as early as February 6, 1992. The Pakistani Inter-Services Intelligence (ISI) agency also was involved in information leading to Yousef's arrest. Iraq was exonerated in complicity in the 1993 attack, with no evidence found to associate Iraq by the Joint Terrorism Task Force in New York, the FBI, the US Attorney's Office for the Southern District of New York, the CIA, the National Security Council, and the US Department of State.

The writing was now very clearly on the wall. The Five Eyes intensified their watch lists for terror suspects globally, and with all their liaison affiliations outside the immediate Five Eyes community. What the 1993 attack showed was that a very small group with minor funding could potentially inflict massive damage in a dense urban area such as New York City. The 1993 attack was to become characterized, with a large range of similar type attacks, as asymmetric warfare, where the attacker uses non-conventional, non-traditional military means to inflict damage on large and structured forces and civilian entities, such as New York City.

The Five Eyes were, in retrospect, not prepared organizationally and culturally for this challenge, and this was exacerbated by divisions within the various key US intelligence agencies, particularly between the CIA and the FBI, who both tended not to share information and were culturally divided, one an overseas covert intelligence collection agency and the other a law enforcement agency focusing on post-criminal event investigations, not collecting, analyzing and sharing internal US intelligence with an organization such as the CIA. In fact, the FBI's counterintelligence division had reasons to remain hands off in order to monitor potential internal CIA betrayal, as well as conducting counterintelligence operations against countries such as the Soviet

Union. This situation was, in hindsight, a recipe for disaster in terms of intelligence sharing and cooperation. This was something that the Five Eyes as a whole could not either change or certainly anticipate, leading to the tragic intelligence failures and consequences of 9/11. However, there was serious change occurring in another part of the United States national security structure, and the United States Navy was at the front end of change, and anticipating and preparing for the new world of asymmetric threats.

We have seen how increasingly precise weapons such as the Tomahawk, first fired in combat during the Persian Gulf War in 1991, can play pivotal roles early in a conflict. Weapons improvements after 1991 made precision ordnance even more effective. However, the 1991 First Gulf War exposed several serious weak links in the chain that the in-situ military commanders recognized very early on. Simply stated: however good the weapon (whatever it might be, from a Tomahawk to a Special Forces unit armed with handheld weapons), they or it can only be as good as the targeting system itself and the timeliness, accuracy, and reliability of the targeting data. Near or real-time data is necessary in fast-moving tactical situations or where units are unknowledgeable of the immediate tactical situation, including the disposition of civilians relative to threat forces, because rules of engagement, the Geneva Conventions, and simple humanitarian issues can quickly come into play in unanticipated tactical events. The significance of these factors for locating, tracking, and targeting terrorist asymmetric attacks should now be borne in mind in the above context.

Intelligence data dissemination to the front-line warfighter, or to covert intelligence field operatives, or to small special forces units is critical. In 1991 several factors inhibited the free flow of key intelligence data, particularly that provided from overhead/satellite sources and methods. Security restrictions prohibited the wider dissemination of very valuable intelligence, and also the timeliness of distribution even to those with the necessary security clearances. By the time intelligence had been collected, analyzed, and distributed through very special channels to just a limited few, it was often time late, and therefore irrelevant to a fast-moving operation or tactical action. In the early 1990s the US NRO was the only unacknowledged and covert agency of the US intelligence community. Disseminating overhead data to a front-line warfighter in or near real time was not only unheard of, it was at total variance with both the culture and organization (and communications systems) of that key part of the intelligence community. To say that intelligence was poor during the First Gulf War is well off the mark, but it certainly was not good enough. Nowhere was the latter truer than in the "Scud hunting" operations by Special Forces, attempts to locate and eliminate Iraqi Scud missiles before they could be fired into Israel and against US and coalition targets. The Iraqis played several games to disguise and deceive Scuds' locations and movements. Placing a precision weapon on a camouflaged and mobile Scud battery is not as simple as it may appear. Threat mobility requires the antidote of real time overhead IMINT, SIGINT, and ELINT to locate and confirm the Scud, and then maintain contact while an attack is prepared. All these factors presuppose satellite availability, the correct positioning via orbital planning, trajectory and swath of the satellite, and its download program, location and timing to download analysis to warfighter command center to the warfighter in need. None of this is easy. As a result, many warfighters were badly served with either inadequate or late intelligence.

Post-First Gulf War Changes and Technological Innovation

The US intelligence community took great pains and significant investment during the 1990s to rectify the situation after the First Gulf War. The architectural and communications solutions were imaginative and technically gifted. In addition, the community recognized the need for other systems besides satellites: the birth of the unmanned aerial vehicle (UAV) and the need for airborne detailed tracking of mobile targets became axiomatic requirements. Systems and platforms such as the Predator and Global Hawk UAVs and the US Air Force's Joint STARS (Surveillance Target Attack Radar System) aircraft have pedigrees that were nurtured by war fighting experience. The Joint STARS' radar is a prodigious system. However, even this aircraft is limited by range and endurance factors, even with in-flight refueling because of crew fatigue factors. Joint STARS can image at considerable ranges from the target area of choice in relatively benign air defense environments, constrained by crew endurance and the availability of in-flight refueling and friendly airfields for maintenance and support.

The First Gulf War taught the intelligence community huge lessons about the need to take massive cultural strides to find ways to sanitize intelligence so that it was usable at the Secret collateral level by any user with a need to know and with a Secret-level clearance. This meant inventing clever ways to change extremely highly classified material so that its inherent value was not denuded while the true capability of the collection system could not be deduced if the material was ever compromised. The impact of this on the Five Eyes proved to be invaluable, intensifying even more after the 9/11 attacks when Five Eyes military forces, particularly special operations forces, were working closely together.

I was directly involved in the key programs that provided the solutions to the weaknesses exposed in the 1991 First Gulf War. One domain that still to this day requires extra attention is Special Forces operations, in the case of the US Navy, the SEALs. SEALs are placed in highly dangerous situations and are very well trained to cope. However, SEALs always need the very best, up-to-the-minute tactical intelligence. Providing this capability is not easy because to carry even the very latest lightweight compact transceivers is both an additional weight and a trade-off for weapons, ammunition, water, and food supplies. In the 1990s there was no available fully field tested and approved means to send a satellite image in real time to a US Navy SEAL. The digital communications era and the iPhone era were developing but only in the most modest ways. The issue was not just compact, light, and secure hard drives and small displays, but bandwidth: an issue that continues to trouble conventional US military communications, particularly satellite systems, to this day.

The next generation successor systems that the Five Eyes will employ in the 2020s and beyond will transmit massive amounts of data, voice, and imagery that will make the intelligence issues of the First Gulf War look almost as antiquated as Nelson firing his famous bouncing "Yorker" shots across the water at his French adversaries. Even when satellite orbits are conveniently reprogrammed to support Special Operations, it has taken the US intelligence community a long time to provide real-time intelligence to SEALs except via satellite voice communications, and these have not always been as efficient as they should. The well-documented, and much written about US SEAL Operation *Red Wings* that began in Afghanistan on June 27, 2005, went wrong for several reasons, but one key reason was poor and unreliable communications systems in an era of excellent commercial communications systems. Receiving images or video of where the threat is located, including numbers, movements, relative positions, and likely weapons, is absolutely critical information for a small SEAL team wishing to avoid a much larger force and, worst case, being surrounded and then attacked in a no-win situation. This applies to ingressing and egressing helicopter lifts for Special Forces.

Threats on the ground need to be identified in plenty of time, not when it is too late. The UAV helps shift this paradigm, and there is no substitute for persistent, reliable, real-time intelligence: IMINT, SIGINT, and ELINT. There were no such networks in the desert in 1991 when British SAS units were up against not just the environment but also the unknown thanks to poor tactical intelligence, and intelligence not delivered in a timely manner. Handheld satellites transceivers can obviate much stress in highly dangerous tactical situations, provided the hardware is reliable, there are back-up systems with enough power when one system fails, and the information needed is actually available: either passed directly or indirectly by voice, or imagery, or video, or some combination.

The British had experienced the same tactical dilemmas in the Falklands campaign (1982) and the operations planned for the Argentine mainland were frustrated by a combination of poor to almost negligible intelligence, and unreliable real-time actionable information, even though satellite voice communications worked. These are ineffective if there is not the actionable information to pass to the front-line unit. The worst of all worlds is a distant command center that may have overall operational command and control (such as for example the Joint Operations Center at Northwood, England) over Special Forces units in the thick of things but who possess no reliable real-time actionable intelligence of value to the very units with whom they are communicating and over whom they ostensibly have operational command and control. From such situations the worst tactical scenarios of all can be born: when the unit on the ground acquires in an untimely manner the local picture as a result of direct contact with the enemy and finds that the intelligence assessments at the last pre-deployment briefing were either inaccurate or incomplete, or both.

It is important to observe at this point a critical shift in the civilian–military/industry–government mix of the past 25 years since the First Gulf War. The Five Eyes governments' acquisition processes and cycles are such that they are now well behind the commercial R&D and acquisition cycles, where businesses can only survive by both keeping up with rapid advances in technology and industrial production processes, and ideally always being ahead of the competition. If the competition is the threat, or possible future enemy, it becomes clear that on the military–government side of relationships the acquisition process cannot be such that procurement time scales invalidate technical leads by simply being too late in reaching initial operational capability (IOC). For example, if it takes ten years or longer to field a system, it may already be out of date.

This is a major issue in the digital era and particularly within the command, control, communications, intelligence, surveillance and targeting domains. Industry will, by definition, be ahead. The Five Eyes governments' procurement agencies, if they continue to follow current acquisition practices, run the great risk of being behind the technological curve. Nothing is truer of communications, particularly with non-commercial satellite systems. Global networked 4G LTE and 5G systems can carry massive data sets of every kind. Contemporary highly secure encrypted networks can provide panoply of cyber protections, indeed built in cyber-offense–defense systems for the Five Eyes agencies.

The US Navy Moves Ahead with Asymmetric Warfare

The US Navy was the first of the Five Eyes to seriously address asymmetric warfare, and its wider terrorist-related manifestations.

At the center of change in the US Navy in the 1990s was the Third Fleet, US Pacific Fleet, headquartered on board the Fleet Flagship, USS *Coronado*, in San Diego, California. Third Fleet was not concerned solely with asymmetric warfare, though this innovative, dynamic and well-led fleet should indeed take much credit for beginning much-needed focus on what would become in the next century the norm rather than the unusual. There were several key people in Third Fleet who were well ahead of the game and who recognized that the US Navy, and indeed US military forces generally, would face asymmetric threats. Central to Third Fleet's thinking were key aspects of intelligence paradigms. The later impact and transference to The Five Eyes was to be game changing.

There was nothing new in itself about the concepts of asymmetric warfare, defined as where two enemies, belligerents, or opposing forces, or factions are different in terms of the warfare resources they control, where the resource weaker player uses tactics and lower-end systems and technologies to offset weaknesses or deficiencies of both quantity and quality. The weaker player resorts to unstructured and informal means to undermine the other party who has a more formal, well-equipped and structured force. Military and naval history have numerous examples of the use of asymmetric warfare—in modern times the American Revolutionary War, actions by Colonel John Mosby during the American Civil War, the methods of the Boers during the Second Boer War in South Africa, Lawrence of Arabia's attacks on Turkish forces, and the brave tactics of the French Resistance and Yugoslav partisans during World War II are illustrative. What Third Fleet recognized, including US Marine Corps staff, was that the world was again changing: in a direction that was asymmetric rather than the structured bipolar world of the Cold War. The evidence for this rested in data collected by reliable global think tanks and organizations such as the International Institute for Strategic Studies (IISS) and the Stockholm International Peace Research Institute (SIPRI), together with government-based intelligence assessments. The so-called Peace Dividend was slowly being eroded as the 1990s passed by a less publicly acknowledged but nonetheless relentless surge from violent extremism in the Near and Middle East. What was emerging had already been experienced in recent years in the UK with the threat from the Irish Republican Army for well over two decades, and in the Middle East with the attack on the US Marine Barracks in Lebanon and countless outrages in the Palestinian–Lebanese–Israeli territories. All had decisive asymmetric characteristics. Later would follow the East African embassy bombings, the routing of US conventional forces in Mogadishu in Somalia (the Blackhawk Down incident) and the attack in Aden on the USS *Cole*, all precursors to denouement on September 11, 2001. Third Fleet staff in their wisdom perceived the shifting balance in the world and the changing nature of warfare and that the Navy must be trained and prepared to counter such threats.

As the 1990s progressed it became clearer that there was no response coming from Washington in terms of funding for training or the more formal doctrinal statements and documentation that would signal a recognition of global change. This observation includes not just the Department of Defense but also the national intelligence community's key three-letter agencies (CIA, NSA, and DIA). Fundamental Islamic extremism was gaining momentum but there was no official answer. What happened in San Diego, in Third Fleet, with the total benefit of hindsight, was quite revolutionary in conceptual as well as action terms. The Third Fleet team did not wait for Washington to show a lead. They initiated and provided the lead. Third Fleet found a way ahead by a combination of leadership, ingenuity, resource capture, and by forming a unique coalition of the willing that fully understood what they advocated. They found two principal means to create change, and they did this without any formal action on the part of the Department of Defense or the US Congress. Their achievements led in due course to massive changes not just in maritime strategy and tactics, alone hugely significant, but also across the intelligence community and, in due course, the Five Eyes as a community.

The means Third Fleet used, were: Fleet Battle Experiments (FBEs) and Limited Objective Experiments (LOEs). These were employed to test new ideas to meet the changing world and to implement doctrinal innovation. No US Navy Fleet could have achieved what they did in the space of the nine years from 1994–2003 without outstanding personal and involved leadership from two extraordinarily capable Third Fleet commanders, Vice Admiral Herbert (Herb) Browne from October 1996 to November 1998, and Vice Admiral Denis (Denny) McGinn from November 1998 to October 2000. Both were the lineal successors of prior great Third Fleet commanders, the father of them all being Admiral William F. "Bull" Halsey. Other illustrious predecessors included Vice Admiral S. (Sam) L. Gravely, Jr (who incidentally I had the honor to serve with at sea when on exchange from the Royal Navy in the nuclear-powered cruiser USS *Bainbridge*), Admiral K. (Ken) R. McKee, and Admiral S. J. Locklear. Both Admirals Browne and McGinn had the total support of their respective Commanders-in-Chief, US Pacific Fleet (an historic designation that would be changed by Defense Secretary Donald Rumsfeld by decree to the title Commander Pacific Fleet, along with all other US C-in-C designees, on the grounds that there was only one Commander-in-Chief, the President of the United States), to whom they reported, and then upwards to the Commander-in-Chief US Pacific Command, historically always a senior four-star US Navy Admiral. There was therefore an impressive lineup of four-star support for these two Third Fleet commanders.

From November 1996 to October 1999 Admiral Archie Clemins was the Commander-in-Chief US Pacific Fleet, with his fleet headquarters at Makalapa, adjacent to the Pearl Harbor naval base on Oahu, Hawaii. Admiral Clemins was himself an innovator, directing his fleet to get into the modern digital era with network centric concepts and technology. He took a personal interest and involvement in implementing change. There was therefore a crucial period before the 9/11 tragedy hit the United States when the US Navy had what can only be called an "A" team in the Pacific Fleet. The downstream impact on the Five Eyes was to be prodigious.

Both Admirals Browne and McGinn were distinguished naval aviators with extraordinarily fine command records, with Admiral Browne winning the Navy Cross in Vietnam and later in his career, before Third Fleet, commanding Navy Space Command. Later he would be the Deputy Commander-in-Chief at US Space Command in Colorado Springs before retiring and becoming the President of the Armed Forces Communications and Electronics Association (AFCEA). Admiral McGinn would leave Third Fleet for a critical position on the Navy Staff in the

Pentagon as Deputy Chief of Naval Operations for Warfare Requirements. He was responsible for all future naval capabilities, a most appropriate position following his innovations at Third Fleet. After retirement, in 2013, he was appointed the Assistant Secretary of the Navy for Energy, Installations and Environment, in the Obama administration, where he employed his knowledge and passion for green energy for the US Navy.

There was no official line item funding for Third Fleet's initiatives in the Navy budget and nor was there any "earmarked" funding through indirect Congressional funding, where key members of the House and Senate Armed Services Committees and Defense Appropriations Sub Committees can insert additional funds as "adds" to the President's official Navy budget for projects that they personally support. The fleet commanders relied on available existing funds from various budget line items that had sufficiently broadly based language in the original budget lines in the annual defense budget to justify expenditure. At the same time key senior Navy flag officers back in Washington DC who were supportive of Third Fleet's goals were proactive in ensuring the swift movement of funds to legitimately support FBEs and LOEs that were not to be found anywhere in the official budget process. One of the key stellar admirals who rendered such support was Vice Admiral Arthur (Art) Cebrowski, who was the N6 on the Navy Staff during this period of innovation. Admiral Cebrowski was the father of Navy transformation at the Washington end of change. As N6 he was responsible for all key future requirements affecting US Navy command, control, communications, computers and related domains across all the Navy warfare specialties. The Five Eyes owe Admiral Cebrowski a debt of gratitude.

While Vice Admiral Cebrowski was the key US Navy catalyst for change back in Washington DC, Vice Admirals Browne and McGinn led at sea. Cebrowski realized that large-scale integrated circuits that would permit the network centric flow of information that he advocated would be a game changer for naval warfare. He saw what the civilian sector was doing technologically and that the Navy, indeed the US military as a whole, needed to get on board and exploit the revolution in information technology. As a member of the Strategic Studies Group in 1981 at the US Naval War College in Newport, Rhode Island, he concluded along with people like another young US Navy Commander, William Owens (later Vice Chairman of the Joint Chiefs of Staff) that innovation was required.

They advocated that the networked environment, with information flowing to the warfighter from multiple sources, would provide a level of information dominance in the battlespace that would lessen the historically overarching need for mass of lethal kinetic force to subdue the enemy. The paper, "Joint Vision 2010," was produced by the US Office of the Joint Chiefs of Staff into the next decade and became the template for how things would work. Not everyone supported this philosophy as a basis for radical change. In fact, when Cebrowski's two leading champions retired in 1998, the Chairman and Vice Chairman of the

Joint Chiefs of Staff, General Shalikashvili and William Owens, respectively, there was a definite push against them from within the Joint Staff and the Navy. Some were skeptical of the new lexicon. Some used more pejorative words such as jargon and buzz words as descriptors of the Cebrowski school of thought. More educated analysis argued that Cebrowski did not see that the technological impetus from the commercial world and its military impact and applications was evolutionary and not revolutionary, and that the Navy should exploit the new capabilities like many prior changes based on technology. On the purely Navy side some compared the information changes that Cebrowski advocated to the change from active sonar to digitally enhanced passive sonar. Cebrowski concluded his military career as a most distinguished President of the US Naval War College on October 1, 2001, and just days after the 9/11 attacks took up the civilian position of Director of the Office of Force Transformation at the personal bequest of Secretary of Defense Donald Rumsfeld, with whom he had considerable personal influence and regular direct access and dialogue. Admiral Cebrowski succumbed to cancer and died on November 12, 2005, aged 63, and before he could consummate his influence over the wider Department of Defense. His positive impact on Five Eyes intelligence downstream has never been properly attributed. What Third Fleet achieved with his direct support would flow to the US intelligence community and thence to the Five Eyes as a whole.

Arthur Cebrowski left behind him an intellectual legacy. He had shown that military power could come from information technology and that this can lead to new strategic thinking, concepts, and advocacy, and that networked forces can be combined with kinetic force to have overwhelming effects, even to the extent that attrition in war would be superseded by the effects of information dominance, thus providing the political leadership with a whole new regime of political–military options. The Cebrowski philosophy championed the notion that information dominance would always win over sheer brute force. The counter arguments emphasized that such change was simply a part of the continuum of military technology evolution and that decisions such as the ones to invade Iraq and pursue nation building strategies as a key component of a political–military strategy were not products of, or related to simple changes in information technology, that strategy in its historic context was unaffected by changes in the information technology base. Some argued that the unleashing of the historical clash between Sunnis and Shi'a in the Middle East Moslem heartland was a vastly separate strategic issue than the nuts and bolts of current and future information technology and the military network architectures that can evolve from such technical bases. Many argued that information dominance was part of classical electronic warfare, evolving in ways that had witnessed over time evolution from direction finding at sea and communications intercept, through the ULTRA and MAGIC era of World War II, to the highly advanced worlds of contemporary SIGINT and ELINT in the digital communications era. The electro-magnetic spectrum has not changed, with technology evolving based on new and clever exploitation of natural phenomena. The same argument was applied to digital communications and the whole microwave environment: evolutionary not revolutionary. However, the impact on the tactical level of naval warfare and operational intelligence for front-line operations was not only significant, it was here to stay.

One key domain that the supporters of change pushed hard for in this period was the need for a reappraisal of how the industrial–military community did business. The status quo of program development, with lengthy acquisition and contracting processes, plus long lead times to initial operational capability, all combined to stifle innovation. The US Department of Defense was simply not running in parallel with commercial information technology developments, in fact, the military was several years behind. In retrospect this seems a powerful case for simply keeping up with the commercial world. However, this issue still overshadows the rapid implementation of technical change based on acquisition processes, and the US Federal Acquisition Regulations as currently employed. Admiral Cebrowski wanted a cadre of naval innovators to emerge from the US Naval War College. This may indeed be his lasting legacy: that education is the true catalyst of change, and that thinking through the implementation of change in an unfettered environment is a powerful ally.

"The Coalition of the Willing in San Diego": The Third Fleet, US Pacific Fleet

On the waterfront at Third Fleet in San Diego there was a different approach, a different tempo, and real action. The coalition of the willing in the Pacific Fleet turned words into deeds. What did they do, how did they do it, and what did they achieve?

Firstly, let me define the "it." Third Fleet was very much aware of network centricity and the three-star leadership was read into the latest highly classified programs at the National Reconnaissance Office. The "it" was to take both new and innovative network concepts and existing systems and command, control, and communications architectures, and translate them into new advanced operational applications.

One key Fleet Battle Experiment (FBE) BRAVO had an additional subtitle added to its phonetic name: "The Ring of Fire." This took place between August and September 1997 and involved the US Navy and the US Marine Corps, and Navy Special Forces. BRAVO was sponsored by the Chief of Naval Operations. The key units involved were the Third Fleet flagship, USS *Coronado*, and two other major surface units, the USS *Peleliu* and the USS *Russell*, with support from the Naval Air Station Fallon (F-18 aircraft), the Naval Air Warfare Center China Lake, and the Naval Air Warfare Center Point Mugu. The National Reconnaissance Office provided key services as did the SEALs. The Concepts of Operation (CONOPS) centered on the use of a new battlespace Local Area Network (LAN) architecture that connected sensors and other information sources in real time via satellite links. The objective was to test and demonstrate that a target could be successfully attacked and destroyed with real-time battle damage assessment by the network architecture.

One such scenario involved a small SEAL reconnaissance team ashore and inland sending real-time intelligence data, including imagery via satellite that was exploited aboard *Coronado* and then transmitted in real time to an F-18 aircraft that successfully destroyed the target with flares indicating a direct hit. The flagship built a command tactical picture (CTP) from multiple sources, including IMINT from the forward air controller (FOFAC) who designated the target. The *Coronado*, many miles out to sea, was able to decide and execute weapon-to-target pairing with several choices available. In this particular case an F-18 aircraft delivered the coup-de-grace. The other options included a SEAL attack, and a TOMAHAWK launch. The US Marines provided the FOFAC from the 13th Marine Expeditionary Unit.

Another subset of BRAVO included Operation *Silent Fury*, a highly successful test and demonstration of a National level C4I architecture with the National Reconnaissance Office providing both systems and direct support. This was a unique event, the first time in naval history that the breadth and magnitude of national satellite systems came to play in naval warfare.

The outcome of this FBE was prodigious and led to major new fleet-wide changes that were to reap dividends very soon after the 9/11 attacks. The use of the new architectures and real-time sensor data via satellite links and the US Navy SIPRNET (Secret Internet Protocol Router Network), the classified variant of the unclassified NIPRNET (Non Classified Internet Protocol Router Network) has borne enormous fruit, and has led to the US Navy having a massive advantage over its potential adversaries. Since 1997 the US Navy has made valiant strides in addition to the huge steps forward that Vice Admiral Browne made, to be followed by his successor at Third Fleet, Vice Admiral Denny McGinn.

New Ways of Doing Business and "Just in Time"

The US Navy implemented new ways of doing business after Fleet Battle Experiment (FBE) ECHO and Limited Objective Experiment (LOE) ZERO in the late 1990s and before 9/11. Vice Admiral McGinn took all this knowledge and experience with him to his next position on the OPNAV staff in Washington, and was in the Pentagon on September 11, 2001, with an office very close to where the aircraft entered the building. He retired in 2002 from the US Navy. His predecessor at Third Fleet, Vice Admiral Browne, did sterling work at the US Space Command Headquarters, and retired from the Navy in 2000. When 9/11 occurred the US Navy was instantly ready to respond by CVN strikes from the sea into Afghanistan and with Navy Special Forces. It would be a senior US Navy SEAL commander who would, alongside other clandestine Five Eyes and US forces, lead the attack on Bin Laden's sanctuary, caves, and training grounds in Afghanistan.

The Five Eyes were the beneficiaries of these seminal changes ushered in by the Third Fleet. The process of change may have been slower internally within the United States, and consequently perhaps even slower in sharing with the Five Eyes as a whole, but 9/11 transformed both thinking and actions.

The period after 9/11 was not unlike the period just before and then after the attack on Pearl Harbor. Minds were suddenly concentrated and improved intelligence became not just the order of the day, it was the lifeblood for survival in a new threat to world order. The United States Navy had led change by showing leadership, innovation, and risk taking. The Five Eyes owe the United States Third Fleet perhaps not just more than most realize, but also more than has ever been officially acknowledged in public forums. Most parts of the US intelligence community had remained static in a dynamically changing world across all domains—politically, theocratically, technically, and in terms of organizational cultures tied to past paradigms. The new asymmetric and terrorist threats coincided with a digital information revolution, communications infrastructure step changes, and the vast expansion of global networks, and all by no means under the direct control of the governments of the Five Eyes.

The 9/11 tragedy ushered in changes that very few in the departments and agencies of the Five Eyes anticipated and acted upon. The US Navy was the one defense organization together with the National Reconnaissance Office that had tried to stay ahead of the game with innovation and change. I am proud and privileged to have been able to work with and for both organizations at this crucial stage in the evolution of the intelligence art and science.

CHAPTER 5

September 11, 2001 and its Aftermath

On September 11, 2001 at 8:45 am, Eastern Daylight Savings Time, on a clear Tuesday morning, a Boeing 767 of American Airlines with 20,000 gallons of jet fuel crashed into the North Tower of the World Trade Center in New York City. Later another aircraft crashed into the Pentagon in Arlington, Virginia, and passenger intervention led to the downing of another aircraft in Stonycreek Township near Shanksville, Pennsylvania. The events of September 11, 2001 changed not just the world as a whole but also ushered in a new set of challenges for the Five Eyes against a backdrop of global technological change in communications and information flow.

The 9/11-related failures both of UK–US intelligence and government as a whole have been well documented in key reports, not least of all the 9/11 report published in 2004 in the United States, and "The Chilcot Report," published much later in the United Kingdom in 2016. The Chilcot report in the UK had a different emphasis and approach, and was a British public inquiry into the nation's role in the Iraq War, announced in 2009 by Prime Minister Gordon Brown.

"The Final Report of the National Commission on Terrorist Attacks upon the United States," mentioned above, was issued on July 22, 2004, with the commission having been established on November 27, 2002. The report has had many critics, not least for an apparent whitewash of many of the government's failings, while blaming the Federal Aviation Administration (FAA), for instance, for failures that were not substantively within its bailiwick or jurisdiction. The FAA is not a counter-terrorist organization. The 9/11 report did not please many in either the public domain, in the media, or in Congress. The missteps in the US intelligence community were not connected just to information but to organizational flaws that led to serious failures in communication, particularly between the CIA and the FBI, and also within the FBI itself, where crucial leads were not acted upon. The UK Chilcot Report offers much more in-depth analysis of the wider political–military–intelligence interactions and their effects on not just policy decisions but much wider strategic issues.

The Five Eyes as a whole could find zero connection between Saddam Hussein and al-Qaeda. In fact, he was known to be a serious threat to any sign of internal terrorist organizations such as al-Qaeda that may threaten his regime. He had ruthlessly stamped out any form of opposition. There was no evidence whatsoever that linked the group that led the attack against the World Trade Center and the Pentagon with Iraq. This situation was then exacerbated by intelligence misrepresentations in both the United States and the United Kingdom regarding whether or not Iraq had weapons of mass destruction. The performance of the US Secretary of State, Colin Powell, in the United Nations General Assembly in New York will forever be a record of the use of false at worst, faulty at best, information to represent a political cause. Powell himself may have been an innocent victim of his own intelligence data, with the Director of the CIA, George Tenet, sitting behind him in the United Nations when he made his momentous speech with visual representations of so-called Iraqi WMD. This was a moment in time, but it involved the catastrophic failure of the integrity of the higher echelons of the US government. Many saw Tenet as a CIA director who had succumbed to the President and his key advisers in order to support their already determined course of action to invade Iraq, whatever the causes and whatever the consequences, without a strategy for a post-war stabilization of a nation culturally split by the Sunni–Shi'a divide.

In the UK senior military advisors cautioned government about a war against Iraq based on legal issues. What legal right under international law did the UK have to invade Iraq without *casus belli* based on historic rights to wage war against a proven threat to the security of the United Kingdom? The Blair government, skating on very thin ice, and wanting no doubt to remain loyal to its American ally, misused intelligence in ways unprecedented in the history of British intelligence. Readers will have their own personal views on the rights and wrongs of the invasion of Iraq and the subsequent expansion of the counter-al Qaeda operations in Afghanistan to a full-blown war against the Taliban and what later became termed ISIS. The argument by many highly reputable scholars that they represent the worst strategic mistakes made by a US government in the history of the United States has to be examined in light of all the intelligence material available to decisions makers, and how such material was employed. Later policy issues are outside the scope of intelligence, whose key duty is to provide unvarnished and the best actionable information on which political decisions may be soundly made. If those decisions do not accurately reflect the intelligence, then this is the responsibility of the political arm of government, the elected representatives of the people, and not the professional members of the UK–US intelligence community and their myriad agencies and departments. The function of intelligence is not to dictate policy but help frame it with dispassionate apolitical data.

Denouement on 9/11 Precipitates Change but it is Not Universal

The subsequent reorganizations in the United States community were not followed multilaterally by the other Five Eyes countries along the same lines as the United

States. To obviate failures in communication and data exchange the Office of Director of National Intelligence (ODNI) was created in 2004 under the US Intelligence Reform and Terrorism Prevention Act with a centralized multi-agency staff functioning in new ways to coordinate the intelligence of the various agencies and departments of US intelligence. In parallel a new National Counter Terrorist Center (NCTC) was created combining representatives and inputs across the US intelligence community, with the flow of Five Eyes information entering at new key focal points. Cooperation and inter-agency cooperation were the new orders of the day. The British and the other three Five Eyes enjoyed the benefits of being smaller and more closely knit. They already had well-established lines of communication and organizations to ensure a more unified approach than the US agencies, many of which did not always wish to necessarily cooperate, and often because of sources and methods issues. The US National Intelligence Estimates were often seen by the other Five Eyes as compromises, and not thoroughly integrated intelligence estimates.

There were in some cases sound arguments in key US agencies for not sharing information, and these were largely related to security and need-to-know. We saw earlier why British and US naval intelligence kept many of their operations and data away from other agencies. The internal changes in the US did have a price. With greater inter-agency cooperation this also meant that more people, both government employees and contractors, had access to more data in unprecedented ways. This meant in essence that highly secure computer systems with discreet passwords for only select users with proven need-to-know were now accessible by a much wider number of people. Many of the latter did not necessarily meet the need-to-know criteria of the past. This led in part to several compromises associated with both intelligence contractors and government employees who could enter highly secure facilities and under the noses of his colleagues, supervisors, and the security staff, and steal valuable intelligence data via thumb drives.

In parallel to this issue was the sheer increase in numbers. Of the Five Eyes the US reacted far more than the other four nations in terms of the number of hires to the intelligence community after 9/11. The Five Eyes as a whole did expand their staffs, particularly in the counter-terrorism domain, but nothing like in the case of the United States where, for instance, the new Department of Homeland Security became a huge bureaucracy, taking under its wing the previously historic connection of the US Coast Guard to the Department of Defense and the Department of the Navy. The US Coast Guard's prior organization, the Revenue Marines, was created by Congress on August 4, 1790, under the auspices of Alexander Hamilton. This organization morphed into the US Coast Guard on January 28, 1915, under the US Department of the Treasury. The move to the Department of Homeland Security though at one level seemingly organizationally sound, seemed to some specialists as an unnecessary tampering with a well-established organization, simply in the name of change and over reaction to the 9/11 tragedy. However, the US

Coast Guard, incidentally the twelfth largest naval force in the world, can be transferred to the Department of the Navy at any time by order of the President or in wartime by the direction of the US Congress. The changes and recruitment of large numbers of new staffs were seen by some as unnecessary reactions when the focus should have been quality intelligence garnered from well-established sources and methods coupled to the new and ever-changing nature of global communications networks.

Who Can Spy on Whom?

In 2000 the digital revolution and the various technological applications across the global communications spectrum was, in relative terms, compared with where the world is in 2020, still in its infancy. However, the communications world of 2000 was nonetheless a completely different paradigm from when the Cold War ended. In 2000 the US and the UK, plus their three key allies, still dominated in terms of control and access to global digital data via satellite, landlines, and undersea cables. Satellite phones were in preponderance for those who could afford a relatively expensive device and service. The day of the cell phone, iPads, and the whole panoply of digital devices now available on the international market, had yet to arrive. The period 2000–2020 has been revolutionary in terms of communications, media, and data flow of all descriptions.

The SIGINT world is based on a very simple premise, in order to intercept someone's communications, they have to communicate. The corollary is also vital: if there are no communications it does not mean bad things are not happening. During the Cold War, if NATO did not intercept Soviet and Warsaw Pact communications regarding a possible attack upon the West it did not necessarily mean that they were not planning this. Likewise, submarines do not like to communicate. They like to receive. The reason is simple. Even the most discreet communications may possibly be intercepted. In the heyday of high-frequency communications there were several extremely sophisticated low probability of intercept (LPI) modes by which submarines could communicate. Even so, the SIGINT mission was to break into these and continue interception and decryption. When Osama Bin Laden and his cohorts realized that their satellite phones may be intercepted, Bin Laden simply turned his personal satellite phone off and did not use it again, reverting to the age old practice of using handheld documentation and verbal instructions, and couriers. The goal then became to locate and track Bin Laden's couriers.

The internet was alive and well in 2000, but not in anything like the complexity of today. However, those who did use the internet and satellite phones could be intercepted by the Five Eyes. The privacy issue and the legal challenges to governments breaking into personal communications and data had not yet arisen, until after 9/11 and the later exposure of government programs intercepting internal communications. The US, UK, Canadian, Australian, and New Zealand governments are not allowed to spy on their own citizens except under well-controlled situations with normally a court order from, in the case of the United States, for example, a Federal Judge. The US Foreign Intelligence Surveillance Act of October 25, 1978 is a federal law that established the legal procedures for the electronic and physical surveillance and intelligence collection of "foreign intelligence information" between "foreign powers" and "agents of foreign powers" suspected of espionage and terrorism. This act created the US Foreign Intelligence Surveillance Court (FISC) to oversee requests from the intelligence community and FBI for surveillance warrants. This act was amended after 9/11 because of the implicit issues associated with the domestic interception of the communications of US citizens. The 1978 Act has been amended several times and in different forms: The US Patriot Act; the 2007 Protect America Act; the 2008 FISA Amendments Act, and the USA Freedom Act. Warrantless domestic wiretapping became a public issue in December 2005 when a *New York Times* article[1] claimed that the National Security Agency had been executing such taps under the orders of President George W. Bush since 2002. A *Bloomberg* article[2] later suggested that such intercepts had started in June 2000.

The Five Eyes have always agreed that they would not spy on each other. There are caveats to this. This general understanding does not mean that one nation may not tell the other about information, for instance, regarding possible internal espionage collected from external sources via another nation's intelligence agencies and passed on to another Five Eyes nation. Similarly, in the post 9/11 era each of the Five Eyes had the technical and organizational means to intercept the internal communications, for example, of US citizens. This point is critical and bears detailed examination.

The very nature of global communications networks and the ways in which information flows means that, for one example, a US citizen may communicate internally in the United States but their communications pass through multiple Five Eyes servers and other non-Five Eyes servers and routers that the Five Eyes do not control, but can access. The point becomes clear. A US citizen could sit say in their home in Wichita, Kansas, and communicate via the web, or one of multiple means of global digital communications, that pass through non-US based telecommunications locations and devices. Those communications, in whatever form, voice, data, and visual, can be intercepted by the Five Eyes. Similarly a British citizen in London can communicate via a US-based server and commercial entity providing the service, and those communications may be intercepted by a non-UK-based intelligence agency such as the US National Security Agency because the data is passing through and controlled by the United States. The global complexity of telecommunications makes the difference between what is a domestic communication, or not, extremely complex both in terms of communications paths, but clearly legally in terms of the burgeoning privacy laws and who controls personal data and what they may do with such data.

Metadata Exploitation

Metadata has become a household term in 2020 when in 2000 no one, other than communications and data specialists, used or indeed understood the term. What is metadata? It is not quite as contemporary as most might assume. It is information that provides data about other data. There are several types of generic metadata. There is basic descriptive data that is a resource for factual discovery and identification of a piece of information by, for example, keywords. In the counter-terrorist context words such as ISIS, radicalization, madrasa, explosives, and so on tend to illicit attention. Structural metadata informs us of the different types, versions, and characteristics of digital data. Purely administrative metadata enables the management of a data resource. For example, when was data created, how was it created, where was it created, the transmit mechanism, type of data (visual, text, voice), and technical aspects, such as who can access data, with for example enabling passwords and other authentication and encryption. Libraries are a good example of metadata storage and accesses. In the pre-digital era simple library card indexes contained metadata.

Today the same data is embedded in computer files. The Five Eyes are able to exploit metadata transmitted via global telecommunications networks, whether voice calls, emails, or data transfers, such as bank transfers. Sought-after relevant information can be located by key words and/or locating and tracking metadata sources that are identified in advance as being of interest. The latter could include, for example, illegal drug trans-shipments, human trafficking data, weapons deals and their movements, and the activities of pirates of various kinds. Keyword traffic analysis at light speeds by robotics can cue Five Eyes operatives into real or near real time activities. As an email is transmitted the content may be intercepted as it passes through servers and routers around the globe or internally in a particular country. Regular telephone calls, web page accesses, video traffic, cell phone calls, and various Internet Protocol (IP) processes that underscore the very workings of the global internet, relaying vast packets of digital data across vast network boundaries are the sources that the Five Eyes agencies exploit. All the other contemporary buzz words of the global telecommunications process—transmission control protocols, computer networks of one sort or another, internet service providers (ISPs), routers, ethernet, local area networks (LANs), voice over IP, domain name systems, hypertext transfer protocols, dynamic host configuration, user datagram protocols, virtual private network (VPN), a network packet, and so on, are just some of the infrastructure capabilities and terminology of what in essence comes down to the ability by the Five Eyes to penetrate this total infrastructure and exploit it for very sound and ethical national security reasons. Suffice it to say at this point that this global telecommunications configuration, even with the most sophisticated security protocols, has vulnerabilities in the very nature of multiple point-to-point communications. Even where a system is never ever connected to an outside electronic source, such as the web, there are other types of vulnerabilities, such as the "insider threat."

It is easy to understand in the context of the above that with the vast amounts of data that governments, particularly the United States government, have sought to grapple the problem has been addressed in part by large-scale recruiting. This seems perfectly logical. However, experience and indeed history has shown that large-scale intelligence organizations, in terms of the number of personnel employed, are not necessarily the right answer. In short, it comes down to a question of quality versus quantity. If a large number of operatives are indeed required to perform routine tasks, then clearly there is justification for large staff numbers. But history has shown that a relatively small number of very exceptional people can make a huge difference, and that indeed too many people, in one sense "getting in the way," may indeed inhibit or slow down good intelligence work.

Bletchley Park and the ONI in World War II and the relatively small cadres of people in British intelligence during the height of the Cold War show that great intelligence work may be performed by small numbers of extremely able people. This certainly may not apply to, for example, counterintelligence surveillance operations, where large numbers of well-trained personnel are required 24/7 to locate and track classical espionage threats or more likely in the current environment, those seeking to steal by surreptitious means, key intellectual property (IP), such as aircraft designs, weapons details, and nuclear technology. Machines can today provide data in ways that humans cannot. Very smart humans may then interact and make use of such data.

Added to this quantity versus quality issue is the question of sheer knowledge and experience. For example, US intelligence did not have a history of deep-rooted knowledge and experience of the Middle East prior to 9/11. The US had outstanding Middle East diplomats in its ranks, but their functions were very different. Area knowledge became critical as the post-9/11 period developed. Few spoke fluent Arabic and Farsi, and the associated dialects, and there was not a truly deep understanding of the political, social, and theocratic makeup of, for example, Iraq, when the decision to invade that country was made. Indeed, the US President at the time had very limited international travel experience in 2001, no fault of his own indeed, but it reflected a systemic lack of understanding of the ways of the Middle East and South West Asia.

The impact on the Sunni–Shi'a divide in Iraq as a result of the US-led invasion was not fully understood by people such as Paul Bremer, who led the Coalition Provisional Authority in Iraq from May 2003 until June 2004, a critical period when many mistakes were made. Even though staff may be smart and well educated, what this demonstrates is that unless there is truly deep knowledge and experience even the best-intentioned people can fail miserably. Good, sound, and responsible intelligence can assuage the making of catastrophic policy decisions. However, as we saw earlier in the case of Secretary of State Colin Powell's presentation to the

United Nations regarding so-called Iraqi WMD, intelligence professionals can only do so much. There comes a point in time when good intelligence either speaks for itself or it is ignored, with the necessary national consequences.

The New Digital Era and its Impact on Security to 2020

Almost everyone and everything is connected to the internet. Such that governments, corporations, and the Five Eyes can create detailed profiles of all of us. The latter are used 24/7 to provide marketing data for vendors, a purely innocent commercial activity that we all either endure or benefit from as a result of our internet interactions. The Five Eyes have had to wrestle with a critical issue—privacy. When can and should government intelligence agency pry into your personal data and internet transactions? Mark Zuckerberg, aged 17 on 9/11, and Google were still in their infancy in 2000. Today the United Kingdom and the European Union have already passed laws that represent the world's most thorough control over state access to their citizens' personal telephone and internet data. The UK's 2016 Investigatory Powers Act (IPA) predated the European Union's General Data Protection Regulations (GDPR) that came into force on May 25, 2018, a piece of major legislation with comprehensive protection for all EU citizens against any form of cyberattack, and made such offences criminal. From a Five Eyes perspective with, in this case, only the UK being involved, and then only until Brexit occurred, this marked the beginning of a new era. Five Eyes citizens required the protection of their intelligence services while at the same time facing the privacy issue that prima facie legally prohibited the mass trawling of citizens' metadata.

The 2010s marked the beginning of a major global telecommunications and information technology revolution, at levels far beyond the original ARPANET and the web. In 2001 the internet still had limited purposes. The mobile tablet and iPad revolution of the 2010s changed everything. The Five Eyes could intercept these new communication devices' data in fiber optic cables and other telecommunications media between not just their domestic telecommunications sources, but globally. For example, a UK user could be communicating internally or internationally in or from the UK for all intents and purposes, when in fact their data was passing through an internet platform and or provider in the United States. This illustrates the inter-connected nature of global communications, immediately complicating the privacy laws mentioned earlier. NSA and GCHQ and the other Five Eyes agencies can legally exploit such foreign-derived information.

In the UK GCHQ had used the 1984 Telecommunications Act to obtain bulk information from the telecommunications companies, and the Five Eyes generally have exploited these commercial relationships in order to function and intercept. This has now changed in the UK legally, with a UK Judicial Commissioner determining whether or not an internet search warrant can be issued. This is a huge change with ramifications. In order for a key member of the Five Eyes now to conduct internal UK internet searches it will require some form of a priori information that will enable such a warrant to be granted. In the past, the internet may well have been the primary source. The dilemma becomes self-evident for the Five Eyes legally. A legal and ethical workaround stems from the nature of global telecommunications and particularly internet connectivity. In the UK case for example, data passing through a US-based server or other non-UK Five Eyes system can be legitimately and legally intercepted. This is where metadata analysis technology becomes critical. The simple fact is that Five Eyes agencies do not have the time or resources to even begin to look at trillions of bits of data per second. What metadata analysis does permit is to narrow the field to just the very key data points that may be linked to national security concerns. The Five Eyes high technology telecommunications giants and the key hardware manufacturers have to play cooperatively with the agencies in order for this to happen. We all live in a borderless digital world with multiple communications nodes globally placed that can be exploited for intelligence purposes. Such data can be used not just for what may be called classical intelligence purposes, but also for key law enforcement operations, such as apprehending internet sexual predators exploiting minors.

The same applies to cybercrime. The Five Eyes are well placed to detect and cause the apprehension of cyber criminals in conjunction with national law enforcement agencies. This applies to assisting Five Eyes allies. In 2017 the German government passed an Enforcement Act with massive 50 million-euro fines for companies and organizations that fail to take down illegal internet material within 24 hours of a complaint being filed with German law enforcement. This is a slightly different issue from classical intelligence, but it shows the extent to which intelligence reciprocity with law enforcement may work jointly to stop both cybercrime and other illicit uses of the internet.

The "Cloud": Exploitation vs. Privacy and Protection

A new strategic paradigm has emerged. This relates to what is now a new version of a very old word in the telecommunications lexicon, the "Cloud." For the cloud to continue to expand exponentially it has to be secure. The cloud is open to cyberattacks. The NSA–GCHQ and Five Eyes dilemma is a classic case of conflicting roles and missions. Is the security of Five Eyes citizens' communications and data more important than exploitation? The UK National Cyber Security Center (NCSC) is part of GCHQ and is tasked with protecting the UK from cyberattacks. Similarly, the European Union GDPR aims at thwarting cybercrime and industrial espionage. This raised a fundamental question about primary Five Eyes roles. Is it more important for the Five Eyes to protect their citizens via cyberdefense or should they concentrate resources in attack and exploitation of those who threaten, or indeed a combination of both?

Many readers may have received in the past fictitious emails from specious sources soliciting your investment funds. These are a thing of the past, together with fictional emails from your best friend in some far away country who has lost all to theft and needs you to send funds urgently. These types of internet fraud are dinosaurs compared with the sophistication of current cyberattacks, though note that these precursors were predicated on the initial theft of your and others' email addresses. The Equifax credit bureau attack was massive, executed by cyber criminals, and ransomware hackers demanded money to unlock files, estimated at $2 billion in 2017. Compromised business email scams cost approximately $9 billion in 2017. Viruses have infected most readers' computers, such as the notorious Not Petya and Bad Rabbit.

Today, attacks are by state-sponsored surrogates (those acting for a foreign government covertly but not as government employees as such, and most often from disparate locations not associated with the nation for whom they are operating), organized criminal hackers, or ill-intentioned individual hackers, many with serious malintent. Does all this affect us? The answer is a resounding "Yes." Most of us live and breathe as individuals, as families, and in the workplace, by internet connections, whether via cell phone, a personal computer, or perhaps a more complex computer network at work. Without secure uninhibited internet communications, the very nature of contemporary life is challenged. Almost everything that most of us do has internet connectivity. The key problem with cyberattacks is that they are all, without exception, discovered "after the event," and this is in spite of password protection, encryption, and other means of electronic authentication. The cost of disruption, loss of information, whether personal data or intellectual property, and the time and cost to repair damage, is massive. State-sponsored cyberattacks rely not just on large armies of highly trained cyberattackers, but also robotics that are operating at machine speeds unthinkable less than five years ago.

We all live within global networks that are dependent on service providers who are vulnerable. For example, one weak link in a local area network (LAN) or even within a so-called highly secure point-to-point data communications system leads to exploitation. The theft of personal information and technical intellectual property comes at a huge cost to the Five Eyes' economies and national security in a much wider sense than traditional definitions of threats. The majority of global data communications is via undersea fiber cables at light speeds and data rates that were unimaginable a decade ago. The US and the UK together no longer dominate the undersea cable domain. The Chinese have moved in surreptitiously and as the world's data demands grow exponentially so is Chinese investment in data communications and control of markets. The US Department of Defense (DOD) alone has about half a million routers. The DOD total global network is larger than the web. Software failures and vulnerabilities, chip malfunctions, design faults, and implants can cause massive disruption. At a personal level our healthcare and financial data are exploitable. At a local and regional level critical infrastructure is vulnerable. At a national level recent events show that elections can be exploited by a range of devious means. As you read this book millions of robotic attacks are occurring constantly, hitting vulnerable systems at machine speeds. The "insider threat" adds to this technical complexity, where employees with systems' accesses exploit vulnerabilities for financial gain, or to betray Five Eyes secrets and intelligence operations.

Specialists argue that it is pointless paying good money for software that fails to protect and is dependent on post-attack forensics and patches. We are also advised that many legacy systems, such as older Windows, are highly vulnerable to backdoor traps exploited by hackers because there are zero in-built capabilities to perform real-time diagnostics. At the strategic level the US has to accept that the "Fortress Model" adopted by US government departments and agencies has failed, relying on password protection, other authentication, and encryption, that has ignored the total system vulnerabilities at the global level. From my perspective what is required is a new generation of Alan Turings (the World War II Bletchley Park computer and code-breaking genius) to create the capabilities that will both enable readers to operate their systems with 100% security while still enabling US manufacturers to sell products globally that cannot be exploited by deconstruction and the usual technology mirror-imaging.

This is all possible. The brain power exists within the Five Eyes. It does not require an army of computers scientists, but a small highly capable elite cadre of mathematicians and computer scientists who are in a class of their own. They are out there. This will persist unless pressure is exerted on Five Eyes political leaders and representatives to invest in innovation before our nations are held total hostage to new threats the like of which we have not experienced. This is not to scaremonger. If a burglar is knocking at your door to see if anyone is at home, you have hopefully already taken every precaution to protect your home. Perhaps electronic devices should be regarded in the same way, except that the burglar may be using not just multiple means to gain access but may already be inside stealing data. The brains exist in the overall Five Eyes community to negate cyberattacks.

In order to achieve the above NSA and GCHQ and their three key Five Eyes allies will have to close ranks even further to ensure secure high-quality cyberdefense while at the same time conducting exploitation for intelligence purposes. Science and technology are calling the tune, and the key to the future is enabling Five Eyes governments to stay abreast of technical change. It is likely correct that Five Eyes agencies that were once dominant in communications exploitation are increasingly behind the curve, in part due to the very nature of government processes, particularly in contracting, and even in those historically more fast-moving classified special access programs. The reason has become very clear since about 2015. Five Eyes government leaders and personnel are behind their industrial bases in terms of both thinking and capabilities. A US DARPA-type solution is unlikely to work because of the sheer speed at which technical change is occurring. The US Department of Defense opened in 2015 the Defense Innovation Unit Experimental (DIUX) in California, founded to help the US military make faster use of emerging commercial technologies. In May 2016 the then US Secretary of Defense, Ash Carter, rebooted DIUX by designating that it reports directly to his office. DIUX has had a galaxy of commercial stars help its endeavors, but its success remains equivocal. Some have argued that large American corporations find its competitive nature inhibiting of their "business as usual" approach with the US Department of Defense, while others claim that DIUX simply has not delivered. Time will tell whether this adventurous and innovative approach will continue to garner political support and funding. It is a sad reflection at one level that there are indeed commercial interests that see fast-moving innovation financially too challenging for existing multi-year programs with heavy duty congressional support that could potentially become unhinged if innovation wins the day.

Staffs at Five Eyes organizations such as the National Security Agency have been challenged to innovate by fine leaders such as former NSA Director, Admiral Mike Rogers, US Navy, who has recognized that to stay ahead in the new world order NSA must innovate ahead of the threat, see it coming and be ready to not just challenge it, but to exploit it and if necessary defeat it.

Through to 2020 there has been much good news in terms of progressive innovation in Five Eyes military command, control, communications, surveillance, and reconnaissance domains. The latter provide overall situational awareness for Five Eyes regular and Special Forces operators, plus clandestine support forces not operating, for instance in the case of the United States, under US Title 10 (the US code that defines and controls the roles, missions, and organizations of the US armed forces), but enjoying the technological benefits of the regular US military. Suffice to say that developments from the early unmanned aerial vehicles (UAVs) such as Predator and Global Hawk have progressed to in 2020 a wide range of drones and further advanced UAVs in terms of payloads, stealth, range and endurance.

Lightweight handheld drones now complement a range of advanced NRO satellites to which the Five Eyes has access. These technologies are complemented by other multi-intelligence intelligence-collection systems and sensors on board not just US satellites but also manned aircraft, ships, and submarines. The US Navy's successor to the venerable P-3 Orion aircraft, the P-8 Poseidon, is a massive step change in capabilities cross the board. State-of-the-art technologies and better situation-awareness planning have obviated some of the worst outcomes for US Special Forces, sometimes overcome in ambush situations caused by faulty situational awareness and poor communications. Operation *Redwings,* June–July 2005, in the Pech District of Afghanistan's Kunar Province is a tragic illustration of the above. The October 4, 2017 Tongo ambush in Niger of US forces by armed Islamic state militants left four brave Americans dead. These and other similar operations require greater situational awareness data not just in real time but ahead of the threat so that special and clandestine forces from all of the Five Eyes can not just avoid ambush but exploit information to the full. Together the Five Eyes community will undoubtedly grow in strength and resilience against ever more artful asymmetric threats. The combined technical and industrial base of the Five Eyes is prodigious. Technology transfer to the clandestine intelligence collection world is necessary as the threat moves more and more away from the conventional battlefield to cyberspace and asymmetric attacks. The Iranian seizure in July 2019 in the Straits of Hormuz of the British tanker *Stena Impero* illustrates how a maligned intentioned adversary can use in this case AIS data to easily locate, track, and intercept an oil tanker exercising its right of innocent passage in international waters. Exactly the same data is available to any civilian if they have an app such as "Marine Traffic" on their digital device.

July 20, 2019 was the 50th anniversary of the US moon landing and, as Charles Fishman's book, *One Giant Leap* (Simon & Schuster, 2019), shows in fine detail, marked also the beginning of the US lead in the digital revolution. The latter was directly catalyzed by the 1960s space program initiated by Presidents Kennedy and Johnson. That program launched a whole new generation of computer and other scientific and engineering innovations on a massive scale. Maybe the 2020s will witness a new technical revolution created from what may be a "Green Revolution" and a whole new set of scientific and engineering discoveries for alternate energies to fossil fuels and their distribution at affordable prices.

Post-2020 Digital Innovations of an Unprecedented Magnitude

Change is already on the way. In 2019 the US Department of Energy selected Argonne National Laboratory and Intel Corporation, with Cray Computing as a subcontractor, to build the United States' first exascale supercomputer. The latter will be able to execute a billion-billion calculations per second and therefore able to deal in real time with unimaginable amounts of data. The applications for the intelligence community are legion, particularly when coupled with advances in artificial intelligence. Similarly, a race is already on in encryption technology. Current ones and zeros' calculations by traditional computing techniques will be challenged by high-capacity quantum computing that may well lead to the real time decryption of current systems. The technology is based on "Qubits" or calculations made relying on photons, protons, and electrons versus current digital techniques. The so-called random number generators in current encryption technology, that are in fact not random because they are generated by human-produced computer algorithms, will be challenged by quantum computing technology. The implications for current so-called secure encryption are huge. The Chinese, in addition to the US, are also investing heavily in quantum sciences. Encryption has been one of the key security pillars for decades. This could all change. The challenge will be to create post-quantum cryptography that creates algorithms that are quantum resistant. The UK–US intelligence community and its three Five Eyes allies cannot be faced with a possible Chinese "Quantum Surprise."

My own involvement during this period from 9/11 until 2018 was in three main areas and three organizations—the Central Intelligence Agency, the National Reconnaissance Office, the Department of the Navy and specifically the Navy's role in counter-terrorism operations. The latter was specifically related to submarine operations and those of US Special Forces, and covert operatives. The work concentrated on locating, tracking and targeting terrorists. Many of the skills, the systems, and the operational knowledge gained in the mid- to late-1990s that I described earlier were harnessed to defeat terrorist groups and individuals. The details are still highly classified. Suffice to say that all such systems and operations must have key underlying political objectives. I witnessed and indeed was proud to be involved in removing threats to the United States and our allies, while recognizing that without an overarching political strategy, the end game would always be in jeopardy. This still applies today, in 2020. Without a clear and precise statement of strategic goals there is a serious danger of terrorism creep that potentially has no end unless key underlying causes and effects are acknowledged, analyzed, and put into the big picture for policy decisions. For example, the underlying fundamental Middle East discord generated by the Palestinian and Israeli disputes over territory and control thereof politically cannot be ignored and must be related to many of the terrorist acts committed in the name of supporting an independent Palestine. After decades of violence in Northern Ireland only a political solution could solve the sectarian butchery that took so many lives. This analogy is very relevant for Iraq, Afghanistan, Iran, the Yemen, and the complexities of the Israel–Palestinian dilemma, the latter igniting as we see constantly Middle East rivalries and agendas. Intelligence can only do so much. That was my experience. At the end of the day political solutions have to be found and it is the role of intelligence to provide unvarnished, apolitical, high-integrity data and assessments.

Parallel to this work, I was proud to serve the US submarine community in advancing the build rate of the *Virginia*-class nuclear-powered attack submarine by showing in fine detail why, from a "Weapon-Target-Centric" vantage point, the United States and British nuclear-attack submarines provide their countries with the most versatile and cost-effective platforms. There is an urgent need to increase the build rate from the two per year that we succeeded in advocating to at least three per year, given the rising potential threat from Chinese submarines in East Asia and to a resurgent Russian submarine program. Numbers count. Even a highly capable submarine such as the US *Virginia*-class and the British *Astute*-class are not ubiquitous. They cannot be everywhere at once and both countries need to expand their build rates, together with emphasis on unmanned underwater vehicles, networked sensors, and coordinated real time intelligence, plus offensive and defensive cyber operations. Work that I led in the 1980s for DARPA[3] gave me knowledge and experience, but most important of all the analytical structure to address the emerging Chinese submarine threat and Russian resurgence. I imparted this skillset to my team, and we helped the US Navy in convincing the Congress of the way ahead. I recall vividly a crucial meeting with Senator John Warner, Chairman of the Senate Armed Services Committee, and a former Secretary of the Navy, together with a much loved and respected retired US Navy submariner, Vice Admiral J. Guy Reynolds, of the absolute wisdom of an increased build rate. He was supportive. I also oversaw the building of a crucial industrial base model to help ensure that the Navy and the Congress could run key programs simultaneously in the 2020s onwards—the expanded *Virginia*-class, the replacement of the *Ohio*-class SSBN by the *Columbia*-class, and key assistance to the United Kingdom in building their replacement to their *Vanguard*-class SSBN, in parallel with the United States. The key to success is the UK and US industrial base, ensuring that the multitudinous contractor base could be coordinated in a cost-effective way to make all these programs not just achievable, but affordable.

The Magnitude of the Cyber Threat across Multiple Domains

My key UK–US colleagues and I agree the most serious threat to our technological lead is the cyber threat, and particularly the threat of industrial intellectual property theft by cyber means. I became part, as the Senior Advisor, of a joint UK–US team based in Cheltenham, England, and in Maryland. It was a unique and unusual team, made up of some people who were in a technical league of their own, one of whom I describe as the "Alan Turing" of the 2010s. The key to success lay in the simple fact that several members had crucial commercial and industrial experience at places such as Microsoft and Google before joining the NSA. Their opposite numbers in the UK were GCHQ gems. The team worked in perfect harmony. One of the British team members had run the technical aspects of cyber and electronic security for the London Olympic Games, July 27–August 12, 2012. The aim was to develop systems that would be well ahead of the global technology base and the key threats.

At a memorable meeting with the then UK ambassador to the United States, Sir Kim Darroch, now Lord Darroch, the senior team members and I laid out both our threat concerns and our technical answers. I still have considerable concerns over the US government's approach to cyberdefense and cyberattack. Much of the problem is a combination of structural leadership issues, such as the continuity of policy led by truly competent government senior officials, and the other is not having the Churchill-like World War II approach: "Action this Day." In other words, do not wait for the problem to get worse, but take immediate action with only the best and the brightest, and at the same time let go any personnel dead wood that is inhibiting innovation and progress. We also found that the competitive contracting laws and the need to let the wide-ranging contractor base have its share of funding inhibited the very best companies and individuals with super talent within them from leading the charge. The ecumenical approach seemed to us to lead to mediocre results and the waste of not just valuable resources, but time. We constantly stressed the need to be many steps ahead of the threat and anticipate their next moves. I and the other key people with whom I worked are deeply concerned that the US has still to find the right paradigms.

My most professionally and personally satisfying time during this period was working with Rear Admiral Mark Kenny, the Director of the US Navy's Counterterrorism Center and his key technical advisor, Mr. Tom Nutter, the legendary person who for many years managed the installation of hugely sensitive and highly classified "Special Fit" on US nuclear-powered attack submarines. The three of us, together with Admiral Kenny's key staff officers, spent much time ensuring that various critical operations were a success. We operated out of the east coast primarily, with several visits to AUTEC, the US Navy's Atlantic Underwater Test and Evaluation Center on Andros Island in the Bahamas.

One of the most memorable of several sea deployments was onboard USS *Florida*, SSGN 728, a converted *Ohio*-class SSBN that can carry 154 BGM-109 Tomahawk cruise missiles, a prodigious capability. We took with us from King's Bay, Georgia, a group of senior US intelligence community officials together with Royal Navy Rear Admiral Paul Lambert, then Commander Operations and Rear Admiral Submarines, who I had helped train as a midshipman in the Dartmouth Training Ship. Paul was later to become Vice Admiral Sir Paul Lambert in his final Royal Navy appointment as Deputy Chief of the Defence Staff (Equipment Capability) in 2009. The UK–US group was simply awe struck by the special capabilities that we demonstrated. Above all it was hugely symbolic of the UK–US special relationship that off the east coast of the United States, underwater, the latest secrets and operations were being shared in order to protect the vital national interests of the US and the UK.

CHAPTER 6

Intelligence Roles, Missions, and Operations, 1990–2018

The character, locations, and roles of US and British intelligence and their three Five Eyes partners in a new era of conflict from 1990 through 2020 varied dramatically, testament to the changing nature of conflict and its resolution. What many of these conflicts showed is that weapons technology is often not enough—overwhelming kinetic force may not be the solution to complex political–military–theocratic and economic scenarios in which military power and the use of force can only be one component. In some scenarios the very threat of the use of force, such as the Iranian oil tanker seizure situation in the Strait of Hormuz in July 2019, may indeed exacerbate it.

What should UK–US and Five Eyes capabilities look like for the next generation and how should these five great nations work together to help preserve both international order and the critical national self-interests of each country?

Intelligence Investment in the post-Soviet Era

The sum of the parts within Five Eyes intelligence are much greater than the individual units themselves. For examples, if we look at Bosnia, Kosovo, Sierra Leone, Libya, the Arab Spring, the major conflicts in Iraq and Afghanistan, plus Syria, and the whole ISIS phenomena in very objective terms we can see how this aggregation of capabilities yields advantages. These events tell us something about how the Five Eyes invest in intelligence and see the return on this investment.

The Bosnian crisis in south-east Europe, 1992–1995, witnessed a wholesale humanitarian tragedy. The main protagonists were the Republic of Bosnia and Herzegovina, and Bosnian Serb and Bosnian Croat entities within that Republic, following the breakup of Yugoslavia and secessions of 1991. The conflict was a clash of ethnic and religious rivalries, overlain by the ambitions of individual leaders, particularly Slobodan Milosevic, the Serbian leader. The worst manifestations and atrocities occurred with the massacre (or ethnic cleansing) of the Bosnian Muslim and Croat population. Five Eyes intelligence reporting was thorough and accurate.

However, there was considerable negative political blow back as a result of US inaction during the unfolding crisis, so close to mainland Europe, and in spite of the mounting intelligence assessments.

The European Union was politically committed to deterring and countering any return to the very causes of European disharmony and bloodshed that had witnessed countless slaughter since the early Middle Ages. The intelligence provided led to the US and its European allies agreeing on intervention. The British government chose the Royal Navy as its symbol of commitment, sending HMS *Invincible, Illustrious*, and *Ark Royal* (the three light through-deck cruisers of Sea Harrier-Carriers) into the Adriatic, conducting sanctions enforcement. Early on in these operations, on April 16, 1994, one of the Royal Navy FA2 Sea Harriers was shot down by a surface-to-air missile fired from a Serbian launcher. Fortunately, the pilot escaped unharmed.

In addition to Royal Navy Sea Harriers the UK also provided 12 Royal Air Force GR7s. It was some time before the US ramped up its direct involvement, with operations in Kosovo starting on March 24, 1999 with Operation *Allied Force*, which was NATO's bombing campaign to halt the internecine hostilities and ethnic slaughter. This in itself was a major milestone insofar as this was the very first time that NATO went to war. The targets of US Navy and Royal Navy strikes were the forces of Slobodan Milosevic. This conflict was also a first in that the Royal Navy SSN, HMS *Splendid*, fired Tomahawk missiles for the first time. Seven Sea Harrier FA2s provided airborne strike, in somewhat stark contrast to the high level of airborne strikes launched by the US Navy. UK–US intelligence provided excellent intelligence that made these strikes effective. The sources and methods employed were across the span of state-of-the-art collection and analysis.

The UK supported an Australian-led operation to stabilize the situation in East Timor in 1999 by sending the destroyer HMS *Glasgow*, a Royal Marines Special Boat Section unit, and a 300-strong Gurkha unit. Intelligence support was not just across UK–Australian boundaries, but the total Five Eyes community. Similarly when the UK intervened in the civil war in Sierra Leone in 2000, with the deployment of HMS *Argyll* and HMS *Chatham*, the assault ship HMS *Ocean*, and the light Sea Harrier carrier HMS *Illustrious* with 13 Sea Harriers on board, the Five Eyes intelligence network shifted into gear. The UK had the full support of Five Eyes intelligence sources and methods. The agility and flexibility of Five Eyes intelligence to support maritime expeditionary warfare operations became increasingly important. The combined expeditionary forces of the five nations is compelling, and when given a legal international mandate, such as United Nations Security Council Resolution 1368, following the 9/11 attacks, the role of Five Eyes intelligence to support these operations becomes evident. This capability is in addition to Article Four of NATO's Charter—that the member nations will assist one another in collective self-defense, an attack upon one is an attack upon all. In this context Five Eyes intelligence works together as always and in addition across

NATO boundaries, with agreed intelligence passed to other non-Five Eyes nations based on the exigencies of the situation.

Five Eyes intelligence was crucial from October 7, 2001 when the UK and US launched key attacks with naval aircraft and cruise missiles against Taliban and al-Qaeda training camps and their communications, and Five Eyes Special Forces played key roles on the ground. On November 16, 2001, the al-Qaeda leader, Mohammed Atef, was killed by a US air strike based on excellent intelligence. On the night of October 4, 2001 USS *Theodore Roosevelt* (with Carrier Air Wing One, CVW-1) launched the initial strikes against al-Qaeda from the northern Arabian Sea. It then spent 159 consecutive days at sea, with zero dependence on shore support, breaking the record longest underway period in the history of the US Navy since World War II. This was an extraordinary achievement and, most importantly, symbolic of the flexibility and sustainability of naval power. Without a constant 24/7 stream of good intelligence from the Five Eyes its mission would have been constrained. Persistent forward-deployed presence during this vital period to destroy what was, in effect, the threat from a relatively small group of Islamic fundamentalists, that had rocked the civilized world, was sustained by round-the-clock Five Eyes intelligence. We will not dwell on the decision by the US and the UK to invade Iraq in 2003. The US House and Senate gave their approval (The Joint Resolution to Authorize the use of United States Armed Forces Against Iraq, October 2, 2002 and enacted October 16, 2002) and the House of Commons voted 412 in favor and 149 against on March 18, 2003, so in effect no one, save a few, are truly blameless regarding what many see in retrospect as strategic blunder. What is relevant here is that Five Eyes intelligence made corrections to these missteps immediately thereafter. Intelligence does not make policy and determine grand strategy. It does not adjudicate on the rights and wrong of "regime change" for example. It is a support function. However, there are many dynamics at work in the Five Eyes intelligence domain other than just providing what is hopefully the best actionable information.

Each of the Five Eyes has facilities in key locations around the globe. For example, the UK's Diego Garcia Island in the Indian Ocean and the UK sovereign base at Akrotiri in Cyprus proved invaluable for intelligence as well as military purposes. Intelligence infrastructure and five-way communications are paramount. The Australian facility at Pine Gap is of enormous importance, together with facilities in the UK itself at places like Menwith Hill in Yorkshire. However good these may be, and they are outstanding, the complexity of political–military–intelligence interactions often may cloud the enormous value that good intelligence provides. This point became clear as the Iraq campaign was waged, with a whole new set of politically unanticipated problems arising, characterized by sectarian upheaval and violence. In more structured scenarios successful outcomes are more predictable. For example, Five Eyes support to counter-piracy operations in the Gulf of Aden and off Somalia can be measured in quantifiable terms. There were 197 pirate attacks in 2009 and by 2013 there were just 13 attacks. At the time of writing the problem has been surmounted if not eliminated, though there will always be pirates in certain regions who are desperate enough, like most criminals, to chance their arm against the odds.

What this again demonstrated was the total overwhelming effectiveness of Five Eyes intelligence support. As 2019 progressed it became clear that full support was required for the preservation of international maritime law in the Persian Gulf/Arabian Sea and the Strait of Hormuz and its approaches in the Gulf of Oman. The seizure by Iran of the British tanker *Stena Impero* was described by British Foreign Secretary Jeremy Hunt as an act of piracy in the House of Commons on July 22, 2019. In order to provide escort protection, reliable real-time intelligence was required so that beneath the surface of diplomatic maneuver was a rock-solid input of current intelligence.

Humanitarian relief and evacuation of nationals and others from hot spots have always been key peacetime missions of the US and the UK. For example, the December 2004 tragic tsunami in South and South-East Asia and the July 2006 Royal Navy evacuations from Lebanon during the Israeli–Hezbollah conflict required intelligence support. In January 2010 came the Haiti earthquake, and in November 2013 the devastating Typhoon Haiyan in the Philippines, all requiring a measure of intelligence support.

In amongst natural disasters came global political change with the "Arab Spring"—a series of anti-government protests and uprisings that spread across the Middle East in early 2011. The beginnings in Tunisia spread across the Middle East, to Egypt, Libya, Yemen, Syria, Bahrain, Kuwait, Lebanon, and Oman, while the governments of Morocco and Jordan preempted revolt by various constitutional reforms knowing that protest could and would escalate. There were protests elsewhere, including Saudi Arabia, Sudan, and Mauritania, but the center of change began on December 18, 2010 in Tunisia with the Tunisian Revolution. By mid-2012 the "Spring" had faded to a "Winter." By spring 2012, rulers had been forced out in Tunisia, Egypt, Libya, and Yemen. There were major civil uprisings in Bahrain and Syria. From a UK–US intelligence perspective the 2011 Libyan revolt required support. On February 26, 2011 the United Nations imposed UN Resolution 1970, an arms embargo, on Libya, together with a UN-mandated No Fly Zone, UN Resolution 1973. UK–US intelligence provided support to Royal Navy Tomahawk strikes from the SSNs HMS *Triumph* and HMS *Turbulent* with similar strikes by US Navy surface ships in Operation *Odyssey Dawn* in March 2011. More than 112 Tomahawk cruise missiles attacked over 20 targets in the first assault: Libyan air-defense missile sites, early warning radar, and key communications facilities, mainly around and in Tripoli, Misratah, and Surt.

The Five Eyes as a whole brought a wealth of intelligence knowledge and experience to these operations, developed over a significant period from the beginning of the

Cold War through to, for example, US operations in the Lebanon in 1982–83, in Grenada in 1983, and in Panama in 1989. These operations, together with operations such as the Falklands, in Sierra Leone, and East Timor build resilience into Five Eyes intelligence coordination. Multi-intelligence sources and methods were used throughout these operations, with, for example, overhead IMINT complementing on the ground special SIGINT capabilities and HUMINT. By 2020 there is very little that the UK–US–Canada–Australia–New Zealand intelligence team has not faced. In some instances, the Five Eyes were powerless in spite of first-class intelligence. The 2008 Russian invasion of Georgia provoked no military response from the US or the West in general. In August 2013 the British House of Commons voted against intervention in the Syrian crisis and civil war, with a resounding withdrawal from concepts of "regime change" as a strategic objective of intervention. The Five Eyes intelligence apparatus is outstanding, but its purpose is not to illicit or encourage political decision making. For example, where there was excellent intelligence but no political response: India's invasion of East Pakistan in 1971 in support of Bangladesh secession invoked no response; similarly the 1978–1979 invasion of Cambodia by Vietnam to destroy the very evil Khmer Rouge regime was simply observed; in 1978–1979 Tanzania intervened in Uganda against the equally evil regime of Idi Amin without Five Eyes nations response. Perhaps tragically, the Five Eyes, and the West as a whole, did not intervene in the terrible 1994 genocide in Rwanda. Shades of the Hungarian uprising and the invasion of Czechoslovakia by the Soviet Union began to emerge in another key location.

In August 1999 Vladimir Putin, a former Soviet KGB officer, became Boris Yeltsin's Prime Minister. Following the Second Chechnya War Putin became President of Russia. In August 2008 Putin launched the invasion of Georgia, a sovereign state, against international norms and the collective positions of the Five Eyes. The occupation of the Crimea by Russia gained more attention. What all this shows is that the Five Eyes nations have picked their interventions.

Intelligence has been in a support role, and only that. In fact, in the past 30 years from 1990 to 2020, most of the interventions globally have been under the auspices and mandates of the United Nations. This observation somewhat undermines the often-misleading notion that the UN remains moribund in the face of challenge. In the early part of the period, between 1989 and 2013, the United Nations directed and supported a total of 53 documented peacekeeping operations, with the Five Eyes nations supporting these actions.

One arena where there has not been so much political differences, rather the nuances of diplomatic position-taking between the US and the other member nations of the Five Eyes, is in regard to the United Nations Convention on the Law of the Sea (UNCLOS). This became effective on November 16, 1994 with 60 nations signing the treaty. At the time of writing 166 countries and the European Union as a whole have joined the convention. International lawyers tend to debate and agree to disagree whether or not the convention has in effect codified what is commonly accepted as customary international law as embodied in prior case law. The United Nations has no role in implementing the convention. Authorities such as the International Maritime Organization, the International Whaling Commission, and the International Seabed Authority (established by the UN Convention) do play very active participatory roles. The United States is a non-party to the UNCLOS.[1] The US did participate in the prior conference on UNCLOS from 1973–1982, and the subsequent negotiations and modifications to the treaty from 1990 to 1994. In essence UNCLOS is a Law of the Sea. It defines rights and responsibilities of nations in the use of the world's oceans, delineates maritime business guidelines, environmental issues, and most significantly it lays down code for the management of marine natural resources. There is a strong legal intellectual movement in the US in support of the US Congress ratifying and the President signing the UNCLOS respectively. Much of the argument has devolved from the current situation in the South and East China Seas.

Intelligence and Nuclear Weapons Agreements

Both Iran and North Korea have challenged the West in the development of their nuclear weapons programs, and in the case of Iran in monitoring their program in light of the 2015 agreement in Lausanne, Switzerland, between Iran and the P5+1, and the EU, namely the permanent members of the United Nations Security Council—the United States, the United Kingdom, Russia, France, and China, plus Germany, and the European Union. On July 14, 2015, the Joint Comprehensive Plan of Action (JCPOA) was announced.

On May 8, 2018 the United States President, Donald Trump, announced that the United States was withdrawing from the agreement.[2] The specificity was extremely well defined as to what Iran would do in order to enjoy lifting of sanctions, with the IAEA (International Atomic Energy Authority) providing the in-country monitoring of Iran's compliance. Both the Secretary General of the United Nations, Ban Ki-moon and the Director-General of the IAEA, Yukiya Amano, welcomed the agreement. The role of intelligence is to supply ideally first-class actionable intelligence. In addition to the work of the IAEA inspectors, all of whom are regarded as highly competent by their peers in the nuclear weapons inspection community, there has been separate and independent intelligence operations by the Five Eyes on a collective basis. There have been no official political pronouncements from the UK, Canada, Australia, or New Zealand political leadership that there is evidence that Iran has violated the agreement. These member countries plus the United States will have employed and coordinated multiple sources and methods to ensure that Iran has not been cheating on the agreement. When the product of these sources and methods is aggregated with the direct in-country work of the IAEA inspectors the probability that Iran is cheating on the agreement is extremely low. The risks for Iran of losing the economic benefits of the agreement are tremendous. This illustrates perhaps better than no other contemporary case in the past five years where intelligence can only go so far. It is rather like the old equine adage, "You may lead a horse to water, but it may not drink." It is never the role of intelligence to directly influence policy. However, conversely, it is always possible, as we saw in the case of the invasion of Iraq, that intelligence can be used by politicians to justify their policies and actions, even when that intelligence is skewed.

Five Eyes intelligence in Iran clearly watches, listens, looks, samples, and follows the discreet paths of the Iranian supply chain. Rather like an analogue with the current Russian and Chinese maritime build up there is a detailed and very observable supply chain that enables a country such as Iran to assemble the infrastructure for developing nuclear capabilities, whether for energy purposes or for weaponry. A country such as Iran, with a GDP in 2017 of US$387,611 million (29th in the global GDP league table in 2017), lying in GDP terms between the state of Indiana, with a GDP of US$361,732 million and the state of Maryland with a GDP of US$397,815 million, cannot on its own produce all the key components for a nuclear weapons program. In 2017 Maryland was the 15th US state in GDP, and Indiana was the 16th US state in GDP.[3] (CIA World Factbook). This data puts Iranian national assets and wealth in the proper context, somewhat like the economic status of Russia. The further imposition of US sanctions has undoubtedly reduced Iran's current GDP in 2020. Various other countries have to be compliant in aiding, and in the past, abetting Iran, a country that we see from the above data, is not wealthy. Similarly, intellectual capital is required of a high order.

Atomic weapons scientists and technologist do not grow on trees. They have to be trained and acquire all the necessary skill sets to manage and develop a nuclear weapons program. Every part and component of a nuclear weapons system is understood by the scientific and technical intelligence community within the Five Eyes, with specialist support for example in the case of the United States, the national laboratories, such as Los Alamos, Lawrence Livermore, and Oak Ridge, where key technical staff are part and parcel of the technical intelligence community. The same is true in the United Kingdom, the other nuclear weapons power within the Five Eyes. The movement of key components and intellectual property are targets for Five Eyes intelligence. This process also indicates who else is compliant with Iran, perhaps more often for financial gain than simply just political allegiance and position taking in the politics of the Middle East. They too are watched, listened to, and closely monitored to establish the technical dependencies and relationships between key individuals. An Iranian nuclear scientist can try to hide from exposure to Five Eyes surveillance, but this is an extremely difficult task, and the more key people try to hide the more they become vulnerable to exposure and their collaboration with second and third parties becomes more and more exposed. One highly competent, knowledgeable, and experienced defector or émigré can yield so much intelligence that a whole hierarchy can be well understood.

A former MI6 HUMINT operation will illustrate just one of multiple ways of gaining access. This operation entered the public domain in November 2010 as a result of a report in the UK's *Guardian* newspaper by Richard Norton-Taylor, the lead staff reporter. This illustrates certain trade craft capabilities of the Five Eyes. MI6 employed two businessmen from a Coventry, UK-based machine tool company, Matrix Churchill, and another company, Ordtec, to spy on Saddam Hussein's nuclear weapons program. The operation only became public knowledge because two key executives, Paul Henderson of Matrix Churchill and John Paul Grecian of Ordtec, were inadvertently accused of breaching various UK trade embargoes on Iraq. One part of the UK government, that was not in the know, did not communicate with another part, the intelligence community that naturally wished to keep its deeply buried program well away from the purview of regular British civil service trade overseers. Both men were actually put on trial at the Old Bailey in London. Both men were later exonerated and well compensated by the British government. What sadly became exposed was the key fact that MI6 had gained inside access by allowing a British company to sell components to Saddam Hussein's program. MI6 gained thereby access to much of what was transpiring in Baghdad.

Today the Five Eyes keep a constant close watch on "Who, what, and where from," as far as the global movement of nuclear-related materials, components, and brain power are concerned. The same applies to non-weapon related radionuclide materials, such Cobalt-60 and Strontium-90 that if used inappropriately can, for example, be combined with various types of high explosives to make a "dirty bomb."

In the digital microwave communications-era the Five Eyes have to contend with the complexities of the electronic spill over from microwave towers, particularly of largely unencrypted communications, in order to sweep up vast volumes of communications. Satellites become crucial in this mission and at the analysis end of the business are highly sophisticated key word search engines sifting the wheat from the chaff. The latter requires constant software upgrades plus the added challenge of multiple dialects in the key languages of interest. The Cray computers of the 1970s are today dinosaurs in comparison with what the Five Eyes require to analyze the vast amount of real-time traffic.

North Korea has presented much more of a challenge for the Five Eyes than Iran at one level. The reasons are well known, particularly as North Korea has been a closed society with no access of note, and for those who have been visitors from the West, always running the risk of arrest and imprisonment. The usual North Korean excuse for such arrests has been espionage. Space becomes very significant regarding North Korea in the absence of HUMINT, very much akin to the Soviet Union during the Cold War and certainly true of China today, where western attachés for example are not permitted to visit certain key military sites inside mainland China.

It is impossible to hide nuclear construction sites from satellites. Similarly, with the North Korean missile facilities and launch sites. Modern commercial satellites are highly capable systems and imagery from these is available for the world to see, together, for example, with Chinese military construction sites on islands and atolls in the South China Sea. Facilities cannot be hidden. However, detailed technical plans and status are less easy to acquire but are nonetheless available to good scientific and technical intelligence analysis. North Korean missile telemetry gives away much valuable information that cannot be hidden. Even with mobile launchers and attempts to conceal and camouflage launch systems, both US national and commercial systems can see such platforms.

The US National Geospatial Agency is most likely ahead of any other non-Five Eyes agency in supporting collection by the US NRO, in terms of processing and presentational techniques and technology. Underground facilities and bunkers are naturally a problem for satellite surveillance, but even these are open to imaging during construction. The Five Eyes together have a wealth of historical knowledge and expertise in collecting against and analyzing nuclear weapons programs that go as far back to the early days of the Soviet programs, and the first Soviet nuclear detonation on August 29, 1949, at the Semipalatinsk nuclear test site in what is modern day Kazakhstan. Technical collection against air burst and underground nuclear tests is extremely well developed amongst the Five Eyes. MASINT or Measurement and Signature Intelligence, is not as new as may appear. The generic title covers multiple domains that have been developed over many decades since World War II. These domains include: Radar Intelligence (RADINT); Acoustic Intelligence (ACINT); Nuclear Intelligence (NUCINT); Radio Frequency and Electromagnetic Pulse Intelligence (RF/EMPINT); Electro-Optical Intelligence (ELECTRO-OPINT); Laser Intelligence (LASINT); Materials Intelligence; and various forms of Radiation Intelligence (RINT). These unclassified domains show the extent to which Five Eyes specialist technical intelligence collection has developed. Along with the science and technology underpinning these developments, the Five Eyes developed specialist clandestine collection ways and means to measure just where in the development cycle, for example, a Soviet nuclear weapons program was.

Decades of experience have been brought to bear on current Iranian and North Korean nuclear systems. An a priori knowledge base is essential for accomplishing all the above. This applies particularly to both the United States and the United Kingdom in their development of both nuclear weapons and nuclear submarine and submarine-launched missile technology, the latter being shared with the United Kingdom by the United States as a result of the agreement signed in December 1962 between President Kennedy and Prime Minister Macmillan.

A major part of the Five Eyes nuclear weapons intelligence posture has been indicators and warning (I&W), applying to the 24/7 watch for a possible nuclear weapons launch by any non UK–US country, and particularly one of the defined "rogue" nations. I&W capabilities require multi-intelligence sources and methods. Clearly one of the most worrisome scenarios is a possible accidental launch as a result of a system failure, a cyber penetration and attack, or a rogue group taking over a launch site together with all the necessary command and control facilities. An accidental missile launch that does not contain a nuclear warhead is a most challenging scenario for very clear reasons. Unannounced test launches have a high priority and require 24/7 watch systems in order to differentiate a test launch from an attack. The Japanese government has, for example, naturally been deeply concerned about North Korean ballistic missile launches passing over Japanese territory. In these situations, every source and every method come into play, particularly if the threat nation employs various deception techniques.

The above illustrates perhaps more than anything the fundamental role of the Five Eyes in maintaining global peace and security, and keeping international order on an even keel.

President Donald Trump's meeting with Kim Jong Un of North Korea in Singapore on Tuesday, June 12, 2018, was the first time a US President met with a sitting North Korean leader, in an attempt to begin negotiations for North Korea to begin de-nuclearization of its nuclear weapons program. The US President met with a man that has been a dictator who has authorized the execution and imprisonment of all who opposed him or offered any form of challenge to his dictatorship. The rocky road ahead, from June 12, 2018 onwards, was analyzed almost into paralysis by the world's media. Every political commentator throughout the globe had their version of what may or may not have transpired in Singapore in terms of likely outcomes. This was followed on June 30, 2019 by the Trump–Kim meeting at the Demilitarized Zone (DMZ) in Korea, followed by President Trump entering North Korea. World media speculation again abounded. One aspect is most certain in the uncertain world that followed June 12, 2018 and June 30, 2019—the Five Eyes intelligence community will be ever vigilant, employing not just the sentinels in space, but all and every one of the sources and methods described above to monitor North Korean moves.

The Microwave and Digital revolution and its Impact on Intelligence

The technical order of the Cold War was changed significantly by the microwave and digital revolution, together with the vastness of contemporary communications in terms of volumes of voice, data, and imagery passing via undersea cables and space. The Five Eyes communications systems have to be both well defended as well as retaining the ability to penetrate threat communications across the spectrum. We saw earlier how cyberattacks have changed the parameters of not just intelligence sources and methods but also those very sources and methods themselves. Threat systems have figured out the one key way to penetrate the Five Eyes intelligence bastion is in the development and acquisition stages, and through cyberattacks. By these means, threats to the Five Eyes can understand in advance what systems are being developed.

Penetration of the Five Eyes industrial base is the key to these operations. This is well illustrated by an article that appeared in *The Washington Post* on June 8, 2018, by Ellen Nakashima and Paul Sonne.[4] This article described how China had hacked into "a Navy contractor and secured a trove of highly sensitive data on submarine warfare" in January and February 2018. According to the article, *The Washington Post* agreed to "withhold certain details about the compromised missile project at the request of the Navy, which argued that their release could harm national security." What this illustrates is a major change in the rules of the game.

Protection of vital Five Eyes systems from cyberattack is crucial, together with protection of space assets and in particular GPS satellites and the infrastructure that support them. GPS is not just the means and end for an almost endless list of military and intelligence systems it is the ways and the means for multiple global applications across every sector of human activity, and not simply the obvious ones related to our daily use of GPS mapping and location finding. GPS underpins the global financial system. Dependable commercial satellite systems are part of the way of life of the global economy. Detecting and countering threats to these systems by the Five Eyes has now risen very high on the list of intelligence missions.

We can look back to the 1880s and the age of Blinker Hall and his father to the communications transformation of the 21st century. During this period one aspect of the intelligence process has not changed. This is open source material, or simply what our fellow human beings write. Within open sources is a wealth of intelligence that relates to, for example, the likely intentions of nation states. It is very easy to neglect this valuable source of information. The amount of valuable information in open sources is simply prodigious.

On Thursday, May 17, 2018 Captain James E. Fanell, US Navy (retired), a former Director of Intelligence and Information Operations, US Pacific Fleet, gave a lengthy and detailed statement to the US House of Representatives Permanent Select Committee on Intelligence (HPSCI), with specific reference to China's worldwide military expansion. Captain Fanell's statement was entitled, "China's Global Naval Strategy and Expanding Force Structure: A Pathway to Hegemony."[5] His statement drew heavily on reliable Chinese open sources. What the Chinese have indeed told us about their future plans and expansion not just in Asia, but beyond. The outer island chain expansion policy has been followed in Chinese literature by Captain Fanell and his former staff. When these open source writings are coupled with what the Chinese have actually done, together with other intelligence sources and methods, a highly reliable intelligence picture emerges.

Listening and reading is invaluable, and this applies across the board of foreign societies, not just key leaders. This encompasses scientific and technical journals, and a whole range of foreign technical, political and economic press and journal sources, together with official governmental statements and speeches. As Captain Fanell wisely demonstrated in great detail, "what the Chinese have said they plan to do, they have indeed done." The open source approach may be sometimes neglected. For example, the foreign and Five Eyes nations' open source literature is regularly addressing the issue of undersea communications cable vulnerability, and reports of foreign undersea intrusions on vital undersea nodes. This is clearly a serious issue, and one that cannot be ignored by not just the Five Eyes intelligence community but the combined political leadership of each member nation.

The world has changed so dramatically in geo-political terms since 9/11 and in technical terms there has been a revolution in digital and microwave technologies. The disparities with the 20th century are enormous. The Five Eyes must not lose, institutionally, culturally, technically, and operationally, some of the key achievements of the 20th century. The last thing that the Five Eyes need to do in the world today is lose the knowledge and experience base that may still be relevant in spite of the dramatic changes that we have examined. Reinvention of the wheel is a costly experience.

On February 27, 1984, Denis Healey, Member of Parliament in the UK House of Commons and former Minister of Defence in the 1960s made the following observation: "GCHQ has been by far the most valuable source of intelligence for the British government ever since it began operating at Bletchley during the last war. British skills in interception and code breaking are unique and highly valued by our allies. GCHQ has been a key element in our relationship with the United States for more than forty years."[6] Denis Healey's words were turned into bricks and mortar 12 years later when between 1996 and 2003 the plans were laid, construction began, and was completed, for the new GCHQ complex near Cheltenham, England. The grand old men of GC&CS, such as Hugh Foss, Dilly Knox, Commander Alastair Denniston, Commander Edward Travis, and the early leaders of SIS, such as Commander Mansfield Cumming (the original "C") and Hugh "Quex" Sinclair, would have been duly proud of the new edifice, the "Doughnut", called such because of its doughnut like shape, that emerged in the English countryside. It is salutary to reflect that on October 21, 1941, four great stalwarts of Bletchley Park, Hugh Alexander, Stuart Milner Barry, Gordon Welchman, and the inimitable Alan Turing, took it upon themselves, without any approval or the knowledge of higher authority, to write to Winston Churchill directly asking for more resources for Bletchley Park. Such was the change from the dark days of October 1941 to the brighter post-Cold War days of the 1990s, with the post-war record of GCHQ and its American and Five Eyes cousins in Canada, Australia, and New Zealand, standing as a record of successful cooperation.

Winston Churchill saw the incredible value of Bletchley and made the necessary investment immediately. We can reflect on Professor Max Newman and Tommy Flowers at the Post Office Research Facility, at Dollis Hill, building the first electronic computer "Colossus" for Bletchley Park. The great cooperation between the United Kingdom and the United States exemplified in the January 1941 agreement to share the MAGIC data with the UK, a quid pro quo for UK ENIGMA data. In September 1942, the Deputy Director of Bletchley, Commander Edward Travis, and the Head of the Naval Section, Frank Birch, traveled to Washington DC to conclude the "Holden Agreement" that initiated full and total UK–US cooperation and integration on German naval traffic, of which ENIGMA was a critical component. This was further expanded in 1944. In May 1943 the UK–US BRUSA Agreement expanded cooperation to German Army and Air Force SIGINT traffic. In 1945 Winston Churchill is reputed to have told King George VI that ENIGMA's product, ULTRA, won the war, according to Gustav Bertrand, the French military intelligence officer who played a key role in deciphering ENIGMA in the 1930s.[7]

After 1945 nothing changed. UK–US cooperation continued in full, with the VENONA Project a great example of successful joint penetration of Soviet KGB message traffic. The latter led to the pinpointing of the British spies Donald MacLean, Guy Burgess, John Cairncross, and the notorious Kim Philby, who caused massive damage to MI6 operations. The British atom spy Klaus Fuchs was similarly detected. As part of the growing involvement and cooperation with Australia, the KGB Moscow–Canberra cable traffic[8] was read in almost real time by GCHQ. The British First Sea Lord, Admiral of the Fleet Andrew Browne Cunningham, First Viscount Cunningham (nicknamed "ABC") wrote in his diary on November 21, 1945, "Much discussion about 100 percent cooperation with the USA about SIGINT. Decided that less than 100 per cent cooperation was not worth having".[9] Admiral Cunningham's words sum up aptly the state of play that has persisted within the Five Eyes after World War II through to our time.

All was not rosy during this period. For example, when North Korea invaded South Korea on Sunday, June 25, 1950, both the US and the UK were taken by surprise. Similarly, when the Chinese entered the Korean War in October 1950, both nations were surprised. In 1956 both GCHQ and NSA had failed to predict the Soviet invasion of Hungary. President Truman was so unimpressed with intelligence's performance that in 1952 he had ordered the classified "Project K" that created the National Security Agency (NSA) at Fort Meade, Maryland. Similarly, in the UK there was disquiet over "our intelligence about Soviet development of atomic weapons is very scanty."[10] On August 21, 1968 the Soviet Union's land forces invaded Czechoslovakia to suppress the "Prague Spring" led by Dubcek. In spite of warnings from highly reliable sources on the ground showing quite clearly that the Soviets and their Warsaw Pact allies were not just preparing but actually moving towards the Czech border with the clear intention of invasion, the British Joint Intelligence

Committee in London failed miserably in its assessment to provide clear direction to the Prime Minister and then to the Five Eyes nations and the NATO allies. There was intense criticism of the Cabinet Office staff by the British Ministry of Defence. The British BRIXMIS team in East Germany gave very loud and clear warnings of an impending invasion. The CIA performed no better. After this debacle there was a power shift in London from the Cabinet Office to the Defence Intelligence Staff.

The Importance of SIGINT

The British Ministry of Defence had its own considerable panoply of collection and analysis assets as the post-Czech invasion period progressed, through into the 1970s and today. On a more positive note Five Eyes SIGINT was forced by circumstances to become ever more critical as tensions erupted in the Middle East, after a gap following the 1967 June War. Egypt and Syria launched what appeared to be a surprise attack on Israel on October 6, 1973, beginning what became known as the Yom Kippur War. Shortly thereafter Turkey invaded Cyprus. Some analysts and historians have ranked this surprise attack as an intelligence failure by the West not dissimilar to the Japanese attack on Pearl Harbor, and even Hitler's invasion of Russia. The evidence is by no means all in on this issue, even 47 years after the event, given the need to still maintain the key sanctity of various Five Eyes sources and methods.

The country that was undoubtedly most surprised was Israel. In effect the attack was a preemptive invasion. There were repercussions in both Washington and London over the timely analysis and distribution of what was, in retrospect, clear evidence of Syrian and Egyptian plans and preparations to attack Israel. In a not dissimilar vein, there was similar disquiet in the corridors of power on both sides of the Atlantic after the February 1979 fall of the Shah of Iran. UK and US SIGINT, out of locations such as Cyprus and Turkey where there were clear collection sites, had not been asleep at the switch, and nor had MI6 and the CIA, together with other collateral sources and methods. There was simply very little that the Western powers could do to change the dynamics on the ground in Iran of a successful revolution.

The failures in the UK in the spring of 1982 as Argentina invaded the Falkland Islands have been addressed elsewhere, but suffice to say that all the evidence existed that the dictator General Leopoldo Galtieri and his cohorts Admiral Jorge Anyana and Air Force General Lami Dozo were planning to invade. The resignation of the British Foreign Secretary, Lord Carrington, says it all, in terms of the political failure to take action as the situation worsened. What these failures brought home to the political leaders of the Five Eyes was that SIGINT and the other key sources and methods had worked admirably. What had failed was analysis and coordination, and in some cases listening to experts lower down in the bureaucratic chain and process, and then addressing what political options were open. As a result of these lessons learned, the leaders of the free world found themselves increasingly dependent on

SIGINT intercepts for timely and accurate intelligence. Once the realities of the Argentinean invasion sunk in within the Whitehall bureaucracy the intelligence community was able to find innovative ways to counter capability discrepancies. For example, the Norwegians intercepted Soviet satellite data containing information on the movement and tracks of Argentinean naval assets. This crucial data was passed to their British ally and fellow NATO member. Also, by contrast, it should be noted that the earlier invasion of Afghanistan by the Soviet Union in 1979 was matched by outstanding prior invasion SIGINT within the Five Eyes. When the British marched into Port Stanley on June 15, 1982, and the Argentinean forces surrendered, the lion's share of intelligence had been by far provided by Five Eyes SIGINT from multiple sources.

The Royal Air Force's NIMROD flights from Ascension Island and operations of specially equipped Nimrod SIGINT aircraft from Punta Arenas in Chile were not significant in the bigger SIGINT picture. Other sources and methods from the Five Eyes SIGINT community dominated. The initial UK SIGINT failures are highlighted by the key fact that it was not until Wednesday, March 31, 1982 that the JIC in London had incontrovertible SIGINT of an impending invasion that then took place on Friday, April 2, 1982. After this major lesson learned the GCHQ Director, Brian Tovey, committed to investing in a dedicated UK GCHQ SIGINT satellite capability. This was long overdue to complement the extensive US space network.

The US had become somewhat leery of the UK's commitment to the classical intelligence agreements when Britain joined the European Economic Community (EEC), the forerunner to the European Union (EU) in 1972. There were some blips on the screen between the two nations during the Kissinger years, but these amounted to nothing in the long term, with Mach 3 SR-71 flights and other even more sensitive operations being conducted from the UK with full US participation. US facilities at Chicksands in Bedfordshire, and at Edsel in Scotland, performed legendary feats at the height of the Cold War, the former tracking Soviet Air Force operations and the latter a US Navy Security Group special communications facility. Highly sensitive UK–US programs were being executed well outside public purview. Kissinger seems to have been sensitive to what the Europeans may do in the future, particularly if the British assisted them, in improving their intelligence collection capabilities. This was a somewhat narrow view of countries that were major NATO allies, irrespective of the French position. Some historians have made much of Henry Kissinger's apparent antagonism towards the UK over intelligence matters. The undeniable fact is that the agreements were not only rock-solid agreements, indeed inviolate treaties, but also the institutional daily round the clock connectivity and personnel exchanges between GCHQ and NSA, the CIA and MI6; and the Canadian, Australian, and New Zealand intelligence equivalent organizations, rendered Kissinger's protestations ineffective. Any symbolic acts by Henry Kissinger were seen by the permanent staffs within the Five Eyes as just one man's somewhat irascible temperament at a time when his President was on the slippery slope towards resignation.

The addition of Canada, Australia, and New Zealand to the special UK–US relationship brought added strength in multiple ways. In Hong Kong alone, the US, UK, and Australia worked round the clock to run SIGINT operations, agent running, and interrogating Chinese defectors. In the 1950s and 1960s as the new post-World War II order solidified the US rapidly came to realize the significance of Hong Kong as a critical overseas intelligence center, together with multiple other locations that were British, Australian, Canadian, and New Zealand territories. The Australians' SIGINT targets included China, Indonesia, and Vietnam. In the 1960s the British and the Australians worked hand in glove in combined SIGINT operations during the Indonesian Confrontation. These operations laid the foundations for the development of special tactics, techniques, and procedures (TTPs) for applying near or real-time SIGINT in support of Special Forces, particularly the British Special Air Service (SAS) and Royal Marines Special Boat Service (SBS), and the Australian SAS.

Many of these TTPs have been expanded and applied since, in multiple operations and locations, including operations against the Irish Republican Army (IRA) in Northern Ireland. Nowhere was the Cold War hotter than in Berlin where the US and the UK worked side by side to break into Soviet communications. The tapping of the underground landlines that was so vital for Soviet communications was vulnerable as it was not encrypted. The Soviets considered it invulnerable as it was "underground." Tunneling as a source of intelligence from underground cables and moving agents across closely guarded, often impassable boundaries and fortifications, such as the Berlin Wall, has been a most effective way to avoid detection.

In the case of the Berlin Wall communications tunnel it was only exposed to the Soviets by the treachery of the British spy George Blake, who in 1956, as an MI6/SIS officer, betrayed the program to his Soviet controllers. However, data gleaned from this one source before Blake's treachery was prolific, including information on Soviet KGB and GRU personnel and operations. Similarly, undersea communications cables, as Blinker Hall had demonstrated so effectively before the outbreak of war in 1914, were equally vulnerable to highly complex operations. The Five Eyes cooperated fully in military airborne reconnaissance and clandestine high-altitude photo reconnaissance and SIGINT and ELINT collection.

Much has been written about the aftereffects of the 1960 shoot down of the U-2 spy plane piloted by Francis Gary Powers, and the subsequent US dependence on satellite SIGINT. The US launched its first SIGINT satellite in 1960, in fact not that long after Powers was shot down. However, the use of highly specialist aircraft by the Five Eyes persists to this day. In fact, the U-2 program gained new life. The US SR-71 Blackbird spy plane performed admirably until it became technically obsolete, as well as not cost effective. However, during its life it operated at a moment's notice from key sites such as RAF station Mildenhall in the UK. Since

1960 the Five Eyes have had multiple aircraft types performing sensitive SIGINT and ELINT operations. Aircraft, like ships and submarines, can gain access in ways and times that satellites cannot. Because of their orbits and constellation programming and footprints, satellites cannot always be in the right place at the right time, nor can they carry various types of highly specialist intelligence collection equipment that cannot be housed in satellites, and also satellites cannot carry personnel for collection operations. The RAF Nimrod RI aircraft, for example, operated out of many different bases around the globe to provide critical SIGINT. RAF station Sharjah in Oman, and clandestine sites in Iran before the fall of the Shah, were also used to launch covert flights. Such flights were necessary when satellite data was either unavailable or the nature of the collection mission predicated an aircraft, not a satellite.

Specialist aircraft, supplemented now by unmanned aerial vehicles and drones, are still key elements of the Five Eyes collection inventory. The attacks on the USS *Liberty* and the USS *Pueblo* dented the Five Eyes confidence in spy ships, however the submarine persists as a critical component of the covert and clandestine collection of the most sensitive intelligence. The only truly dead spot in all these years before the break-up of the Soviet Union, and the digital and communications revolution of the 21st century, was probably the Suez crisis of 1956, a sad blemish on an otherwise outstanding record of cooperation. On October 29, 1956 the British Prime Minister, Anthony Eden, ordered the launch of Operation *Musketeer* to capture the Suez Canal from the Nasser regime in Egypt. British SIGINT played a crucial role in this operation. Eden decided to share neither his plans nor GCHQ SIGINT with President Eisenhower in the United States. Eden made a fateful mistake by not consulting and working with Eisenhower in the resolution of Nasser's take-over of the Suez Canal. The positive aspects are that lessons were learned and the intelligence sharing that had persisted during and after World War II was soon back in fine fettle. Harmony had only temporarily been ruffled.

Has There Been a "Poor Relations Syndrome"?

There has never been what might possibly be construed as a "Poor Relations Syndrome" between the US on one hand and the other members of the Five Eyes family on the other, the UK, Canada, Australia, and New Zealand, based on massive US investment in intelligence compared with the other four nations. In spite of the irascibility of Henry Kissinger mentioned earlier, the Five Eyes have universally recognized one critical aspect of their relationship, that the sum of the individual parts is much greater than the individual national capabilities. This is the sustaining mantra of the Five Eyes, joined together in the dark days of World War II and sustained during the Cold War to our times. Like a well-knit family that may occasionally have an issue, the Five Eyes remains a coherent whole.

As we look back on this from the modern era, we have to ask ourselves, "Have we forgotten the past at the expense of being absorbed with the present?" Technological advances have certainly changed the physical collection environment, but are the challenges and innovations of the past being lost in the noise of contemporary technical change?

Landlines are just as important today as they were when buried under Berlin at the height of the Cold War. Similarly undersea cables, with fiber optic cables today carrying per millisecond more data internationally than is possible to comprehend in terms of conventional numbers, are as vulnerable and exploitable today as when Blinker Hall ordered the cutting of the German undersea cable in 1914. Mail was an 18th-century means of interception, predated by the Tudor and Stuart periods in the UK that had the British monarchy's agents locating and tracking couriers of undesirable nations, such as Spain and France, and intercepting the written word. Drugs today are increasingly being transferred and sold by mail to reduce the interception of drug dealers, street peddlers, and their higher-up drug lords. Mail has new roles in the Five Eyes world, and it will require new technologies to detect and track mail, together with their senders and receivers. The more the criminal community and foreign intelligence agencies become fearful of email and cell phone intercepts the more reliance will be made of former means including, for example, "word of mouth," via couriers. Detecting and tracking the latter will require additional technological expertise. Old-fashioned code systems, long used by the British and other European nations to communicate with their agents overseas, have a new life in deeply buried couriers' identities.

Uncovering money laundering schemes by terrorist and other criminal elements is prima facie a task for highly sophisticated contemporary computer networks, achievable in a global economic and banking network where trillions of dollars are transferred daily. Clandestine or covert arms deals have to be paid for across borders. Russian weapons bought by Iran, for example, for Hezbollah, however much hidden in the murky world of burying identities and shipments, have to be paid for at key points. Russian Mafia and oligarchic controllers want their money. Identifying and stopping those payments are vital. By the same token transfer evasion by covertly shipping large cash sums (in the tens of millions of US dollars or equivalent) have to be located and tracked. There is nothing new here. The British Navy and its merchantmen regularly intercepted and effectively stole the equivalent of billions of dollars' worth of gold from the Spanish in particular.

Intercepting terrorist and criminal groups' cash payments is critical, together with state-sponsored money laundering and clandestine shipments to fund arms, agents, and other activities, such as communications centers and propaganda machines. Cyber hackers and criminals have to be paid. Locating, tracking, and intercepting their funds is paramount as more conventional international bank transfers are derailed.

Deception and New Innovative Intelligence Opportunities

Deception is as old as the hills in terms of intelligence practice. The art of deception can be easily lost in the haze of trillions of bits of intercepted communications, video, and other data. The brilliance of the "Double-cross System" that was masterminded by the British in World War II has been lost in the noise of contemporary communications cleverness. Controlled and extremely well-designed false information can be created and passed by multiple channels, and not just the obvious modern media tools. Data mining and analysis enables perpetrators, such as the attacks on the US election in 2016, to determine who to hit with information, indeed propaganda, to persuade and influence.

On a larger scale the tragedy at Pearl Harbor had its recompense with the brilliance of the American code breakers at the battle of Midway, the key turning point in the Pacific war. Technology can sometimes blur the vision of the art of the possible, as if only sheer technology itself is the answer. Asking the critical question, "what do we want to achieve?" is crucial, before marching down the all-expensive technological path. By the same token the Five Eyes need to be ever vigilant about what possible adversaries may do in this domain to deceive and cajole the allies into fateful states of mind that pronounce, "all is well." For example, can Iran and North Korea execute workarounds to deceive the allies over arms-control issues? Diplomacy can suddenly become moribund in the face of sudden recognition that friendly nations have been duped.

Both Germany and Japan were skillful in evading their arms programs in the 1930s, so that by the time the Chamberlain government woke up and the Prime Minister headed to Munich to try to negotiate with Hitler, Neville Chamberlain was very much in the situation that Winston Churchill so aptly described on becoming Prime Minister: "You cannot negotiate with a tiger when your head is in its mouth." The Soviet acquiescence over nuclear arms control was deeply investigated by the Five Eyes to ensure that American negotiators were truly talking with well-intentioned opposite numbers, and not being drawn into the tiger's mouth, to quote Winston Churchill. The MAD (Mutual Assured Destruction) doctrine was working and both sides were indeed acting in total good faith to the benefit of global security from nuclear warfare.

The Five Eyes all collectively participate in the management of and use of the international maritime Automatic Identification System (AIS), an outstanding piece of modern communications and data architecture that is managed by the IMO (International Maritime Organization), a specialist agency of the United Nations responsible for regulating shipping, with headquarters in London. Its antecedent organization (Inter-Government Maritime Consultative Organization) was founded in Geneva on March 17, 1948, with changes in organizational structure occurring in 1959 and 1982. There are currently 174 member states and three associate members. IMO has a comprehensive full-time staff and UN secretariat. Its headquarters are located on the Albert Embankment in London. The Secretaries General of IMO have been international. All members have ratified the Convention on the International Maritime Organization. The three associate members are the Faroe Islands, Hong Kong, and Macao. Most non-members are land locked, except for the Federated States of Micronesia and Nauru, which are island nations in the Pacific Ocean. IMO controls approximately 60 legal instruments binding on member nations. Secretaries General of IMO have come from the UK, Denmark, France, India, Canada, Greece, Japan, and South Korea.

IMO has multiple technical and safety committees and many more sub committees. Its work and organization are far too voluminous to describe here. AIS is an outstanding service and capability of IMO, used extensively by the Five Eyes to augment information on the identity and precise movement of all merchant ships of member nations. Information includes current speed and direction, together with details on port of departure, intended arrival port, cargo, technical details of each ship, all passed in real time to any other AIS ship that must have an AIS/GPS receiver/transmitter. AIS helps guarantee safety at sea, particularly collision avoidance. AIS ships now rely heavily on AIS as a key addition to radar as well as the mark one eyeball. AIS data is provided by a constellation of commercial satellites in or very near real time.

My sailboat that has been ported in Annapolis, Maryland, for many years has an AIS integrated with the navigation systems and GPS display. I can examine detailed information on all AIS fitted shipping within any area of navigational concern. Rogue ships that are mandated to be fitted with AIS, because of their size, and are not transmitting AIS data, even when fitted with AIS, become clear targets for surveillance and tracking. Such ships are marked as possible vessels with non-commercial intent, including possible piracy, gun running, drug and human trafficking, and acting as an intelligence gatherer. Such rogue ships may then be tracked by other covert means. If such ships are transmitting on AIS and are on the rogue ship list, then they will be watched by the Five Eyes. This was impossible in the pre-commercial satellite years when the US National Reconnaissance Office and the Soviet Union, followed later by the Chinese, and indeed the British with their SIGINT satellites, dominated satellite intelligence. Today IMO-controlled satellite data, and multiple other commercial systems provide outstanding imagery. There is nothing that the Chinese can hide from such commercial satellites on the reefs and atolls in the South China Sea, and the disputed Paracel and Spratly Islands. Anyone with a laptop computer or similar device can look at commercial data of Chinese military installations in the South China Sea.

The Five Eyes have a golden opportunity to transcend the nature of hitherto highly classified government satellite imagery by combining commercial satellite data, and where and when necessary, releasing this for public consumption in those circumstances where it is in the public interest to raise awareness of unfriendly and threatening acts by those who intend to disrupt the international order. This can apply to all manner of situations, not just the more ominous scenarios, such as a possible Chinese threat to Taiwan, and at worst, preparation for and execution of a covert invasion plan.

Very little can be hidden from commercial satellites today. As the 2020s progress such data will become even better. Public knowledge and awareness are better served if information is shared by the Five Eyes in a responsible agreed manner, rather than commercial satellite companies and private individuals pointing out worrisome data. This applies equally to other issues, for example IMO concerns for ships depositing trash in coastal and international waters, illegal fishing and over-fishing, and contraband of many kinds. Assistance to local national law enforcement agencies and coast guards can only do good. On a more insidious level international hackers, both state and non-state sponsored, together with criminal gangs and mafia-sponsored entities, have penetrated global maritime companies with serious financial effects. This is achieved by disrupting key maritime terminal operations and the detailed workings of large-scale companies such as Maersk. Ships' physical equipment has been hacked causing for example dangerous effects on Ro-Ro ships' ballasting systems. Cyber security in the maritime domain has to be of key national interest to the Five Eyes as well as IMO members.

The same cyber threats apply to offshore oil and gas rigs, and most of all to the huge oil and gas merchant ships that are the life blood of the Western and Asian nations. Economic disruption can occur therefore without sinking a single ship, re-emphasizing the concept of the defense of maritime trade. This type of cyberattack is also a form of both blockade and embargo if it prevents the free passage of ships and goods. Mining may be unnecessary in the Straits of Hormuz, for example, if effective cyberattacks can leave port handling systems in disarray and the actual working machinery spaces and navigation systems of ships out of control and dysfunctional. A most insidious threat is to the actual electronic charts on which all modern ships, with very limited crews because of extensive automation, rely for their navigation. Penetration of these systems, particularly the GPS data itself, can be potentially catastrophic particularly when ships are on autopilot. In 2019 I was given a briefing and demonstration of the latest unclassified commercial technology. After the demonstration I held a small highly capable GPS disruption device that can operate within a limited but nonetheless effective range of ships, and other key locations and assets. This also applies to airfields and the effects on aircraft systems. GPS signals are very vulnerable because of the nature of their transmission modes. The threat to seaborne trade has taken on not just new meaning in the 21st century but a whole new complexion of threats. The Five Eyes will need to consolidate their capabilities in the defense of maritime trade, the lifeblood of the world.

The one area of international business that has a direct financial interest and security concern in these realms is maritime insurance. Shipping insurance can come at a high price when the risks increase to a global insurance company such as Lloyds of London, founded in 1686 by Edward Lloyd. Lloyds is not an insurance company as such. It is a corporate body governed by the Lloyds Act of 1871 and other acts of the British Parliament. Lloyds is a group of financial backers grouped in "syndicates" that come together in order to "spread risk." These are the famous Lloyds underwriters. They can be both individuals and corporations. In 2017 the annual value was 33.6 billion pounds sterling according to published annual reports. The relevance of this is that Lloyds List Intelligence is an extremely capable maritime intelligence service. The database alone is extraordinarily detailed, up to date with real-time data, and provides detailed insight into global shipping and commercial maritime operations. The Five Eyes have an ever-present interest in its data and data sources. In the event of a crisis in, for example, the Persian Gulf (Arabian Sea) situation involving Iran in 2019 and threats to merchant shipping, Lloyds can have a major impact insofar as insurance rates may immediately rise, or Lloyds may forbid transit through various sea areas in order to mitigate risk. Ships that ignore such restrictions may proceed at their own risk without insurance, a huge risk for say a 100,000- to 500,000-ton oil tanker. In the current environment risks from cyberattacks are equally if not more threatening than, for example, clandestine mining. The interface between the Five Eyes, their respective navies, and Lloyds' data is therefore an enduring capability.

Institutional Memory Loss

Shifting away from modern electronics and cyber warfare we should likely rethink lessons learned from both World War II and the early post-war years when the British and their Commonwealth allies within the Five Eyes successfully practiced unconventional warfare, infiltration, and espionage that was different from what may be described as organized special warfare forces. This refers not to covert CIA-type agents or Seal Team Six-type operatives, or MI6 agent runners, or any of the several cadres of US Special Forces units (Green Berets, Rangers), or by comparison with the former Soviet Union, Russian Spetsnaz. The Five Eyes institutionally have forgotten how British SOE (Special Operations Executive) recruited, trained, and operated in Nazi-occupied Europe during World War II. The institutional memory has been lost and much of it resides in the British National Archives, and some highly important written narratives by operatives who are long gone, a very salutary thought.

The US Office of Strategic Services (OSS), founded by William Joseph "Wild Bill" Donovan, predecessor to the CIA, never really caught up with the British SOE, mainly because the US joined the European war later, effectively not until well into 1942. The Five Eyes may wish to reevaluate why and how SOE was so successful, not just in following Winston Churchill's explicit order to "set Europe ablaze," but in the extremely subtle, deceptive, and capable ways in which SOE operatives, many of whom were not at all the typical Special Forces and MI6 types, were so successful in clandestinely disrupting the Nazi occupation. The SOE operative used many subtler means than just kinetic attacks, with a whole range of penetration skills that have been lost in the passage of time. This is not just about deep cover and identity obscuration. It is about a whole range of cultural, linguistic, technical, and psychological knowledge-based skills that are not easily imbibed in the specialist schools run today by CIA, MI6, and their sister organizations in Canada, Australia, and New Zealand. The types of people involved were indeed very special, and extremely capable. Women made excellent SOE operatives. The SOE people were different, the skill sets were different, and the modus operandi was different from classical agent running and HUMINT operations.

In the modern era various media sources play well to the latter-day SOE trainee and operative, supported by the most covert communications capabilities. Take one scenario: we have observed earlier that without nuclear weapons and a large cyberattack force, the Putin regime supported by the Russian oligarchs and mafia would be nothing in the great international scheme of things. With a GDP less than the state of California, the state of Russia is poor, and relies on energy exports for its lifeblood. Nuclear weapons and cyber capabilities make Russia a serious threat to global stability. Agent running in Russia belongs in my opinion to a bygone age, unless of course a Russian citizen decides of their own free will to come over. In the latter situation, an SOE-type asset is the best in-situ handler. Russia, China, North Korea, Iran, and several less worrisome nations, have intensive national security and counterintelligence organizations, an army of dedicated and loyal specialists supported by thousands of minions, and, in the case of Russia and China, targeting not just foreign nationals but indigenous disaffection and opposition. Classical CIA-type operations using diplomatic cover are more and more in the moribund category. Regular diplomatic contacts, observation on the ground, photography, and electronic eavesdropping are much more productive than seducing nationals to give away secrets. The SOE-type operative is a different person, and will be far more effective in this new world order and, most of all, in terms of personal security and survivability, is almost guaranteed not to be detected and arrested, interrogated, tortured, and murdered.

The Five Eyes may need to collectively analyze this requirement and rethink the past. There are within these overarching capabilities skill sets that must be left only to the day of reckoning, when it is critical for their use. The new Hitlers and the Waffen-SS are with us, but in different forms. There are still brutal dictatorships, but they cannot be addressed by kinetic force unless they first do things that require only one response. Much more subtle, safer, and over time far more effective techniques and procedures are required from people with different skill sets than the traditional CIA and MI6 recruit of the past. All the above refers not to the SOE operatives who were indeed committed to kinetic operations in fulfilment of Winston Churchill's directive, such as sabotage, assassination of Gestapo leaders (Geheime Staatspolizei), and amassing weapons in readiness for the liberation of Europe. It refers to the much more complex tasks of total insinuation and infiltration and total undetected acceptance in society for long-term intelligence gathering and warning and indicators, none of which involve high-risk agent recruitment or exposure to counterintelligence operations.

***

Tagging, tracking, and locating technologies and concepts of operation became paramount in the pre- and post-9/11 eras. Knowing where the threat was is one thing, being able to continuously monitor it was another. The large Joint Stars USAF aircraft (a converted Boeing 707) is able to track a vast number of mobile ground targets and relay the data, but it has endurance limitations in terms of both fuel and crew. The large UAVs such as Global Hawk have considerable range and endurance and successor systems in a stealthy mode can provide persistent round-the-clock data to complement satellite IMINT, ELINT, and SIGINT systems. I worked both ends of this problem as a program lead after the first Gulf War ended in 1991 until very recently (acquiring data and then distributing it in a timely fashion) and a key achievement of the team that I have worked with was the operational introduction of integrating all the above and many other tactical and theater sensor systems into one single multi-intelligence collection and distribution system in virtual real time, a huge leap forward compared with the situation in the First Gulf War. We gained operational experience and developed CONOPS (Concepts of Operation) for users by rigorous and realistic FBEs (Fleet Battle Experiments) and LOEs (Limited Objective Experiments), using very realistic threats played by SEAL teams. The unclassified title Distributed Common Ground Station (DCGS) eventually entered the lexicon many years later, providing an unclassified insight into what we achieved.

Behind the sensor systems, HUMINT reporting, and clever integration and distribution technologies lay answers to major problems when intelligence data was either too scant or the data was overwhelming. How could one make reliable decisions from disparate and often confusing data? "How do you know what you don't know?" to coin a well-known intelligence adage. How can you make sound decisions from imprecise data when traditional statistical means based on well-used probability theory cannot apply? I worked with teams that employed advanced Bayesian log likelihood mathematical techniques that enabled us to sort the wheat from the chaff. My colleagues Carl "Tony" Barlow and Dr. Theodore "Ted" Kadota are exemplars of solving almost intractable intelligence problems using unique applications of Bayes' original theory. Thomas Bayes was an English statistician, philosopher, and Presbyterian minister, 1701–1761, educated at Edinburgh University, and one of those incredible unknown geniuses during his lifetime. His notes and key theory were published after his death by Richard Price. Bayes' work enabled my colleagues and me to resolve several major problems for US intelligence. These problems involved, for example, locating and tracking sensitive targets in complex physical environments. Targets included materials and equipment as well as people.

Operational field work instilled in me the need to always bear in mind the operative on the ground, often in difficult and dangerous circumstances, and to provide the best means of secure undetectable communication and the best real-time data. Weather comprises a vast array of information. To couple terrain data with weather and the other "Multi INTS" referred to earlier became an imperative. Weather, compromising both meteorological and oceanographic data, is not as easy to access and provide in formats that fit the operational needs of those on the ground, or for example a SEAL team being launched from a submarine at night in difficult sea conditions. A colleague, Jay Rosenthal, came up with a perfect scientific solution. As a distinguished former Navy METOC specialist Jay worked with us to integrate the complexities of ocean, land, and air weather with 3-dimensional terrain data provided by the National Geospatial Agency and overlain with all the "INTS" that are relevant for any particular location, scenario, and operational intelligence requirement, a huge step forward for clandestine operatives and Special Forces.

Targeting is a very generic term in the intelligence community. It has many and varied connotations depending on the scenario. Most readers may link targeting to a kinetic solution, placing a Tomahawk missile from a submarine or a Hellfire missile from say a Predator UAV on a terrorist target. This is correct but it may also vary to include an electronic target such as an individual's computer in an another country, a highly technical R&D program in a less friendly nation, an individual or group that are laundering money, running drugs, or are engaged in human trafficking, and more recently for example, attacking the election infrastructure in the United States. These are all targets and require different collection techniques. The legendary CIA operative Theodore "Ted" Shackley (1927–2002), known to all operatives in the CIA Directorate of Operations as the "Blond Ghost" had enormous clandestine experience before becoming the Deputy Director of the CIA's Directorate of Operations (the "DO"), second in command, in other words, for all covert operations. When Admiral Stansfield Turner became Director of the CIA in 1979 in the Carter administration, he cleaned house in the DO, arguing that clandestine operations had a poor track record and NSA provided better intelligence. Shackley was relieved with many others and he retired in 1979. The Reagan administration took a different view under its new Director, William J. Casey (director from January 1981 to January 1987), and clandestine operations were reborn, though many key personnel had either retired, left, or found reemployment in other parts of the US government.

Shackley did retire, but he never really left. He contacted me to visit him in his Rosslyn office, in Arlington, and asked me to perform a covert operation for the Agency on behalf of the President in a country I cannot name for obvious reasons.

The reason was most sensitive and there were major risks. I fulfilled the mission and was duly remunerated and thanked but only after I had narrowly escaped and spent several days in a foreign hospital, not in the target country, recovering from a poisoning attempt on my life. The information I collected went straight to the Oval Office. What this shows is that very occasionally HUMINT is invaluable when all the other myriad collection systems just cannot do the job in a timely manner. But this is rare.

Special Support to SUBPAC (Submarine Forces, US Pacific Fleet) was always one of the most enjoyable and rewarding professionally, with output that made a difference to keeping the United States on top in the Pacific region in what at the time was just the emergence of a resurgent China and its PLAN (People's Liberation Army Navy). Submarines are not ubiquitous, and the US Pacific Fleet has naturally a finite number of nuclear-powered attack submarines forward deployed, on station, at any moment in time. The team that I led provided best means to optimize deployments and to ensure that in the likelihood of rising tension or, worst case, hostilities, that the Pacific Command could obtain the optimum military utility from these incredibly capable platforms.

I have alluded to the disparate value of HUMINT. However, this can be complemented by invaluable "open sources," whether political statements, highly technical foreign reports on new and innovative technologies, economic and logistics intelligence, or internet-based source material of a myriad kind, all of which may be linked to more often than not government collected unclassified information such as customs' data (those entering and leaving the UK and US, where did they come from, where are they going, did they take circuitous routes, false or legal passports, and so on), fingerprint and eye scan data, video collection in real time, airline and ship passenger information, and the analysis of internet metadata that yields much about individuals as well as technical information. There are multiple key open-source databases, such as the Lloyds of London insurance database and ship movements, with cargo and end user data, that complement global AIS data. All of these types of information colleagues used to link with HUMINT as well as highly classified SIGINT, MASINT, and ELINT. The compounding of all this information often constituted pure gold when run through the discreet sieves of UK–US computer systems and we as teams analyzed discreet data sets of interest from the above types of sources.

New and innovative quantum computing techniques will permit the deciphering of vast amounts of real-time information that my generation could not handle because of sheer volume and complexity. At a more tactical level the US Special Operations Command, for example, is developing smartphone apps for operatives that will permit the real-time collection, transmission, and distribution of biometric data, such as fingerprints, ruggedized to cope with austere locations and challenging temperatures, humidity, and scenarios, and where covertness is at a premium.

My generation had similar capabilities, all to be supplanted with the march of technology and innovation in the digital era.

The Walker spy ring in the United States gave away vast amounts of invaluable intelligence to the Soviet Union. The team that I led in the UK, and then followed up with in various initiatives when I came back to the United States as an immigrant, stayed ahead of Soviet programs. The latter was achieved by both outstanding collection and very capable analysis of data, thereby enabling the UK–US to, for example, figure out how to counter Soviet improvements in acoustics, non-acoustics, noise quieting, and command, control, and communications. It is my very best assessment that in the early days of any major confrontation (short of any kind of nuclear escalation) with the Soviet Union and its Warsaw Pact allies, the UK–US team, with its NATO allies and those in Asia, would have disabled Soviet capabilities. In my opinion, from a purely intelligence collection (sources and methods) perspective, GCHQ and NSA produced during this 50-year period the most valuable of all intelligence on a consistent basis. Neither MI6 nor the CIA's DO were in the same league. However, the CIA's analytical organization was outstanding as have been several of the services' intelligence organizations such as the National Maritime Intelligence Center (NMIC) and what was once the Foreign Technology Division of the US Air Force at Wright Patterson Air Force Base in Dayton, Ohio.

In the 2020s the new generation of MI6 and CIA personnel will have to be "data geeks" as much as luring foreign nationals over clandestine meetings to betray their nations' secrets. "Walk-ins" and sources "turned" after multiple encounters may still yield valuable information but it is equally likely that it will be highly fashionable and operationally cost effective to be termed with the slang sobriquet, "geek," as much as someone who just turned an important source. The analysis of data may become far more significant than the endless endeavor to find the perfect agent to betray their country. However, one cautionary note, that the likes of Kim Philby in the UK and Aldrich Ames in the US betrayed a whole network of UK–US agents respectively. One bad apple can indeed ruin the whole barrel. "Insider threats" are just as dangerous in any intelligence organization, whether it is a HUMINT or SIGINT collector, or any other. My experience of dealing with HUMINT operations, and the analysis of such intelligence, can be hugely lucrative, but it is very random, not consistent, and therefore does not have the overall efficacy of the other combined "INTs"

Indicators and warning (I&W) is a much-underrated UK–US intelligence function. In the digital era, I&W is just as critical as it was during the Cold War to alert the political leadership to not just a rising threat but to the very serious likelihood of kinetic confrontation or the possibility of cyber penetration, whether it is election interference, infrastructure attack across a whole range of vulnerabilities, or the disruption of vital national security capabilities. I&W will have to be addressed in a concerted highly integrated way across all domains by the US Directorate of

National Intelligence and the British Joint Intelligence Committee and their key customers in their National Security Councils, the White House, and 10 Downing Street.

I still regard as the golden thread of collection and analysis over the past 50 years, the relentless and highly classified combined and individual intelligence operations executed by the US Navy and the Royal Navy, during and after World War II. They still stand as a beacon and testament to their illustrious forebears such as Admiral "Blinker" Hall, Royal Navy, and Captain Joseph Rochefort, United States Navy, both pivotal war winners.

CHAPTER 7

Current and Emerging Threats

The growing power of China and the development of what is clearly a "Grand Maritime Strategy" will play out in support of not just China's Belt and Road policy but China's overall strategic national security goals. This will affect not just the Five Eyes as a whole but increasingly their unilateral, bilateral, and multilateral relations with India, a crucial nation in the Indo-Pacific region. China's key policy statement issued in July 2019, "In the New Era" (issued by the State Council Information Office of the People's Republic of China) makes it abundantly clear where China is headed, with the Chinese Navy becoming the centerpiece and instrument of China's power and influence.

Insider Threats

The years since 9/11 have seen the development of "insider threats" to not just the Five Eyes community but also all the main democratic nations in the West. This has come through the march of technology and for which new paradigms and technologies will be required in the post-2020 period to counter those who wish to penetrate the daily lives of individuals, businesses, and governments by electronic means. However, there is also the enduring factor of the more traditional insider threat posed by classical traitors and spies, and also those who betray sensitive and classified information in the name of the public good, and the protection of privacy. New forms of propaganda, subliminal opinion forming, and disinformation are now commonplace in the digital era when so much information can be accumulated by the very nature of the internet and its vast information gathering capabilities.

The large internet providers' huge data collection engines, analysis and storage capacity know as much about each individual subscriber, user, or customer as the governments of the countries in which they are located. Advertising and commercial transactions are drivers and the offshoots of this massive amount of data. The concept of privacy is moot when all of us as individuals make daily selections on the internet for news, products, and information searches that both define us and characterize our needs, likes, and dislikes. We are then naturally targeted by commercial entities, having provided a very detailed profile of our lifestyles, likes and dislikes at myriad different levels, including political persuasion.

Classic spies gave away highly classified information on UK–US intelligence operations and personnel. Some gave away valuable technical information. The British GCHQ spy Geoffrey Prime was not unlike the Walkers in the United States, giving away extremely sensitive Navy operational and technical intelligence. Prime betrayed data on UK–US efforts to track Soviet strategic submarines, and various means by which the US Navy and Royal Navy used SIGINT and SOSUS. 1985 became the "Year of the Spy" in the United States. Ronald Pelton was exposed at the National Security Agency; the Walker spy ring was broken up; at the CIA Edward Lee Howard was caught spying, and in November 1985 Jonathan Pollard was arrested for spying for the Israeli Mossad. After 1985 Aldrich Ames was exposed at the CIA, and Robert Hanssen at the FBI, both giving critical information on CIA HUMINT operations and counterintelligence operations to the Soviet Union. Much later the case of Edward Snowden, who copied and leaked classified information from NSA. He did this, so he claimed, in the name of "Liberty versus Security," exposing several key global surveillance programs run by NSA and the Five Eyes, with cooperation from various telecommunications companies and European governments. Many of these spies' modus operandi may have been penetrated not by just better physical security checks and vetting procedures, in addition to covert review of bank accounts and personal communications, but also and very importantly by better and sophisticated monitoring of access to computer data. There are very good tools available with real-time checks for not just regular access to sensitive data, but unwarranted and out-of-hours computer access, and certainly the removal of data via a thumb drive, disc, and hard copy printer and reproduction. Programs can immediately alert security personnel to unusual and or out of routine access. For example, anyone accessing Five Eyes data using a thumb drive should sound an alarm immediately if there is no prior approval for such action.

The current threat situation in 2020 is more insidious than the above type of espionage threats. The internet poses the greatest challenge to Five Eyes intelligence since the dawn of SIGINT. The cooperation of the Five Eyes in a concerted technical and operational effort to develop new ways to cope with the overwhelming amount of data transmitted every millisecond on the internet is paramount. No one country can claim dominance and certainly all the brain power and skills of New Zealand, Canada, Australia, the UK, and the US are required. Cyberattacks have and will continue to take multiple forms. Long before the current wave of cyberattacks there had been, for example in the 1990s, attacks on the New Zealand power grid in Auckland and the London banking system. In parallel, companies began to provide privacy protection via encryption technologies fairly early on. The renowned PEP (Pretty Good Privacy) 1993 case in the United States is an exemplar of the march of commercial innovation that complicated Five Eyes' SIGINT operations. The American Phil Zimmermann provided the public worldwide with "Public Key Cryptography," and the case against him by the US government failed miserably. As the British government was investing in building the "Doughnut" to house GCHQ in the late 1990s, at the time the largest construction program in both the UK and Europe, both GCHQ and NSA were increasingly facing the daunting challenge of intercepting unprecedented volumes of data that even with the most advanced "keyword" searches could not keep up in situations where, for example, likely targets were using coded words in Pashtu, Farsi, and multiple obscure dialects, making life extremely challenging for the dedicated Five Eyes listeners and analysts. Traffic analysis became the order of the day as a quick and easy way to attempt to isolate threat data. In light of this observation it becomes clear that Five Eyes governments, in their urgent need to protect their citizens and those of their closest allies from burgeoning terrorism, faced the challenge of "Liberty versus Security," in the vernacular of the debate over the mass trawling of personal data from the internet and phone calls. In retrospect it is very easy to discern that the Five Eyes were up against intractable odds, with terrorist groups changing their cell phones and SIM cards regularly, often every few days, and transmitting in worded codes and dialects.

At the operational intelligence level in the field these challenges were faced over time very effectively by robust and highly intelligent tactical SIGINT systems, such as those used in Afghanistan. None of these systems depended on NSA- or GCHQ-derived data, unlike, for example, in earlier years when United States Air Force targets against Serbia were derived directly from GCHQ and NSA data. There was no highly reliable SIGINT that, for example, confirmed or denied the existence, location, and possible types of WMD in Iraq in 2003. The head of the United Nations investigative team in Iraq, Hans Blix, kept his team on the ball looking for hidden WMD. Data mining and using "Voice Prints" or the recordings of likely suspects for matching with vast amounts of intercepted communications were still in their infancy. Drone technology was barely off the ground in 2003. In fact, as late as 2010 countries such as the UK did not have any effective drones for surveillance and reconnaissance.

Computer Innovations and their Impact on Intelligence

The revolutionary Cray supercomputers[1] first designed in 1972 by Seymour Cray were subsequently supplanted by a series of massive parallel computers built by a large number of companies in the 1980s. However, by 2000 Cray was the only remaining supercomputing provider in the Western market, with its one rival, NEC Corporation.[2] Ordinary mainframe computers were still very much the order of the day at most large corporate and Five Eyes intelligence centers. Cray went into Chapter 11 bankruptcy in March 1995, and in February 1996 Cray Research merged with Silicon Graphics (SGI). SGI's Cray Research Business Unit was subsequently sold to Tera Computing Company in March 2000. In April 2008 Cray and Intel joined to collaborate on future computing systems. By 2009 they produced the fastest computer in the world for the National Center for Computational Sciences at the Oak Ridge National Laboratories. Fast forwarding to October 2017 Cray, together with partner Microsoft Azure, brought supercomputing to "the cloud," and in the same year built two new Cray CS-Storm systems for artificial intelligence workloads and on April 18, 2018, Cray announced the development of the most advanced processors to the Cray CS500 product line. At the time of writing Cray continues to make more revolutionary advances. The next decade will witness limitless advances that will make the great innovations of the 1970–2000 timeframe seem like computing dinosaurs.

By its very nature, the US and the UK and their Five Eyes partners from the turn of the century onwards have faced an uphill battle of keeping up with the march of technology. Private commercial companies have been far ahead of the UK–US governments in innovation and introduction to the commercial marketplace. A company such as Google is ahead of the game compared with NSA, GCHQ, and the Canadian, Australian, and New Zealand equivalents. Part of the problem is the very nature of the acquisition and contracting culture, particularly in the UK and US, with regimes that are slow and ponderous and not quick to adjust to changing technological circumstances. Added to this procurement plight is the inability to deal with vibrant and innovative startups with often critical disruptive technology that may challenge the secure multi-year contracts of large companies whose products are, in effect, already obsolete. This critical problem will have to be faced by all the Five Eyes, and in particulate the United States Departments of Defense and Homeland Security, plus their intelligence agencies, as the 2020s progress. On Thursday, July 7, 2005 the UK had its tragic and devastating wake up call, with the suicide bomber attacks in central London. This was the deadliest attack on British soil, and by British nationals, since World War II. This presented GCHQ with the need to rethink its total surveillance strategy. The worrisome thing is that between 2005 and today the pace and scale of technological change has been greater than could ever have been anticipated. The ability to process data has to be accompanied by advanced decision aids that convert vast amounts of information to relatively tiny amounts of critically important actionable intelligence that will enable decision makers to be ahead of the threat.

Intelligence and Drugs

There is a heroin–opioid epidemic in the United States, and to a lesser extent in the other four Five Eyes countries. Heroin is a highly addictive drug processed from morphine, a naturally occurring substance from the seed pod of poppy plant varieties. When sold as a drug it appears as a white or brownish powder. Opium is refined to make morphine, and then further refined, with various additives (some extraordinarily destructive to the body) into different forms of "street heroin." Opioids act on the human opioid receptors and have similar effects to morphine, in essence pain killers. Opioids have legitimate medical applications regularly prescribed by medical practitioners. Some experts claim that less professional practitioners either overprescribe or unnecessarily prescribe opioids instead of using other therapies—the pill-popping syndrome. Used non-medically without proper control they produce euphoric effects like an illegal drug. Excessive use leads to dependence, withdrawal symptoms and, particularly when combined with other depressant drugs, results in death from respiratory failure. By 2020 a combination of recreational use, addiction, and over prescription, plus illicit inexpensive heroin, has led to millions of Americans, young and old, dependent and dying in large numbers.

Narcan is the brand name for "Naloxone," and is used medically, indeed it is vital for paramedics in US rescue squads, to block the effects of opioid overdose. Rescue squads and emergency rooms administer intravenously and by injection. Often multiple doses are required to save the patient. If a US rescue squad runs out of Narcan this becomes a critical situation for a patient in need of urgent life support. By the time a unit arrives at an emergency room it may be too late. In the US, West Virginia, for example, has a nationally excessively high addiction rate. West Virginia rescue squad units often have to attend the same victims, indeed whole families, on more than one occasion during a 24-hour period. The overall impact of this is not good if rescue units are not available for trauma cases (traffic accidents and so on) and medical emergencies (heart attack, stroke, emergency childbirth and so on).

Heroin arrives in the US and the other nations via a discreet distribution chain. Breaking that chain and arresting the criminals who make millions at the top end of this chain, and more modest sums at the bottom ends, and preventing distribution to our vulnerable fellow citizens, are clear Five Eyes operational intelligence objectives. The drug cartels that manage and operate the initial distribution depend on international shipping, in addition to the fast speed Caribbean shipments and small submarine operations that have been documented in the media. The Five Eyes tracking of drug shipments requires multi-intelligence sources and methods. The tracking of rogue ships is not new to the Five Eyes. Each of the nations contribute to a 24/7 global tracking network relying on satellite intercepts, SIGINT, AIS (Automatic Identification System)-related data, and key HUMINT at places such as production sites and ports of embarkation. The heroin routes can be monitored from poppy fields to port delivery. Drug forensics permit obtaining the details of specific batches of the heroin's origin. Breaking into the money chain is as important as tracking illicit international shipping. The laundering of international drug money requires intensive analysis of offshore accounts, covert cover up schemes to hide drug operations and payments and at the lower level the ways and means by which drug pusher suspects' financials can be accessed. This requires the most intensive Five Eyes cooperation from ship tracking to financial analysis. Coastguards, or their equivalents, are important in the final stages of ship transits once vessels enter territorial waters, to board and search suspect vessels.

The US Coast Guard Foundation Calendar states: "Every day the Coast Guard screens an average of 360 merchant ships for potential risks before they arrive in US ports," and: "Each day, vigilant Coast Guard patrols prevent over 1,000 pounds of illegal drugs from reaching our communities."[3] In international waters the navies of the Five Eyes and their close allies can legally board and search suspect vessels. The additive materials used in the manufacture of heroin, particularly the more virulent varieties, are well known and their manufacture and distribution to locations where the "mixing" takes place can be traced. This process requires the involvement of multiple national agencies beside the traditional intelligence agencies of the Five Eyes. In tracking heroin from poppy fields to street "pushers" requires drug enforcement agencies, local and federal/central government law enforcement agencies, sheriff departments, and customs authorities. The law enforcement task is further complicated by heroin distribution via mail, as opposed to by hand. Data "Fusion Centers" that combine the resources of both the intelligence agencies and law enforcement agencies at all levels (federal/government to local) with specialist drug enforcement agencies are crucial in the fight against heroin and other drugs' distribution. The same problems exist with breaking into drug cartels' communications that exist with terrorist organizations where awareness has made the bad guys much more resilient and cunning in their communications' evasion and deception techniques.

If there was one single weak point in the distribution chain it is in the shipping/transport process, whatever form that takes. The big cartels want to make major shipments, not dribs and drabs over protracted periods, because of the loss of revenue. Shipment delays to avoid and confuse interception require more complex planning and execution. A chain with a weak link is vulnerable, and as the 2020s progress more and more effort will be required in this interception phase based on good intelligence of the total system, not just one part. Knowledge of where and when shipments will be made, and their ports of embarkation, are crucial data points. Corruption will be an ongoing problem, particularly in the law enforcement side of counter drug operations. The best Five Eyes intelligence can be thwarted by corrupt law enforcement and customs officials turning a blind eye to shipments and distribution. This will continue to require stricter vetting procedures and in the case of discreet high-level classified intelligence, restricting access not only to limited need-to-know personnel, but also providing the type of computer and data security discussed earlier. In the digital era it is possible to not just restrict access but to know what, when, and how each individual had access to data, and what uses were made of data. Counterintelligence can focus quite intensively on data paths and usage, particularly timing and other associations with highly specific data sets.

Artificial intelligence techniques combined with, for example, advanced Bayesian mathematics employing the most sophisticated log likelihood theory applications, can be used to analyze large real-time intelligence data sets in ways that were impossible for individual analysts striving to not just make sense of massive amounts of data, but deliver answers for users in very constrained time lines.

Today relatively simple AI applications can make the intelligence analyst's job faster, less stressful, and vitally more productive. AI can quickly visually recognize people across international boundaries, recognize speech, and instantly translate the most daunting languages and dialects, while executing sophisticated tasks allied to machines processing data from a vast amount of accumulated experience and learning built into the AI systems that will then adjust to new changing inputs in or near real time. Machines can therefore demonstrate intelligence when the computer copies or mimics human cognitive functions that we all normally associate with how we learn and solve problems. The evolutionary algorithms are however created by human beings, not in any way self-generated by the machine, a popular misconception. If the machine and the operator can work together as if the machine is another human being then the machine has passed the "Turing Test" developed by the famous Bletchley Park code breaker Alan Turing in 1950.[4] AI is progressing by leaps and bounds and will undoubtedly add an extraordinary dimension to Five Eyes intelligence, which at the time of writing in 2020 is almost impossible to predict. One fact does undoubtedly remain. Alan Turing was a genius. The Five Eyes require more like him to revolutionize the intelligence process. Finding them is the challenge but they are out there in the bright new generation of computer scientists and mathematicians.

Global Terrorism, Human Trafficking, Piracy, Illicit Arms Transfers and Money Laundering

Global terrorism, human trafficking, piracy, gun running, illicit arms transfers, and the associated money laundering with these activities, have ushered in new challenges for the Five Eyes, not dissimilar to international drug trafficking. The common thread that runs through all these operations is money. They all require the acquisition, transfer, and dispersal of funds in order to function. "Following the money" is an appropriate adage. The other common thread, with the possible exception of human trafficking, is weaponry. Weapons are required in order for these operations to function. Money and weapons are the lifeblood of these evil activities. Preventing and or disrupting the flow is a key goal. A multi-source intelligence approach is required. Added to this mix is the crucial task of locating and tracking the means and methods of transnational recruitment and training, particularly in the terrorist domain, and in those other domains that are more of an international criminal nature where individuals are lured in, corrupted, or wittingly join the ranks, trained, and paid for their wrongdoing. The means are as important therefore as the individuals and knowing the nature and dimensions of these means is paramount for successful intelligence operations in the future.

Since 9/11, cooperation has been the order of the day. Long gone the days when, for instance, in the 1980s an NSA Director, Lieutenant General William Odom, US Army, decided to cut off NSA intelligence flow to New Zealand because of New Zealand's ban on US nuclear warships and submarines entering New Zealand ports. This was short lived, with GCHQ and the Australians supplying the New Zealand GCSB (Government Communications Security Bureau) with SIGINT and other intelligence. In fact, NSA working personnel surreptitiously worked around Odom's ban, such is the core strength and relationships within the Five Eyes. Nothing in the future, and particularly the whims and fancies of political change within each of the Five member states, should jeopardize the continuum of Five Eyes 24/7 working cooperation.

Arms dealers and the middlemen, who operate in the shadows, often acting sub rosa for governments, are key targets since they mastermind the deals and transfers of funds to those who provide and those who receive weapons.[5] Israel's operations and arms deals with Russia and Iran, in light of contemporary international relations, are eye openers. What they provide is a template for thwarting arms deals that are clearly and unambiguously dangerous for the global order. This requires close collaboration rather than unilateral dealings. The sort of operations that CIA officers such as the legendary, perhaps infamous, James Jesus Angleton (1917–1987) ran at the CIA in the early Cold War decades with little or no cooperation with the other Five Eyes, is perhaps an object lesson in how to both create a certain amount of chaos but more important seriously jeopardize the joint collection, analysis, and sharing of Five Eyes intelligence.

The key motivation driving both illicit and clandestine arms deals and the appalling consequences of human trafficking is money. However, out-of-control covert intelligence operations without proper oversight can and has led to disastrous political repercussions. The Iran–Contra affair illustrates this well. The intersection of intelligence as an arm of political policy is clearly a most troubling scenario. As the 2020s progress the US and the UK together with the other three Five Eyes will have to pool their total resources. Based on a complete review of stand-alone clandestine intelligence operations since 1947 by the United States, it is recommended that unless there are overwhelming reasons for a stand-alone US covert intelligence operation, then the Five Eyes should work together in collaboratively tracking money, people, and weapons. This covers not only 24/7 electronic and other means of exchanging data, but the constant interaction of Five Eyes personnel not just through the various personnel exchange programs but through constant meetings.

The March 11, 2004 Atocha railway station bombings in Madrid, Spain, with 192 killed and approximately 2000 people injured, showed that in tracking the al-Qaeda terrorist cell involved there had been insufficient close working relations between the various European intelligence and law enforcement agencies. The bombings were the deadliest terrorist attacks carried out in the history of Spain and Western Europe. Close working-level meetings between the agencies may well have improved considerably the Spanish understanding and interpretation of the available intelligence data. As the 2020s progress more and more close working meetings will be required to address not just weapon and human trafficking, but also the wider strategic intelligence issues.

The end games for both illicit and illegal arms deals, weapons movements and human trafficking are well understood—the motivation, the locations, the customers, and the likely possible routes. Take for example the AR-15 and AK-47 Kalashnikov weapons that are used extensively on the global markets, both legally and illegally. Like almost every weapon, including those weapons that are manufactured ostensibly for official government military purposes, the Five Eyes know where they are manufactured, both overtly and covertly. Tracking their sale and distribution is an art and a science of modern intelligence operations. The political context is the art, and the science involves the myriad technical intelligence sources and methods to track their movements and end users. Large weapons present an easier profile—tanks and armored personnel carriers are easier to track than Uzi submachine guns or RPGs (rocket propelled grenades). Part of the problem is that nation states indulge in clandestine arms deals. Corrupt money deals often underly the reasons for purchase, with paybacks for the key top people in the process, with hard cash passing between the principals, not via international banking. International relationships are not always what they appear to be. Today it may seem a total disconnect that major Western European countries and Israel were major arms suppliers to Iran, and that countries that could not necessarily go direct to the arms manufacturer or middlemen would use surrogates.

In the early days of the Cold War, Israel was a major source of intelligence on the Soviet Union because of the large number of Jews still in Russia and other Soviet states, and the backwards and forwards of Russian Jews, while at the same time that Israel was collecting intelligence it was also buying arms from eastern bloc sources, particularly Czechoslovakia, with the full knowledge of their Soviet masters. This apparent symbiosis is likely to continue, and the Five Eyes will have to not just work much more closely together in tracking and inhibiting weapon and human trafficking, they will have to be open about mutual political agendas. Outstanding intelligence organizations are communities of very talented and mostly hugely ethical people serving common purposes of protecting critical national interests. The United States in particular may have to adjust some of its modus operandi in terms of greater transparency and sharing, though all under total security.

Money laundering tends to accompany terrorist weapons and explosives purchases, drug cartels, human trafficking, piracy financials, and gun running, together with more opaque weapons procurements. The technological edge can defeat these operations. In addition to the types of technologies that we have already discussed, new technologies will augment the massive search and analysis engines being developed for both GCHQ and NSA, with technology sharing with the Canadians, the Australians, and New Zealanders. Two examples will suffice: artificial intelligence (AI) can add to the sources and methods mix in hitherto unexplored domains, particularly when using a holistic approach to say gun running and arms transfers with very clever cognitive tools, that will automatically provide the sort of warnings and indicators that lead to interception, arrest, and seizure. Similarly, shared drone technology will enhance Five Eyes surveillance with stealth, improved power to density propulsion systems that will extend range and endurance, and ever-increasing sophisticated SIGINT and IMINT payloads with real time low probability of intercept data links. These new techniques will be added to the classical armory of SIGINT, IMINT, HUMINT, GEOINT, ACINT, and MASINT in all their myriad forms, and used in a fully integrated way so that the speed and accuracy of initial detection and location are enhanced.

Drones are here to stay. The more sophisticated stealthy covert drones with long endurance and highly capable sensors will augment the more lightweight tactical drones in adding to the SIGINT, ELINT, ELECTRO-OPINT/INFRA-RED, and IMINT capabilities of airborne and space systems, whose whereabouts are often known by the threat. Drones are very versatile, and in money terms, hugely cost effective. They can be launched from ships and submarines, from friendly territories using surrogates, and not so friendly nations clandestinely. They can self-destruct in the worst scenarios. Locating and tracking portside activities using drones can become both more efficient and less risky than employing covert human operatives. Paramount in this technological leap forward still remains the key collective strengths of the Five Eyes. In my 50 years of intelligence experience, there can be no hiding vital information that is of mutual benefit. For example, Canada may not have the same historic and current SIGINT organization of the British at GCHQ and the Americans at NSA, but the Canadians have a vast network through their embassies that augment their traditional CSE covert collection operations. The same applies to the Australians and New Zealanders. The sum of all parts will be more and more crucial as we move into the second quarter of the 21st century.

The combined navies of the Five Eyes represent a prodigious round-the-clock forward-deployed presence to counter the international trade in illicit arms. These five navies are complemented by the navies of friendly and allied powers. The Five Eyes share data with and through the US National Maritime Intelligence Center (NMIC) and the associated echelons in the other four countries. Locating and tracking rogue ships transporting illicit arms is today a hallmark of the Five Eyes navies. For example: on March 28, 2016, USS *Sirocco* intercepted a dhow[6] in the Arabian Sea and confiscated 1,500 AK-47s, 200 RPGs, and 21 .50 caliber machine guns (these are manufactured by several nations including the Russians and Chinese); on August 27, 2018, USS *Jason Dunham* tracked and intercepted a stateless dhow (not flying a national flag) in international waters in the Gulf of Aden off the coast of Yemen. Aerial surveillance showed the crew throwing packages of AK-47s into a skiff. The following day, August 28, 2018, USS *Jason Dunham* boarded and seized the weapons that included more than a 1000 AK-47s. The above illustrates countless at-sea operations. Five Eyes shared intelligence and cooperation with other friendly navies has paid serious dividends.

Intelligence and the Middle East: Will the Past Be Prologue?

It is not the purpose here to reexamine the intelligence failures that occurred prior to and after the invasion of Iraq. These issues have been addressed by many authors and much of the product is axiomatic. From a Five Eyes intelligence perspective however there remains one key overriding issue. This is the separation of individual single state policy (that is the policies of the United States, the United Kingdom, Canada, Australia, and New Zealand) from both individual state-sponsored intelligence collection and analysis from collective Five Eyes intelligence collection and analysis. This is an important issue and it involves total Five Eyes agreements and also the separate bi-lateral and multi-lateral intelligence agreements and intelligence exchanges that exist between the Five Eyes nations. The United States has, for example, pursued different policies in the Middle East than the other four nations, sometimes contentiously, with disagreement, as is clear from Five Eyes ambassadorial statements and votes in the United Nations. As has been stated several times, intelligence products, particularly key assessments from the various Five Eyes Joint Intelligence Committees, or their equivalent, should not be subject to any form of political pressure or influence. Intelligence's role is to provide the highest quality unvarnished information for policy makers without any skewing of data to support either national policy or the political motives or intentions of political parties and national leadership. Intelligence should be at arms' length. It is never the role of intelligence to make policy. In this regard the Five Eyes therefore hold collectively the moral high ground. The intelligence agencies and departments of the Five Eyes have an ethical standard to maintain, insofar as they cannot be swayed in their assessments by political exigencies, notwithstanding that there may at times be disagreement or varying interpretations of intelligence data. The latter is a different issue, and can be a sign of a healthy, vibrant, and professional organization. As the 2020s progress it is crucial that the cohesiveness of the Five Eyes endures and adheres in spite of national political policy differences to the above ethical considerations.

The Five Eyes have known one enduring fact since the 1950s, and the consequences of the 1967 June War that has led to many contentions ever since. This is the need for intelligence collectors and analysts to truly know and understand the Middle East in detail, from every dimension, and not just in terms of classical political and international relations and diplomacy as practiced in the West, but in terms of the deep history, culture, political origins and developments since World War II; religions, economies, educational systems, traditions, family structure and community organization; diverse languages and dialects, and the origins of current and likely future political alignments and intentions—both internally, regionally, and internationally. Without that knowledge and experience Five Eyes intelligence can, potentially, be clutching at straws in spite of the very best intelligence collection systems. There has to be greater awareness of the various shifts in all these variables as many external international players, some at total odds with Five Eyes interests, seek to pursue their national self-interests in what is likely the most conflicted region in the world, and one from which can emit the worst of consequences. History and culture come together in abundant strength in the Middle East. Understanding these is a prerequisite.

The aftermath of the occupation–invasion of Iraq in 2003 was clearly not adequately assessed prior to military operations, a huge lesson in itself. At the core of this issue most likely lay a fundamental lack of understanding of the history and culture of the Middle East. The latter were not fully understood and factored into decision making in the White House. Herewith lay a potential recipe for strategic disaster. We must have collective understanding not just of why we are where we are today in the Middle East, but also the systemic underpinnings that are driving regional politics in ways that no one in Washington would have predicted in 2001.

Over the past 19 years there have been many academic analyses and intelligence assessments regarding the rise of ISIS and its apparent successes. Interpretations have varied, in some cases quite significantly. Some researchers have attributed responsibility to Washington, while the others have seen al-Qaeda in Iraq (AQI) as the driving force behind the emergence and growth of ISIS. The overall fall-out of these varying views is that it is a far more difficult and complex process to comprehend what caused the emergence of ISIS in 2006 and its claims to be a state. Despite various US political pronouncements, ISIS today, in 2020, is far from eliminated. Although it has suffered serious military defeats and many of its leaders have been eliminated, it has a most unfortunate ability to regenerate and garner more supporters. ISIS has been declared defeated on several occasions only to reappear. The internet plays a role in the ISIS recruitment process and although the Five Eyes very successfully tracks much of this, there remains the challenge of countering the recruitment process, training, and the supply of weapons.

Syria and Iraq lie at a geo-strategic crossroads, where the Sunni and the Shi'a worlds intersect. From the south to the north there is the main Sunni line, from the Gulf countries to Turkey. The Shi'a area stretches from the east to the west and consists primarily of Iran and Hezbollah. Syria and Iraq have mixed populations, and until the beginning of the 20th century both these countries had secular regimes, with mixed populations of Sunni and Shi'a communities coexisting in similar economic and sociopolitical conditions.

The role of ideology and doctrine in the Middle East should never be underestimated. The struggle between Shi'a and Sunni Muslims has not ceased since the 7th century. The ruling regime, whether Sunni or Shi'a, is what determines outcomes, irrespective of population and Moslem demographics—Bahrain, for example, is a Sunni state, though it has a Shi'a majority. This key overlay should drive both intelligence collection and analysis.

ISIS appeared just after the Iraq parliamentary elections of 2005, initially in January. The Shi'ites obtained the overwhelming majority in the National Assembly. In January 2005 the two main Shi'a parties obtained 180 seats (the Kurds receiving 75 seats, the rest, 20). These results led to a wave of criticism, and the elections were repeated. In spite of an increasing number of Sunni votes, the Shi'a United Iraqi Alliance got 128 seats out of 275 (Kurds 53, the Sunnis altogether 58).

The civil war began, as the Sunni population would not acknowledge the legitimacy of the elections. The main role was played by terrorist groups that had evolved from breakup of the Iraqi army and what became AQI, and later ISIS. In June 2005 Washington began a "Together Forward" operation, which finished in October. Immediately after that, ISIS appeared. This precipitated a reaction by those in Iraq not disposed to the US occupation, uniting them in a common purpose, to challenge the United States. ISIS consisted of some elements of the terrorist groups defeated in the civil war, including AQI, and other subdivisions and generals of Saddam Hussein's army. Though distinct entities, these groups displayed similarities. They combined to fight a common enemy, the Americans, and their aim was to expel the US from Iraq. What is much more important to observe is that they are all Sunnis. The very name of a new group, Islamic State of Iraq, marked a key common and unifying claim: to create a Sunni state by a Sunni political elite. To ignore this crucial fact is to blindside Five Eyes intelligence operations and assessments.

Sponsorship from the Gulf countries helped them to join together. ISIS's early emergence therefore is not directly related to the Washington government, to AQI, or to economic factors such as poverty, but rather support from the Gulf and, in particular, from Saudi Arabia and Qatar. Saudi Arabia has always claimed to be an indisputable leader between the Sunni communities, and is a Sunni regional leader. Although Qatar had intensified its connections with European countries in order to increase its GDP, Qatar still needed to have a Sunni key relationship to the north. Syria was ruled by the Alawi kin and showed political affinity for Iran, and Iraq had a strictly secular regime and a Shi'a majority in population. As a consequence, the Gulf countries such as Qatar felt a strong need for a separate Sunni state. If these fundamental facts are ignored it is clearly possible for the Five Eyes as a whole to go astray in making assessments.

The First Gulf War, Iraq, August 1990

The invasion of Kuwait by Saddam Hussein, August 2–4, 1990, eliminated a chance for the US and its allies to cooperate with his regime, while good relations between the Assad family and the Iranian government opened the door to challenges to US influence. Readers should bear in mind one key aspect that a former head of the Israeli Mossad, Efraim Halevy, points out in his book, *Man in the Shadows*: "The beginning of our journey in this book took us to Baghdad and to the key player, Saddam Hussein—confronting the Shiite revolutionary hurricane emanating from Iran. Hussein was then the savior of the modern Arab world and the vital interests of the United States in the region."[7] The tragic irony that the Mossad chief points out underscores a crucial fact that, much as Saddam Hussein was a well-proven extremely evil man in many ways, he was the regional bulwark against Iran and indeed the dire enemy of an emergent threat from al-Qaeda. Much earlier in his book Halevy points out that it was Saudi Arabia, not in any shape or form Iraq, that supported Moslem extremism and provided most of the manpower for the 9/11 attacks.[8] Moderate Arab leaders had always indicated to the West that Hussein, bad person that he was, provided the best defense against both Iran and Islamic extremism. Halevy towards the end of his book makes a significant statement regarding WMD, and particularly the nuclear element, that Islamic extremists are much more likely to use WMD, including nuclear weapons,[9] and by implication when revisiting his assessment of Hussein and Iraq, pose far more of a threat than ever Hussein did. Halevy shows how moderate and loyal allies of the West, such as King Hussein of Jordan, followed a position of neutrality and a tilt towards Iraq in 1991 and the First Gulf War because he realized that Saddam Hussein kept the region safe from Iranian intrusion and a Shi'ite resurgence. Halevy states regarding Hizbollah: "However, it has one more characteristic that distinguished it from Khammas and Al Qaeda: It is the Shiite movement allied with Iran … in these respects Hizbollah will have to renounce much more than Khammas if it wishes its dreams of respectability to come true."[10] These quotes from a distinguished former Mossad chief show an analysis of the region that was tragically either forgotten, ignored, or never appreciated in the first instance, in the headlong haste to invade Iraq.

After the invasion the political instability created in Iraq, particularly from 2006, allowed a Sunni organization with a clear political course to gain momentum towards, potentially, the creation of its own state. The Sunni state lying between the Gulf and Turkey had to facilitate laying a gas pipeline from Qatar to Europe and also divide the Shi'a geopolitical and theocratic space into two unconnected parts. This view of a new Sunni state also solved the Saudi problem of political leadership. Syria, primarily agrarian, and Iraq, an oil producer, would not challenge Saudi and Gulf state economic supremacy. It is important to recall that ISIS had been waiting near the Syrian–Iraqi borders and began its expansion in 2013–2014. Why did it wait so long to act? The answer is that ISIS could not establish itself solidly in the Sunni territories of Iraq, as it would have to face surrounding forces, both the Shi'as of southern Iraq and neighboring countries, and the Kurds. Also, it could not connect directly to Turkey, or any sea, so from a strategic viewpoint ISIS, while solely in Iraq, had strategic limitations. However, ISIS saw an opportunity in Syria.

When the Western intervention in Syria began, after two years of civil war, when all conflicting parties and the population became exhausted, ISIS crossed the border and interfered in the war. ISIS needed support from the local population. The idea of a Caliphate was created in order to win over peoples in the newly controlled territories. Syria became therefore a critical factor in ISIS's survival and possible growth.

In retrospect it is clear that the main aim of ISIS was in fact to establish a state, a serious challenge for the West, the region, and the Five Eyes intelligence apparatus, and one that had to be internally stable and could in fact be used by the Gulf countries as a bridge between them and the West. The early success of ISIS militarily can be explained not by military superiority but rather the total fatigue of Syria and Iraq caused by civil disorders and external intervention by Russia and the West, and occasional incursions by Israeli air strikes. However, this very scenario also militated in the other direction, preventing ISIS from gaining stable control in a hugely volatile environment that remains to this day. The chief political–military objective of the United States and the United Kingdom has been to contain and at best eliminate ISIS in Syria, while creating an environment in which the Assad regime will negotiate. The latter has been exacerbated by Russian support for the Assad regime and the very complexity of the ethnic–political–religious diversity that divides Syria. By the spring of 2019 ISIS had suffered major military defeats in Syria. The question remains about the future of the remaining ISIS fighters and their families and supporters in Syria. Will they disperse, and if so, where to? Will they be integrated? Will they be interned in camps? At the time of writing the situation is still ambivalent. Moreover, what will happen to the many foreign nationals who were fighting for the defeated ISIS in Syria? These people remain in transit. Will their countries of origin accept them back and attempt cultural rehabilitation? In some cases, countries of origin may charge returning ISIS fighters with terrorist offences. For those ISIS supporters who are not Syrian nationals what is their economic and social future? Time has shown too that ISIS regenerates. It is crucial, naturally, that this is not allowed to occur. Intelligence is crucial in this process of identifying where and how such regeneration is occurring.

We know that the so-called "domestic" strategy of ISIS was centered on creating a state, a propagandist tool if unrealistic. ISIS has never tried to break into Shi'a territories, and in both Iraq and Syria they have claimed to want to control only Sunni lands. They have, however, tried to capture some parts of Kurdistan in order to reach the Turkish border. ISIS's direct territorial control strategy, most likely a pipe-dream, appears to have been the basis for developing a caliphate ideology that would allow Syrians and Iraqis to tolerate their loss of sovereignty and influence, by creating a theocratic self-identity as an Umar-like[11] caliphate. Fortunately, none of this has been achieved, while the current situation in Syria remains volatile, unpredictable, with massive dislocation, intense suffering, and a massive refugee problem for Jordan in particular. From an intelligence perspective it is important to place ISIS within the much bigger Islamic framework outside of current state structures. ISIS has been criticized severely for direct violations of sharia law by various groups within Islam. However, none of the key theologians or religious leaders have dared as yet to publish fatwa against the ISIS regime. The Moslem intelligentsia, within the religious leadership, has come out in direct criticism in light of ISIS atrocities of massive proportions. The latter has been exemplified by the violent treatment of non-Muslim women. Intelligence can provide data that will show how to ideologically target those populations and communities most vulnerable to ISIS recruitment propaganda by using well-constructed counter propaganda, employing all the subtleties of dialect and local culture.

Prior to the mid-2010s ISIS could claim some success by creating state-like institutions. The ISIS regime has provided in areas where they have or had control electricity, water, and facilitated building schools and hospitals, roads, and mosques. Five Eyes intelligence collection has and remains important in the ways in which ISIS seeks to control perception of itself, and especially where ISIS wishes to be perceived by the local populations as an organization that tends to do best for its people. ISIS would like to have itself perceived by its grass-roots followers, and those who are caught innocently in the turmoil of theocratic cross-fire, as the political conjunction of the material and spiritual, in fulfilment of its people's needs for stability.

As the 2020s progress the US and the UK in particular will need to exploit more effectively ISIS technical and theocratic vulnerabilities in coercing populations and particularly paramilitary recruits to its ranks. There is a requirement for a more sophisticated approach to media interactions by the Five Eyes, far more capable than for example "The Voice of America" during the Cold War. As we observed above, dealing with ISIS propaganda and recruitment requires detailed sophisticated insight into local cultures and dialects. One key ISIS vulnerability is open to penetration: the reality and the perception that ISIS has spiraled into atrocity after atrocity, driven by an evil creed of violence and mayhem, has now been clearly seen for what it is in Syria. This provides the Five Eyes with an open door to influence those who are vulnerable, threatened, and have some hope of being saved from ISIS oppression if the West stays engaged militarily, particularly with the presence of Five Eyes special forces in non-Assad controlled enclaves. The latter are political–military decisions but should be underscored by sound intelligence that indicates where and how the most effective counter-ISIS propaganda and recruitment tools and funds can be employed.

One area where UK–US intelligence intervention can be most efficacious in the 2020s is in the countering of ISIS recruitment of professionals, such as scientists, administrators, engineers, technologists, and economists, to manage ISIS-controlled industry, agriculture, and trade wherever it appears and that is clearly under ISIS direct control. For example, ISIS was able with external financial support from the other Sunni-dominated states in the region, to operate the dam on the Assad Lake, a thermal power plant near Aleppo, petroleum enterprises, and claims by ISIS that it issues its own currency. Future ISIS-related critical infrastructure and logistics can be thwarted by UK–US intelligence operations in conjunction with political–military–diplomatic actions. Many ISIS specialists and consultants have come from Western countries. The Five Eyes as a whole have the means to identify such people, isolate them, and dissuade them from association with a terrorist organization, a serious crime in Western states, and certainly in the Five Eyes countries.

UK–US intelligence will also have to divert energy to collection and analysis of internal ISIS perspectives and self-assessments, as ISIS continues to face internal problems. These are difficult to gauge unless serious programs are initiated to both assess and then disrupt ISIS internal theocratic propaganda and its core organization, especially funding, weapon supplies, and recruitment media. HUMINT has a serious role in this process and collaborative operations with non-Five Eyes collectors will be important. If internal dissent is created within ISIS, then it may lose most of its territorial ambitions under pressure from regional forces. Jordan, for example, joined the Kurds and independent elements in Syria and Iraq in their struggle. Sowing disagreements between ISIS's leaders is potentially as valuable as alienating them in drone strikes and other kinetic means. To date neither Saudi Arabia nor Qatar has been able to control ISIS leaders. The creation of rifts by the Five Eyes community together with pressure from both the West, the United Nations, and the Sunni Islamic states could aggregate to undermine the ISIS leadership, and ultimately lead to its capitulation.

ISIS's main objective to conjoin the Sunni space will have been undermined if, in the 2020s, well-organized and coordinated Western opposition with regional allies contains ISIS's spread. ISIS's "future map" of the 2010s will look like a pipedream. If the right things are executed, it is very unlikely that ISIS will be able to have a major support base beyond Syria and Iraq. However, if the Five Eyes intelligence infrastructure does not maintain a major intelligence collection and assessment capability in this key region in support of national policies, then the future will remain ambiguous.

If ISIS regenerates a foothold of any kind in Syria it is very unlikely to make inroads in the face of President Bashar al-Assad's forces, supported by the Russian Army, Special Forces, and Air Force, arms supply, and other covert Russian operations. The main aim of the Bashar al-Assad regime has been to exterminate local radical terrorist groups and to stabilize the remaining territories, and then to recover the economy in the context of a lost Euphrates. All this remains to be seen. The Syrian scenario is further complicated by relations between Syria and Israel, and their primary supporters and military benefactors, Russia and the United States respectively.

The Five Eyes and their Western allies need to exploit relations between ISIS, Saudi Arabia and Qatar. ISIS atrocities and a clear divergence from fundamental Moslem teaching can polarize opposition to ISIS, leaving the Islamists isolated and surrounded, facing a demise akin to those 20th-century tyrannies that sought to impose their will by brutal suppression and atrocities. ISIS will have hopefully masterminded its own downfall, by brutally violating all the norms of human conduct and indeed the very essence of the prophet's words. Cruelty, inhumanity, and sheer violent atrocity have no place in the civilized world and the UK and US should play their key intelligence roles in ensuring that ISIS reaps the whirlwind of its own making. The Five Eyes together with political initiatives by the United States, the United Kingdom, Jordan, and their allies in the Middle East and Europe have a clear moral and "just war" mandate to destroy the backbone of ISIS that has masterminded atrocities.

At the end of World War II, the US pursued one of the most far-seeing strategies to turn around a country that had perpetrated the worst kind of atrocities and war crimes in history. This model, the reverse of the Versailles Treaty model, signed on June 28, 1919, was created by George Marshall and the American leadership. Once ISIS is defeated, indeed obliterated, the extraordinarily demanding challenge will be for the US and its allies to find just and equitable ways to resolve the complexities of the Sunni–Shi'a territorial and theocratic space. It will require immense humanity to steer through the vastly troubled waters of Sunni and Shi'a rivalries and centuries of theocratic divergence. This is at the very heart of the issues in the Middle East. The lost opportunity after the Iraq intervention-invasion to separate Sunni, Shi'a, and Kurd into defined geographic and theocratic political territories may have been lost, resulting in an ancient sectarian divide that then engaged in bloody conflict, but all things are possible in the Middle East, and the Five Eyes community will have a critical role in supplying highly reliable intelligence to frame what will have to be new and innovative diplomatic initiatives.

The Israel–Palestinian Challenge

During his presidency (2009–2017), Barack Obama proclaimed that he wished to see Israel return to the pre-1967 June War boundaries in accordance with United Nations Security Council Resolution 242, passed at the end of the 1967 June War. President Obama argued that this was a critical prerequisite to begin a truly long-term solution to the Israel–Palestinian situation. His administration's position rested on the fundamental UN concept embodied in Resolution 242 that Israel took land that was not Israel's by force and that in order to meet Palestinian rights to nationhood and wider Arab demands, that the Golan Heights and the West Bank be restored to their lawful owners. These were strident demands and were in keeping with United Nation's resolutions. It should be noted that according to the Department of Peace and Conflict Research in Uppsala, Sweden, Israel has been sanctioned in 45 resolutions by the UN Human Rights Council for various violations regarding the Palestinian situation. Much earlier, between 1967 (shortly after the end of the 1967 June War) and 1989 the UN Security Council adopted 131 resolutions directly addressing the Arab–Israeli conflict. What this demonstrates is the need for constant accurate Five Eyes intelligence across all domains affecting the ongoing Israel–Palestinian situation. This is complicated by the United States' unique relationship with Israel, making an already complex situation for the other four nations of the Five Eyes intelligence agencies even more sensitive. The United Nations General Assembly has adopted a number of resolutions stating that the United States' relationship with Israel encourages Israeli expansionist policies, particularly in the West Bank.

This complicates life for the UK, Canadian, Australian, and New Zealand intelligence agencies and the political systems that they support individually and collectively. For example, the 9th Emergency Session of the UN General Assembly was convened at the request of the UN Security Council because the United States refused to adopt sanctions against Israel. The US has tended to follow what became called the "Negroponte Doctrine" (after John Negroponte, US Ambassador to the United Nations, September 2001–June 2004) that opposes any Security Council resolutions that criticize or sanction Israel without also denouncing militant Palestinian activities by Hamas and Hezbollah. Collecting and analyzing impartial intelligence in this environment becomes demanding not so much because of the sources and methods involved but because of relationships within the Five Eyes that are driven by the national foreign policies of each of the individual countries. For example, at the same time that the Five Eyes are tracking illicit arms transfers from Iran to Hamas and Hezbollah, they also have to keep close watch on Israeli covert operations in the United States and the other Five Eyes countries for conducting both classical espionage and also intellectual property penetration and collection, particularly of sensitive military technology or other commercial technology that Israel deems desirable for sustaining and expanding its economy. There are inherent conflicts in this complex scenario, particularly in even more conflicting scenarios where for instance Israeli military intelligence and clandestine service (the Mossad) may from time to time provide timely and valuable intelligence. For example, the latter may include Iranian sanction violations, covert arms shipments, and Russian–Syrian operations. The overall situation since the 1967 June War has been exacerbated more recently by more proactive US policies in favor of Israel and the Trump administration's withdrawal of substantial aid to the Palestinians.

The move of the US Embassy from Tel Aviv to Jerusalem also caused friction within the Five Eyes political–diplomatic community. The Trump administration's announcement on March 25, 2019 to support Israel's claims to permanent sovereignty and possession of the Golan Heights drew global anger. The fall-out remains to be seen. Syria's ally, Russia, will likely not stand by and do nothing, with an extant UN resolution in their favor that may give both countries legitimacy in a range of possible options. Obama had already used this resolution as a basis for Israel returning territory occupied since the 1967 June War. This situation is a potential tinderbox waiting to be ignited by perhaps reckless adventurism by all the key protagonists. However, the intelligence agencies have to remain aloof in the future from such differences and produce unvarnished and impartial intelligence reports.

President Netanyahu of Israel reacted vehemently to several Obama White House statements, stressing to multiple international audiences that in any two-state solution to the Israeli–Palestinian situation, Israel must have what he defines as "defensible boundaries." He saw a return to the 1967 status quo as giving up territory that is vital for Israel's survival in the event of various military and economic scenarios. His opposite number, President Abbas, and several US Secretaries of State have fully understood the reasons for his declarations. However, many independent international relations specialists on Middle East affairs have stated that if the peace process is ever to enter a substantively new era from the prior decades, and if the Palestinians are indeed ever to accede, as Israel did, to become a nation state within the community of nations, clearly more has to happen than declarations, whether rhetorical or otherwise.

The UN Resolution 242

There has been considerable analysis over the years since 1967 of the intent of the wording of Resolution 242, drafted by the then British Ambassador to the United Nations, Lord Caradon. The resolution is to most lawyers and international specialists quite explicit, precise and well worded with no ambiguity. However, the wording that has caused most analysis is the section of the resolution that says, in affirmation of Article 2 of the UN Charter, the United Nations Security Council affirms: "Termination of all claims or states of belligerency and respect for and acknowledgment of the sovereignty, territorial integrity and political independence of every state in the area and their right to live in peace within secure and recognized boundaries free from threats or acts of force." Within this section the words that cause most disagreement are, "rights to live in peace within secure and recognized boundaries." The Israelis and President Netanyahu have been explicit in stating that any redrawing of the pre-1967 June War boundaries, now essentially the West Bank of the Jordan River and the Golan Heights, since Israel has withdrawn from the Sinai, must be so that Israel can be secure. The latter has been defined by President

Netanyahu as being "defensible boundaries." To most military and Five Eyes intelligence personnel this phrase has significant and very definable connotations.

In looking back briefly to the 1960s, the Middle East was a critical part of the Cold War stand off and a hot bed for playing out the international rivalries between the United States and the Soviet Union. Israel felt naturally threatened and surrounded by potential belligerents that were encouraged and supported by Moscow. By June of 1967 the situation reached boiling point. The sudden preemptive strikes made by Israel to seize territory from Egypt, Syria, and Jordan to extend its boundaries and create defensive barriers were extremely successful. Israel's actions precipitated a crisis that all but plunged the United States into a conflict with the Soviet Union. This could have occurred if Israel advanced beyond the Golan Heights towards Damascus, followed by Soviet intervention. Very well-documented research has shown how the Soviet Union would have launched forces against Israel if they had continued in their march towards Damascus from the Golan Heights. The world has changed with the demise of the Soviet Union, and in its aftermath have emerged equally compelling threats to Middle East stability, not least the rise of Iran and the emergence of several parties and groups that espouse terrorism as a vehicle for achieving political goals. Other state and non-state players have become either directly or indirectly involved through the supply of arms, training, and other equipment.

It is very easy to forget that terrorism is not a recent phenomenon. It has been a vehicle for change in the Middle East since World War II. President Menachem Begin of Israel was a member of Irgun, an organization dubbed by the international community as a violent and extremist terrorist organization and described by David Ben-Gurion, national founder and first Prime Minister of the state of Israel, as the "enemy of the Jewish people." Begin saw himself as a freedom fighter, not a terrorist. It is easy to forget that in the Middle East the past is often prologue. Hamas and Hezbollah pursue political goals often by unacceptable violent means, most often dubbed terrorist acts by the international community. Such factions cite the same principles in working for the creation of an independent Palestinian state that the post-war Israeli "terrorists" cited to justify their violent actions in seeking the creation of the independent state of Israel. It is very easy to lose this perspective, while at the same time condemning, as the international community should indeed do, any acts of terrorism, whatever the goal. In 1977, Menachem Begin, the man born a Russian Jew and persecuted by both the Nazis and the Soviets, became Prime Minister of Israel. Begin was responsible for the peace treaty with Anwar Sadat of Egypt that returned the Sinai to Egypt, and which led to both men winning the Nobel Peace Prize. What this demonstrates is that all things are possible, even though in 1946 Begin had led the bombing of the King David Hotel in Jerusalem, and in March 1952 the attempt on the life of Chancellor Konrad Adenauer of West Germany. UK–US intelligence has to operate within this hugely complex historic backdrop, providing intelligence that will help both maintain Middle East stability and providing the warnings and indicators that certain events may precipitate potentially catastrophic consequences that may impact the global peace and economy.

Intelligence and Politics: The Clear Need for Separation

Today the Sunni Islamist group Hamas that has run the Gaza portion of the Palestinian Territories, and Hezbollah, the Shi'a Muslim militant group and political party in Lebanon, appear very much like how Irgun looked in 1942 when it split from the Haganah, launching from 1944–1948 a campaign against the British in Palestine. On May 14, 1948 the State of Israel was created. The relevance and poignancy are clear: Israel was fundamentally born out of terrorism. The key for UK–US intelligence is to have collection systems in place today that will help in providing accurate information to guide international policies to prevent the spread of terrorism, while clearly finding a solution to the above policy dilemmas. Some analysts see the answer perhaps lying with Jordan and Israel, supported by the United States and its key allies. However, the ever more volatile situation in Syria, aided and abetted by Russia, adds another regional complexity, plus the ongoing crisis in the Yemen, and a range of Saudi-led activities and operations that have caused not just discord within the United Nations, but also within the Five Eyes foreign policy elites, both inside and outside their current governments. The Five Eyes intelligence community has to remain aloof from controversy in order to perform effectively. Moreover, the Five Eyes have to choose their intelligence allies not just wisely, but with continuous circumspection based on the detailed exigencies of a particular scenario.

The 2018 book, *Rise and Kill: The Secret History of Israel's Targeted Assassinations*, (Random House, New York) by Ronen Bergman shows how decades of covert Israeli assassination operations, mainly by the Mossad, pre- and post-independence in 1948, may appear to have temporary short-term gains but in the long term fail to address the ultimate key strategic considerations, particularly a solution to the Israel–Palestinian territorial dilemma. This is the root cause perhaps of all Israel's problems that galvanize the international community, other than perhaps the United States, against its policies and operations, while the advanced democracies equally condemn the continuous bloodshed by both sides' clandestine and terrorist forces.

President Netanyahu's strategic concerns for the "defensive boundaries" of Israel are clearly demarcated by geography, the distance between key locations in Israel and the West Bank are on the order of six to nine miles, with a huge concentration of the Israeli population on the coastal strip where most of Israel's commercial and industrial life resides. His perfectly reasonable concern is that the West Bank provides a buffer area and site for defensive missile systems that will ward off an attack. The key to helping President Netanyahu and the Israeli people find both peace and security some argue may lie with Jordan.

Jordan is perhaps the most stable political regime in the Arab world. King Abdullah leads a nation that is making significant progress in both democratization and improvement in the lives of the ordinary Jordanian, while providing bedrock security against outside extremist influences. Israel has to both respect and trust Jordan, and Jordan's security against outside threats has to be underpinned by equal aid from the United States, just as the United States provides aid to Israel. The likelihood of a destabilizing and anti-Israel regime emerging in Jordan is at present very remote. UK–US intelligence in the 2020s will have to monitor carefully Jordanian stability. The threats to Israel lie much further to the east in Iran, and that country's extremist associations with other state and non-state actors. By the same token Jordan is equally threatened by extremist groups from outside that will try to destabilize an otherwise progressive regime, with the vast majority of Jordanians loyal both to their political processes and their head of state.

Modern cruise and ballistic missile technology are such that the West Bank buffer zone is not relevant for Israel in terms of a ground-attack invasion from the east, particularly given relationships with both Jordan and the underpinnings provided by the United States. The major threats to both countries, other than extremist attacks from terrorist groups, are most likely to come from missile attacks. The very worst scenario for Israel would be a preemptive ballistic missile attack from Iran. In this and other missile scenarios the West Bank does not play as a key geographic entity because of speed, times, and distance issues associated with the location of key targets in both Jordan and Israel if attacked by cruise and ballistic missiles. Some strategists argue that the West Bank can play a role insofar as it could be the site for a layered defensive missile network.

What the above illustrates is the critical intelligence underpinnings for both warnings and indicators but also for supporting policy decisions and military planning. Some argue that a settlement with Jordan over the West Bank can include the following: Jordan regains control of the West Bank and with United States oversight begins the management of both Palestinian and Israeli settlements in the area. In return, Jordan should grant to Israel several key sovereign air base sites in the West Bank where Israel may have full rights, permanent access for its military to man 24/7 defensive missile batteries and provide early warning radar systems. Such sites and systems will be of equal value to Jordan. In addition, it is argued that the United States could provide other key layers of defensive systems for both Jordan and Israel, in addition to the military systems that it provides under the various aid agreements. If these sorts of solution options are both realistic, achievable, and some form of progress is made in the 2020s, then UK–US intelligence will be critical for establishing highly reliable intelligence systems to ensure that risks are mitigated.

From President Netanyahu's perspective the issue of the strategic role of the West Bank has now taken on a whole new complexion, and one that guarantees Israeli access and presence for the above defensive systems. This is all hypothesis, but whatever does occur in the Middle East in the next ten-plus years will require a significant intelligence input that is not driven solely by US interests. The United States will also want to minimize deployment costs, except at times of rising tension in the region. The independence and capabilities of the other four nations of the Five Eyes intelligence community will be hugely significant in terms of independent and unvarnished assessments. Intelligence sharing is critical in any negotiation and agreement and both Jordan and Israel will need to build confidence with themselves and mutually with the United States in order to share time-sensitive intelligence, complicated by the roles of Russia and China intervening at all levels of political–diplomatic–military–economic–arms sales activities. Put simply, good intelligence is about providing information to the user that enables them to make well-informed decisions well ahead of a decision point, never to be surprised, and always to have the upper-hand knowledge base over one's actual or potential adversary.

The Global Challenge from China

The emerging global power of China and its challenge to US military strength in East Asia pose fundamental questions about the nature and goals of Chinese policy for the long term, and how the Five Eyes can provide intelligence to help craft a strategy both in their best interests and in those of its friends and allies, not just in the region but worldwide. In July 2019 the Chinese government published "China's National Defense in the New Era".[12] This articulates China's public version of its defense policy. It is explicit about Taiwan and its "One China principle" and that if necessary, it will fight for Taiwan. These are words to heed. China's stated GDP expenditures on defense and as a percentage of Chinese government spending are revealing, if accurate, and when compared with the GDP defense expenditures that the Chinese quote between 2012–2017 of the US (3.5%), Russia (4.4%), India (2.5%), the UK (2%), France (2.3%), Japan (1%), and Germany (1.2%). China states it spends 1.3% of GDP on defense. There is one statement that also resonates: "China firmly believes that hegemony and expansion are doomed to failure." We assume that China means territorial expansion by aggressive means. This is at odds with China's militarization of the Spratly Islands. So, the question is, "Quo Vadis China?"

The rise of China is self-evident, but the huge question exists as to what are China's long-and short-term goals, whose economic drivers, let alone military expansion, are reshaping the international security land and seascapes? At the same time the United States has currently rejected the multilateral economic and political framework, witnessed by withdrawal from the Trans-Pacific Partnership, renegotiation of NAFTA, and threats to leave the World Trade Organization, compounded by punitive tariffs on China and US allies, and rejection of the Iran Nuclear Agreement signed by our key European allies, Russia, and China. The effect of all this has been to draw nations into the Chinese orbit, create disharmony with US NATO allies, and draw Russia and China closer. Punitive US sanctions have led to hugely negative consequences. Most of all is the extraordinary successful growth of China's "Belt and Road Initiative" (BRI), a 21st-century "Silk Road" started in 2013, a trillion dollar investment that embraces about 80 countries, strategically designed to guarantee that China will not only secure its own energy, trade routes, and key natural resources, but also expand its investment in global port infrastructure and sea routes across all the world's oceans, stimulating demand for Chinese products and acquiring economic control through massive investments and loans that will not be repaid in some cases this century.

China has also articulated a "Polar Silk Road," stating that it is a "Near Arctic State." The means to achieve what are clearly stated Chinese goals is a "Maritime Grand Strategy," with the Chinese Navy the key centerpiece. China seeks to gain access to and control of precious metal extraction and production in Russia, Central Asia, Latin America, and Africa. China's "Debt Diplomacy" is reaping benefits at the expense of the United States and its key allies. It enables China to soften hitherto strained relations with Japan, the Philippines, and Vietnam, lessening the friction resulting from Chinese occupation and militarization of the Spratly and Paracel islands in the South China Sea. The latter is overtly geared to creating a presence to counter the US Seventh Fleet, while enabling China 200 nautical-mile territorial claims to fishing and undersea resource rights around each and every atoll and island, in spite of the International Court of Arbitration's declaration that China has no such legal or historic claims. The US has not attempted to enforce the ruling of the court in The Hague. Meanwhile China is building naval facilities across the Indian Ocean in Gwadar, Pakistan, in Hambantota in Sri Lanka, and Djibouti, with long-term port agreements with Cambodia, Indonesia, Malaysia, Brunei, Myanmar, Bangladesh, Tanzania, Namibia, Greece, and Italy.

Two successive US National Security Advisors, Tom Donilon, a Washington lawyer, (2010–2013) and Susan Rice, a policy aficionado (2013–2017), let all this happen with zero US counter actions with the hawkish John Bolton, more preoccupied with provoking conflict with Iran rather than paying attention to the detail that James Fanell provided in his briefing of the House Permanent Select Committee on Intelligence in May 2018.[13] A trade and resource conflict is inevitable unless the United States shifts gears to a political–diplomatic–economic turn-around strategy, underwritten by the power of the United States Navy and Marine Corps, the forward-deployed round-the-clock presence that guarantees freedom of the seas, a rule-based international order, and the prevention of conflict over trade, resources, and those critical minerals deemed vital for not just national security but the very heart and soul of the continuing digital revolution and its massive product line.

China is following the British maritime strategy and economic model that it pursued for centuries—the defense of seaborne trade and its support of overseas acquisitions and influence. China is investing "Without Risk," with zero shareholders to please. Investment in African mines brings nothing like the risk to US and European investors. China is stealing technology not just through well-known cyber penetration and espionage but a simple and successful economic strategy—US and other foreign investors have and are going to China, investing, and then finding that China replicates their technology, production, and engineering plans, and then creates home-grown industries and companies. Foreign investment has and will die on the vine in due course. The response from the United States and its key NATO allies has been appallingly paltry. Former Secretary of Defense, Jim Mattis, a wise and wonderfully astute US Marine General, has rightly observed that one key counterbalance is the "strategic convergence" of India and the United States, together with other key US allies, because otherwise Chinese hegemony in the Indo-Pacific region at the economic, political, and strategic levels, will predominate. The huge danger of this is a 21st-century version and tragic specter of the 1930s economic implosion in East Asia that set Japan on not just a conflict course at sea but territorial aggrandizement that led to catastrophe for the world and dénouement on December 7, 1941. The global economy, the world, simply cannot afford to witness another conflict on this scale. There will be no winners, only losers all round. The United States and its allies, including convergence with India, must face this challenge with unprecedented diplomatic, economic, and political–military skill and fortitude.

Some of James Fanell's testimony[14] was challenged by other experts, particularly his prognosis that China may invade Taiwan at some point in the 2020s. Notwithstanding this aspect, his detailed description of China's expansionist policies and actions were thoroughly grounded in accurate intelligence. Moreover, he made the salient point that much of what China has done in the past 10 years was clearly stated in their open literature. In other words, the Chinese have not attempted to hide their plans and programs. They have told us in no uncertain terms what they plan to do. It is possible for the United States in particular to slip into a position of action and reaction vis-à-vis increased Chinese military capabilities and operations seemingly intent on challenging the United States. China is overtly demonstrating what Chinese official writings convey, namely that the American East Asian presence will be challenged and that China sees itself as the preeminent Asian power, with an intent to create a hegemony that will in due course extend to the outer island chains of the Western Pacific.

Action and reaction were very much phenomena of the Cold War: The Soviet Union would develop a capability, or extend its influence in various areas, or establish a new base, and the United States and NATO would counter such activities. The great game played itself out until the demise of the Soviet Union. What the United States and its allies must seriously consider now are the potentially negative impacts of following a similar pattern of behavior with China, of being led astray into costly and complex situations at all levels of political–military strategy. There are alternative ways to address the issues, problems, and challenges that lie ahead for the new generation of American leaders, who cannot afford the luxury of a Cold War standoff with massive economic implications. However, what the above does show quite clearly is that UK–US intelligence and their Five Eyes partners will need to be extremely vigilant in the warnings and indicators domain, such that their political leaderships cannot be caught unawares by sudden and perhaps unprecedented drastic actions by China.

It is wise initially to revert to first principles when beginning the analysis that will lead to creating an enduring strategy for the US and its allies in East Asia. Does China resemble, or has it begun to replicate, the patterns of activities that have characterized the growth, and decline, of imperial powers and those nations that sought regional hegemony? Do the imperial models of ancient Greece and Rome, the Spanish, British, Hapsburg, Turkish, and Russian empires resemble and apply to what we see evolving in China? Do the militarist, expansionist territorial goals of Napoleon, the Nazis, Fascist Italy, and Imperial Japan connect with what we observe happening with a growing Chinese military capability, an economic juggernaut that is by no means yet in top gear, and with massive resource needs, particularly oil, that require overseas Chinese investment, foreign port facilities, and overseas political–military infrastructure?

The answer to much of the above is that China has led an extremely non-invasive approach to international relations in modern times, with certain exceptions. The past 500 years, since the European powers began their outward growth, exploration, colonization, and empire building, have witnessed China on a very different track. In that time, China has never invaded and permanently occupied a sovereign state or shown imperial intent. Since the Chinese revolution and the conclusion of World War II, China has for the most part lived inwardly. But there have been exceptions.

General Douglas MacArthur's 1950 foray northwards into North Korea and to the Yalu River provoked a response from China that was not surprising: Its forces invaded south across the Yalu River and drove the United States back to the 39th parallel. From the Chinese perspective, the United States posed a threat to Chinese sovereignty and to a communist client state. In 1962, during the short Sino-Indian War, China invaded India briefly as a means of letting Jawaharlal Nehru's government know that China disapproved of India's support for the Dalai Lama and the Tibetan independence movement. After India suffered a defeat, China quickly withdrew, having made its point.

However, the Chinese invasion of Vietnam in February 1979, to signal Chinese disapproval of Vietnam's invasion of Cambodia to suppress China's client regime, the Khmer Rouge, led to an ignominious defeat. The war lasted just one month. China lost about 20,000 troops, more in a matter of weeks than the United States lost in a single year of fighting in Vietnam. Moreover, a Vietnamese force of 100,000 border troops bloodied a Chinese army of 250,000, a humiliating defeat. The impact on China's leader, Deng Xiaoping, was dramatic.

China has supplied weapons and technology to nation-states that run counter to US and its allies' interests. China has distinctive and clear-cut policies regarding all major international issues, whether it is UN policy in the Middle East or policy toward rogue nations (of which North Korea is a leading example). China, like any other country, pursues what it believes to be its national self-interest. The Five Eyes intelligence community will have to monitor carefully Chinese pronouncements and actions so that changes do not come as surprises.

What China has *not* done is provide indications that it sees territorial expansion by invasion of other nations territories as a way to extend Chinese power and influence. It has mostly followed international law and agreements. There is no question that China could have marched into Hong Kong or Macau at any time without resistance. Instead, China waited until the legal expiration of treaty agreements that, in 21st-century hindsight, amounted to the blunt use of 19th-century imperial power by Portugal and Britain. Both territories were transitioned peacefully to Chinese rule. By contrast, an Argentinian dictatorship decided in 1982 to challenge Britain's long-standing rights and ownership of the Falkland Islands, and suffered the consequences. China has never made such moves. If there is a deviation from this trend, it may be economic and not militarist, and could in due course prove to be the seed of serious discord, the resource-hungry dragon. However, there are intelligence signs that the above may be too rosy a prognosis, that the Grand Maritime Strategy which China is clearly pursuing is a potential precursor to denouement. The Five Eyes as a whole is pivotal in this regard.

China has repeatedly indicated that its inherent needs and destiny are bound to economic hegemony in East Asia. To that end, the People's Republic has begun a systematic set of claims, based on perceived historic rights, to key uninhabited reefs, atolls, and small islands in the South China Sea. China is now a self-evident economic Goliath. At some point its gross national product will equal and likely surpass those of the United States, Japan, and Germany. The danger is not economic competition, which is healthy and beneficial in the context of a well-managed, globally interconnected marketplace, but resource needs. China's massive population requires to be fed and sustained in keeping with its world economic position. China has a serious hold on key precious metals, particularly in the semiconductor and space industries, but in other areas it is woefully dependent. Oil is the largest problem. The exponential growth of Chinese oil demand could reach a possible supply and demand crisis situation in the mid to late 2020s. The country's planners are constantly looking for alternative suppliers and areas for investment and exploration. China is still using coal as a major energy source. The Western powers with green energy and conservation issues high on their national agendas see the Paris Accord as critical for all nations, and especially the two huge-population states of China and India, requiring increasing large investments in green solar, wind, and hydro energy sources. There is no question that potentially both these nations can convert with the right leadership and investment to alternative energy sources. Five Eyes intelligence will have to increasingly invest in economic intelligence, coupling their sources and methods with highly capable analyses from industry and especially the more prestigious academic institutions tracking global energy sources and distribution. The specter of a resource-hungry China replicating the Japanese resource-driven expansion policies of the 1930s which culminated in the attack on Pearl Harbor, is not in sight in any shape of form at present or the foreseeable future. The Five Eyes will have to increasingly devote more resources to economic intelligence in the strategic sense.

Chinese seizure of small islands and atolls in the South China Sea, and the militarization of these with runways, missile sites, radar and communications, exacerbated by aggressive naval posturing underpinning what the international legal community has declared as illegal claims to the Spratly and Paracel islands, are clearly matters of very serious concern. The Five Eyes have collected extensive intelligence on all these developments and the public domain commercial satellite imagery of the Chinese South China Sea sites has made it evident to the world community what the Chinese have done in construction terms, showing in global media sources their clear intent. This is in flagrant violation of the of the International Court of Arbitration in The Hague, finding against Chinese claims in the South China Sea as not based on any legitimate historic rights or antecedents. To the Five Eyes community these actions reflect a likely Chinese policy to continue militarization and claims not founded in the United Nations Convention on the Law of the Sea. All this indicates willful intent to ignore international law, a most worrisome posture. The US Navy and its allies are currently challenging all Chinese claims in the South China Sea by exercising regularly the rights of innocent passage within the historic international limits in all the areas claimed to be Chinese territory, by sailing cruisers and destroyers into those waters that the Chinese claim as sovereign. This has led to near collisions at sea of Chinese and US warships and other hostile Chinese acts, such as intercepting US aircraft in international airspace that the Chinese claim as their national airspace. None of this bodes well for the future as the Chinese expand their navy in both numbers and capabilities, far exceeding what may be regarded as the classic naval mission of the protection of seaborne trade.

The legal concept of a 200-mile economic zone has been generally accepted into the body of international law, but that zone and the law of the sea are the least developed and codified legalisms within the international community. Drawing 200-mile economic zones around the disputed island chains of the South China Sea creates major challenges for dispute resolution. Vietnam has been at odds with China over island sovereignty issues for some time, and the geopolitics of the region place Japan, the Philippines, South Korea, Malaysia, Thailand, Singapore, and Indonesia in potential conflict with China over such claims as well. The wider issue of Chinese resource needs will not fade away. There are no signs of major green energy programs that will solve China's problems any time soon. Coupled to China's increasing thirst for oil is its parallel policy of hard-currency accumulation and owning foreign indebtedness.

What then, may China really want to achieve, given its military buildup, its naval exercises, and its posturing regarding Taiwan? What does China hope to gain by its ability to field new weapons systems that the Five Eyes have assiduously monitored and analyzed? The latter include anti-carrier, anti-access ballistic missiles, and anti-satellite systems, together with a considerable investment in electronic and cyber warfare skills and technology, and a growing fleet of submarines, both nuclear and non-nuclear, along with increasing moves into space and other intelligence/surveillance/reconnaissance domains. The Five Eyes community is concerned that China may, very simply, be planning on winning a war that it never fights. What is the essence of this analysis?

Such a war is about countervailing power, raising the order of battle of key assets to high levels, and creating constant challenges that require persistent US and allied presence, deployments, and basing at very high cost. At one level it may be regarded as a war of attrition by other means, underpinned by sustainable economic growth and a Chinese military–industrial complex based on the new Chinese State capitalist model, which even some distinguished American economists have cited as being more efficient than the free-market capitalist model. The Five Eyes community analysts then have to ask, is this is a new form of hegemony, or a unique Chinese version? The threat is not just the military buildup per se, but the underlying single weakness in the otherwise rosy Chinese future: resource limitations and the increasing demand for oil, and what is already being witnessed in Africa, with massive Chinese investment that is clearly resource oriented, particularly minerals. By beefing up its military strength, China wins the war it never fights by checkmating the United States, specifically the US Seventh Fleet, the key forward-deployed Asian representative of American presence, intent, technology, and firepower.

The intelligence to date does not bode well. China is pursuing quite simply a massive military modernization, with naval operations across the whole Indo-Pacific region, and put very directly, predatory economics. China is constantly strengthening the "Maritime Silk Road" in the Indian Ocean and demonstrating preparations for both combat and non-combat operations in the Indian Ocean, a huge change from pre-2010. In January 2016 China signed a ten-year agreement with Djibouti for port access and basing rights, ostensibly to protect Chinese commercial interests and citizens in Africa, and support counter-terrorist operations. At the same time this base provides China with a strategic posture adjacent to the critical Bab-el-Mandab Strait. Similarly, with Chinese basing rights at the deep-water port of Gwadar, Pakistan, at Salalah in Oman, and in the Seychelles. In May 2019 China indicated that it would invest \$10.7 billion in Oman. China will undoubtedly create "listening stations" in all these locations, as well as becoming a major arms supplier to the former US ally, Pakistan. All the ports in which China is investing are or will become "dual use" ports for commercial shipping and Chinese Navy port visits, repair and maintenance, and as key logistics hubs distant from mainland China. By the early 2020s China will have the world's largest navy, signaling that China is no longer a land power but a maritime power whose trade is currently about 41% of GDP, and of that trade about 95% is seaborne. In 2020 China has about 5,000 known registered ships.

So, what is the best strategy for the United States and its allies, and what requirements will be placed on the Five Eyes community? First, none of the Five Eyes nations can contemplate a war with China. However, no responsible US leader can abide China creating an East Asian economic–political–military hegemony that may witness the demise of US influence, and with it, critical American economic interests. The Five Eyes navies led by the United States Navy plus other key regional allies such as Japan and South Korea will have to return to a more regular and expansive presence in Far Eastern waters. This is critical to keeping the economic arteries healthy by the wise use of naval power. The Five Eyes become the centerpiece of the intelligence gathering and analysis to support these operations.

The solution may perhaps lie within the problem itself. While the United States reacts to Chinese moves—planning, for example, ways to implement new air-sea anti–access tactics and capabilities—essential points are possibly being missed. China's quest for economic hegemony by political–military means, in essence its Grand Maritime Strategy, can be addressed at the strategic level, because the United States and its allies have several critical factors in their favor. In the strategy that evolves from these factors, the US Navy, the other Five Eyes navies and major Asian allies, are important players. All will require coherent, accurate, and timely intelligence.

East and Southeast Asia and the wider Indo-Pacific region, stretching from the Malacca Straits across the Indian Ocean to east Africa and the key entry points to the Persian Gulf and the Red Sea, are joined economically, and therefore politically, by one medium—the sea. It is the means by which most of the trade of Asia, and thus the world, takes place.

Seaborne commerce is the enduring thread that runs through the history of the world since the age of discovery and expansion. Without oceanic trade, the global economy would collapse. The sea routes connecting all the Asian countries with the rest of the world are vital arteries. If, for whatever reason, they cease to function, the world will hemorrhage economically. The disparate Asian nations are interconnected and interdependent in this regard. The vital passages of the Malacca Straits and the Indonesian Archipelago run the routes that take trade onward through the South China Sea, the East China Sea, the Yellow Sea, the Sea of Japan, the Pacific Islands, and the trans-Pacific routes; those aquatic pathways are the lifelines of the world's trading nations. The protection of that trade, the maintenance of the freedom of the seas, and the enforcement of the laws of the sea present a huge strategic opportunity to bring together the Five Eyes nations and their allies in the region. Such a common effort can foster long-term peace and prosperity for all, and ensure that East Asia is not destabilized by misplaced Chinese hegemonic intentions, underwritten by a clearly articulated Grand Maritime Strategy. China does not win a war that it never fights, and Asia can grow in wealth and prosperity with its Five Eyes and other key trading partners. This can be the genesis of a new strategy in Asia, one based on trade-route protection, maritime power, shared efforts based on shared interests, and supported in all regards by high-quality Five Eyes intelligence sources, methods, and analysis. This strategy's key ingredients include freedom of navigation, freedom of the seas, protection of seaborne trade, and rights of passage. What is required is a new "Asian Law of the Sea," either written or declaratory. Such a law would:

- Guarantee various maritime rights, including defining territorial rights, rights of access and passage, fishing and resource rights, and codify maritime conduct.
- Provide unified policing and enforcement.
- Provide agreement-based (and, in due course, treaty-based) means for regular international gatherings of the member states.
- Take the Association of Southeast Asian Nations and other multi- and bilateral agreements to a new organization and forum for organizing and implementing a maritime code of conduct.

This new organization would be the vehicle for resolving issues associated with 200-mile economic zones and disputes over island chains; for enforcing international law and human rights; and for combating piracy, smuggling, and terrorism. That is a formidable array of international activities that the Five Eyes nations can carry out with their regional partners. Such a cooperative undertaking can be the means to bring China into the family of Asian nations in ways that are neither belligerent nor challenging to the status quo. The strategy clearly places markers in the sand. To be a non-participant is to take one's country out of the community of nations. If China chooses a less cooperative, continual hegemonic course, then its Asian neighbors will have built themselves a fortified maritime community, linked by various agreements and obligations that will be formidable. In this environment intelligence becomes absolutely vital. The most recent development of China creating bases and airfields from uninhabited reefs in disputed island areas in the South China Sea is a case in point. Open-source satellite imagery shows a clear Chinese intent to militarize these areas.

The alliance aspects are crucial. The good news is that the region's nations are on board. The Australians, the Malaysians, the Indonesians, the Thais, the South Koreans, the Japanese, the Philippines, and now the Vietnamese, signaled originally by US Secretary of Defense Robert Gates' successful groundbreaking visit back in late 2010, are increasingly joined in a common bond. At the center, in discreet fashion, has to be Five Eyes intelligence as the guardian against change, and worst case, surprise.

The Five Eyes Navies and their close Asian allies are unique for multiple reasons, and one of them is the unifying force of the brotherhood of the sea that navies show toward one another. Sailors are gregarious people who are diplomats in myriad ways, and nothing is more unifying than port visits after joint exercises, rescue missions, disaster relief, and successful operations against drug runners and terrorists. Navies by themselves can implement policies that no amount of conventional diplomacy can hope to achieve. The United States in particular has existing resources that require little additional investment to make security-force assistance with all the participating nations a permanent and persistent feature of US naval diplomacy. Those should be the watchwords of this strategy: "US naval diplomacy," supported by Five Eyes intelligence and complemented by the intelligence services of key regional allies, particularly Japan and South Korea. Vietnam may increasingly become an intelligence player in the above mix. Joint international protection of maritime trade, economic rights, and the enforcement of a new emerging law of the sea for Asia can be the means to peaceful ends. If China balks and insists on an open standoff characterized by "benign aggression," then there is little that the United States and its friends and allies can do, other than to make it very clear that they will never tolerate any form of overt aggression. The olive branch can be continuously offered, and hopefully at some stage will be accepted with magnanimity.

No one can successfully predict regime change in China. At present this seems unlikely. What one can perhaps hypothesize is that the confluence of generational change, the very international trade that is making China great, cultural and travel exchanges, the internet, and technological sharing will overcome the inward-lookingness and control mechanisms of the Chinese leadership. The specter of Tiananmen Square still looms large. China demonstrates a ruthless streak from time to time, and the concern for human rights are not part of China's political make-up. Only time will tell if this will evolve. The virtues of youth and the global economy combined eventually may make certain political transformations inevitable in China. However, this may be a rose-tinted view given that China today monitors every citizen's personal telephones, the internet, and restricts communications in keeping with a 1930s-style dictatorship, while suppressing any form of dissent or opposition to policies such as the treatment of ethnic and religious minorities.

One scenario can illustrate implementation of the new regional collective effort. Regular joint exercises, guided by excellent current intelligence and projections, can be executed to protect shipping following the routes from the Southeast Asian straits to the Japanese Islands and South Korea. Such exercises can develop and train the region's nations in all domains of maritime warfare and seaborne trade protection. For instance, in the antisubmarine-warfare and anti-surface modes, those nations can show both capability and will, and if China elects to be a thorn in the side of its neighbors by offering up a belligerent passive-aggressiveness, then it will merely be providing training targets for the combined nations honing their skills. Hopefully this will not occur, and China will show respect for and observance of the rights of free passage and the various economic zones. Indeed, China has as much at stake as any nation, increasingly dependent itself on the freedom of the seas for imported resources.

Change for the better in East Asia has been illustrated by the transformation of Vietnam, a nation that at the conclusion of the Vietnam War could barely sustain its population at the poverty level. Today, it has rejected the Marxist-Leninist model and pursues a state capitalist economy. Nothing is more symbolic of change than the $1.3 billion investment made by Intel outside Ho Chi Minh City. Vietnam's 95.54 million people are now at a new level of prosperity and growth, perhaps unthinkable at the time of another symbolic memory, the last US helicopter departing the empty Saigon embassy in 1975. Vietnam can become a close ally and major trading partner with the United States and its Five Eyes allies, and be integrated with the other Asian nations in a new Asian maritime strategy.

The United States with its Five Eyes intelligence allies should be strident in implementing the new strategy. It combines the maintaining of vital US and allied national interests, even to the extent of keeping the peace by preparing for war, with an internationalist maritime strategy that focuses on the enduring significance of the sea. The sea is both the means and the end in a modern US and Five Eyes Asian strategy.

Peace in the Indo-Pacific Region and the Relationship with India

Back in the 1960s US Secretary of State Dean Rusk advised President Kennedy that "India is key to countering China." The US went in an opposite direction, investing huge support across a broad spectrum of civil–military aid to Pakistan, driving India towards Russia for most of the Cold War, with the Soviet Union becoming India's chief arms supplier. Experience has shown that Pakistan cannot be trusted, in fact is duplicitous in many regards, as shown by the key Pakistani facility at Gwadar for China to have a naval base for the foreseeable future, with China now providing major arms supplies to Pakistan. US diplomacy with India has fortunately shown most positive signs. In 2015 President Obama issued a "US–India Joint Strategic Vision for the Asia–Pacific and the Indian Ocean region." On April 11, 2016 in the *Times* of India, US Secretary Ashton Carter wrote a key lead article entitled, "A Firm Strategic handshake: The India–US Partnership is moving to embrace defense tech transfers and maritime cooperation." On June 7, 2016 the White House issued a joint statement: "The United States and India: Enduring Global Partners in the 21st century." All this was converted to hard legislative fact in the US Congress. In 2016 India was formally declared a "Major Defense Partner" (MDP), and this was underwritten in the US Defense Authorization Act 2017, cementing the MDP into US law.[15] The Asia Reassurance Act of 2018 further solidified this. On June 8, 2016 Prime Minister Narendra Modi of India gave a groundbreaking "Address to a Joint Meeting of Congress." The so called "trust deficit" between India and the US that had persisted since the US–Pakistan alliance was slowly and effectively being eroded, though it is still not quite there. With a population in 2018 of 1,349,217, 956 (versus in China in 2019 1,409,517,397), India is not just the largest democracy in the world, it also faces off against a single party communist state that is now supporting India's chief political–military problem, Pakistan, exacerbated by China's presence next door in Gwadar, Pakistan.

To overcome decades of US–India mistrust characterized by India's desire to both appear and actually to be nonaligned, India's sense of US diplomatic ambiguities, its own internal bureaucratic inertia and sense of not wanting to move into another quasi "colonial orbit," albeit it the United States, there has to be several years of confidence building. Intelligence can be key to this because India needs all the help it can get given the Kashmir scenario, and China's support for and alignment with Pakistan. A combination of intelligence cooperation and sharing, plus a steady increase in naval cooperation can go hand-in-hand. The two are complementary. In addition, the Five Eyes can extend intelligence relations beyond the maritime to assist India over its border disputes with Pakistan and likely Chinese operations with Pakistan against Indian key national security interests. The US Army and those of its Five Eyes allies may provide specialist technical support, complemented by ground, space, and other sources and methods that the Five Eyes have in spades.

On the critical maritime scene Five Eyes navies can provide, over time, confidence-building intelligence support and across-the-board cooperation for both collection and analyses against China and its surrogates. The Indian Ocean is a maritime highway and the type of intelligence that the UK and US can provide with the other three nations will help India better define its future naval force structure and investment. This has to be an incremental confidence-building process because all those nations not aligned with either China or Russia will need a strong Indian Navy. It is likely that by the mid-2020s India will have a 160-ship navy that will include 3 aircraft carriers, 60 major surface combatants, and 400 aircraft. As a value of the Indian defense budget the navy will have increased from a mere 4% in 1960 to 8% in 1970, to 11% in 1992, and to 18% in 2009,[16] and although this increase is laudable an even higher percentage will be required to take the Indian Navy from its sobriquet of the "Cinderella" service to the next level of operational performance, so that it can operate unilaterally with the US Navy and multilaterally with the Five Eyes navies. This interoperability between navies will require establishing secure intelligence links, discreet encrypted communications, and critical data links such as Link 16, a tactical data link network used by NATO, and all the attendant satellite communication connections. Common seamanship standards and protocols such as replenishment at sea, vertical replenishment, ammunition replenishments, and a host of key seamanship drills and maneuvers will have to become ingrained as second nature in a new generation of Indian naval personnel. To underpin these developments India will need a "Grand Strategic" direction to enable the Indian Navy's future leadership and its political oversight to move in unison to reduce US–Indian political ambiguities, achieve expectation goals, and slowly move India into the realm as the major maritime power in the Indian Ocean. Assisting India with the India–Pakistan scenario will help considerably through US mechanisms such as the Defense Technology and Trade Initiative (DTTI) to leverage for example US Special Forces and rapid reaction cell capabilities in India's border disputes. The sales of P-8 Poseidon maritime reconnaissance and ASW aircraft, SH-3 ASW helicopters, and aircraft carrier and jet engine technologies has helped reaffirm US commitment to India's growing navy. All this is good, and at the heart of change will be Five Eyes intelligence cooperation and collaboration.

The Russia of Vladimir Putin

Russia has clearly violated the norms of international behavior by its annexation of the Crimea and its support for further destabilization in eastern Ukraine. Russia's avowed objectives are not difficult to ascertain, whatever the pleadings of its leader. Without its oil and gas productions and the exports that flow from these, the Russian economy would be in seriously worse shape than at present. The oligarchic nature of the Russian communist party, the roles of small controlling economic elites, and the Russian Mafia, plus the very nature of Vladimir Putin's background as a former KGB operative that makes him secretive and authoritarian, could add up to a recipe for long-term failure, particularly if at some point both the opposition groups and Russian masses coalesce into an effective alternative. The huge personal wealth accumulated by a tiny Russian minority must at some point come back to haunt them, but the exact nature and timing of such denouement is difficult to predict. Vladimir Putin's personal treasure trove cannot be ignored by the Russian people and web users indefinitely. However, the converse of this is a perpetual Putin led dictatorship with opposition groups stifled or worst case removed.

Two fundamental facts need to be stated. First, Russia's GDP, US$1,578 trillion in 2017–2018, is significantly less than that of the state of California, US$2.448 in 2015–2016. California had a population of 39.54 million in 2017, Russia 144.5 million in 2017.[17] These core facts say an enormous amount. Second, Russia has nuclear weapons. Without these weapons readers are encouraged to assess for themselves where they think that Russia would be in the international order, notwithstanding that Russia is a member of the United Nations Security Council and has veto power. Without nuclear weapons, and its oil and gas, it is likely that Russia would not have a lead place in the international order for the foreseeable future.

During the Cold War the Soviet Navy was a serious challenge. The whole NATO edifice kept the Soviet Navy in check by and large. However, we should also note that the Berlin Wall could not have come down soon enough, given the technical strides that the Soviets appeared to have been making, with their ship and submarine build rates most worrisome. Glasnost and Perestroika changed all that, with Mikhail Gorbachev becoming General Secretary of the Central Committee of the Communist Party of the Soviet Union in March 1985. How far Vladimir Putin wishes to put the clock back remains to be seen—indeed whether this is at all credible is an open question, given Russia's financial situation.

On the strategic missile submarine side of the equation the Russians have, after a moribund period following the collapse of the Soviet Union, begun a program to rebuild its SSBN Fleet, with four Borei-class SSBNs in the fleet and, according to the Russian News Agency Tass, another 11 expected to be built by 2020. The three remaining Delta III-class SSBNs and six Delta VI-class SSBNs will be gone from the inventory by the 2020s. The Russians are building the Yasen-class SSGN, with eight ordered so far, and an SSN class that is purported to begin building in 2016, with perhaps fifteen completed by 2035. News reports state that after the improved Kilo-class of six for the Black Sea Fleet is completed the Russians will build a new air independent improved Lada-class – perhaps 14–18 of these over a 15-year period, with most of the class commissioned in the 2020s.

Safety is a huge issue. Since 2000 the Russians had seven major nuclear submarine accidents. The worst of these was the *Kursk* that exploded and sank with the loss of all hands. The nuclear incident in 2019 that killed a group of senior Russian scientists is still being analyzed at the time of writing though it is suspected that a test nuclear propulsion unit became out of control. Russia's submarine force, until the recent resurgence, was older than 30 years. However, by positioning its remaining more capable submarines and new SSNs and SSBNs, together with its nuclear-capable bombers and land-based missiles, Putin's Russia can send unfavorable messages to the West, for example, moving nuclear weapons near to the Polish border, and certainly moving nuclear weapons into the Crimea will be seen by NATO as an aggressive act. The sustainment of Five Eyes intelligence is crucial in this environment to support NATO.

The Russian surface navy is not in good shape, much worse than perhaps media sources relate, with perhaps too grandiose plans for possible aircraft carriers, frigates, corvettes, and large destroyers on the order of 15,000 tons, together with a cruiser modernization program for the Kirov- and Slava-classes, and the Udaloy destroyers, though the *Sovremennyy*-class destroyers will be retired. In spite of the French Mistral-class amphibious ship debacle, it looks like the Russians may build two to three 14,000–16,000-ton amphibious ships, and four *Ivan Gren*-class amphibious ships in each of the Black Sea and Baltic Fleets. All of the above is very much dependent on both Russian yard capacity and finances. If all the above happened by about

2030 the Russian navy could in effect be back in serious business. The question for Five Eyes intelligence is: is this at all achievable? To date unclassified Five Eyes data shows that the Russians have fallen behind almost every program with delays and major difficulties. The overall picture is reasonably clear: the Russian Navy will concentrate on strategic deterrence, the SSBN force, and coastal defense, with the blue water navy of the Cold War era still to be determined. Russian incursions, for example, near to UK air space are by relatively aging moribund aircraft and have the aura of defunct Cold War saber rattling to very little effect.

The question for the West and specifically the Five Eyes intelligence community is how to counter and modify Russian aggressive moves, short of direct confrontation. Where, for example, does the maritime mix play in this? Sanctions and diplomacy have impacted Russia, though the former have negative economic connotations for the West, particularly the European nations dependent on Russian energy sources. Germany has made it very clear to both its EU partners and the United States that it needs Russian gas and the undersea gas pipeline from Russia to Germany is the critical infrastructure. The US argument that Germany could be held hostage to Russian supply is countered by those analysts that argue that Putin's Russia desperately needs the income from German gas sales, and that the relationship is complementary, not potentially an economic hostage situation. Naval power in both the Baltic and Black Seas, judiciously applied with the forward-deployed allied presence of multi-national naval forces, together with classical diplomacy, can send a clear message that aggression will not be rewarded. A US Navy and US Marine Corps MEF (Marine Expeditionary Force)-level surge into either or both seas, supported by the NATO navies, and supported by all elements of the Five Eyes intelligence community, sends not just a clear message of intent and deterrence. It shows solidarity of purpose and the clear military ability to stop aggression in its tracks. A further incursion into the Ukraine by direct or surrogate Russian forces, and a worst-case threat to NATO allies in the Baltic States can be met with an unequivocal display of overwhelming naval and marine/amphibious power. US and other key NATO forces can display, by forward deployed and persistent presence, a similar capability that was shown, for instance, at Inchon in the Korean War. A large and flexible amphibious force that is deployed from the sea, at short notice, with no requirements for shore support, can send a key message, along with diplomacy, in support of the allied cause. This involves therefore the classic display of naval expeditionary warfare based on three main tenets: forward-persistent presence, flexibility to use those forces in terms of the mix and combination of naval forces, and maneuver from the sea at a time and places of one's choosing. These abiding principles will be underpinned by Five Eyes intelligence sources and methods, indicators and warnings, and collective sustained analysis.

The psychological make up of our adversaries and those who wish the United Kingdom and the United States and their allies' ill intent is a critical component of any analysis of their plans and operations. Intelligence that ignores or does not include such analysis is likely built on shifting sand. In the contemporary context take the classic example of Vladimir Putin. Vladimir Putin is a Yuri Andropov[18] lookalike, with Andropov later attaining the General Secretaryship of the Soviet Communist Party, not unlike how Putin acceded to power. Everything Putin thinks and does is characterized by his KGB beginnings, his training, his actions, and therefore how he can be predicted to behave. This is vital in any Five Eyes intelligence assessment of Russian intentions, plans, and operations. Personality is critical. We should look at Russia through the Putin lens and that of his key oligarchs. The Five Eyes have to understand and analyze the inner mindset of Putin and his FSB operatives, his oligarchic friends, his security system, his deception techniques, and his electronic eavesdropping capabilities and procedures, of which cyber penetration for example of the US 2016 election, is merely one amongst many. He and his closest staff, plus the trusted foot soldiers that make up Putin's coterie and do the real work on the ground, always have a strategy and plan. Unraveling that strategy and plan is step one. It is clear to the layperson that Putin very much wants sanctions lifted with the West and, at a more grandiose level, he has a desire to restore mother Russia to another level of recognition and self-aggrandizement for himself, at the expense whenever and wherever possible of what he sees as the old adversaries in NATO and their associated allies. Vladimir Putin sees the Five Eyes as adversaries.

The secret of Putin's success, as most likely measured by his criteria and KGB/FSB standards, is to be not directly exposed to direct evidence of his personal involvement in Russian intelligence operations. Putin's operatives' trade craft is not to communicate while others listen, to launder money through multiple channels with no traceable fingerprints, to hold several passports and identities, to always guard their back and personal weaknesses whenever possible, and to disarm and dissemble with consummate urbanity. This is what the FSB and its surrogates in both the Russian mafia and the wealthy oligarchs are very simply all about. The cultural and historical underpinnings are all there to be analyzed. The psychological make-up of the Russian leader and his immediate entourage holds the key to predicting Russian policies and their likely outcomes. There is clear and perceptible lineal descent at one level from the post-World War II Soviet leadership to Vladimir Putin. The lives and careers of Georgy Malenkov, Nikita Khrushchev, Leonid Brezhnev, Yuri Andropov, Konstantin Chernenko, to the great changes brought about by Mikhail Gorbachev, reveal aspects of their mindsets, behavior, and policies that enabled us to predict with reasonable accuracy their likely reaction to changing global geo-strategic realities in the context of domestic Soviet politics and economics. The same applies to Vladimir Putin and his regime. The Five Eyes will be able to unravel many of Putin authorized asymmetric and apparently non state sponsored covert operations and cyber space initiatives by examining both his past and current dependence on means that run contrary to the maintenance of international order. Putin is not difficult to predict. The secret for the Five Eyes is to penetrate and contain the operations generated by this old-style KGB operative who has grasped the significance of the digital era.

Emerging Threats, Challenges and Impact on Intelligence Collection and Analysis

In some instances, the past may remain prologue in terms of the collection technologies and assessments that were employed successfully during the Cold War being applied to emerging post 2020 military threat systems of potential aggressor states. This is particularly true of ELINT and MASINT collection against new systems and technologies, and to assess when they will gain initial operational capability (IOC) as they appear from the production lines of China, Russia, North Korea, Iran, and, to some extent, Israel. It is salutatory to recall that Israel supplied Argentina with various key military assets both during and after the Falklands conflict. For example, after the conflict Israel refitted three Boeing 707 aircraft with advanced SIGINT equipment that was clearly not in the best interests of the Five Eyes community. The counterintelligence services of all the Five Eyes monitor commercial and military technology gathering by Israel and its surrogates and technical representatives, knowing that Israel has commercial and financial interests in understanding and garnering the latest Western technologies that it can use in its own industrial base. The motive is very simply economic wellbeing, that is not unreasonable, except that it involves in essence taking Five Eyes technology, reproducing it, and then selling on the international markets.

Of course, China and Russia are much bigger and more serious targets for counterintelligence against classical technical espionage as well as perfectly legal acquisition of Western technology by surrogate means. The open societies of the Five Eyes are much more vulnerable than the closed and heavily secret and pervasive societies of China, Russia, North Korea, and Iran, where human rights have no legal standing. Penetration of programs in the very early stages of R&D through initial design and production of emerging advanced technologies in threat countries will require new and innovative collection methodologies. Take for example the development of hypervelocity weapons with speeds and ranges not contemplated during the Cold War. Similarly, with situational awareness, targeting, and space systems technologies, where there is in the case of the latter a growing need to deploy defensive counterspace systems because of adversary offensive counterspace systems. The Five Eyes require more resilient and defendable space assets. Similarly with networked, AI-intensive, and fully integrated advanced UUV (Unmanned Underwater Vehicle) and UAV/UCAS systems there will be major requirements to use the latest AI tools to enhance real-time intelligence collection and secure distribution without any possibility of interception and/or jamming.

All major threats see Five Eyes space assets as huge threats to their ability to cover up technical developments, initial testing, and then deployment. For instance, Five Eyes advanced space-based infrared systems have the capability to unmask myriad different threat developments. As AI becomes more and more commonplace within the interlaced Five Eyes collection networks the overall ability of the major threats will be increasingly fraught to deceive and surprise. GPS vulnerability has been an issue for many years. Between October 16 and November 7, 2018 it was alleged by the Norwegian Ministry of Defence that the Russian military jammed NATO GPS signals during the largest NATO military exercise since the Cold War, Trident Juncture, in Norway, that involved 50,000 US and NATO forces. Jamming evidently occurred in the Kola Peninsula. None of this is surprising, and of course it does tip NATO's hand to what the threat constitutes. I was shown in 2018 and held a GPS jamming device manufactured in China that could jam local commercial GPS signals within about a 10-mile radius. This is daunting if such devices are in the wrong hands, whether criminals, terrorists, malcontents, mentally unstable persons, or worst-case intelligence agents and deep-rooted undercover plants awaiting instructions in the event of hostilities. In 2013, a New Jersey man bought an illegal GPS jammer to thwart the tracking device in his company vehicle. His GPS jammer, bought online for less than $100, interfered with a new GPS guidance system called Smartpath being tested at Newark Liberty airport. Federal agents tracked his jamming signal to his truck. He received a very heavy fine, as well as losing his job.[19]

In the past seven years since the incident above, jamming technology has improved considerably. Military- and intelligence-grade jammers are in a league of their own from commercially accessible devices. The Five Eyes have the capability to collectively design and employ the most advanced anti-jam GPS devices that will undoubtedly both confuse and deceive the threat, while indeed homing weapons onto the source. The essential parameters of electronic warfare persist. Those who seek to do bad things with what may appear to be state-of-the-art offensive tools often become their own worst enemy.

Modern HUMINT

Perhaps the single biggest challenge facing those who manage clandestine HUMINT operations in the digital era is how to securely and covertly maintain contact with HUMINT sources without counterintelligence services detecting an agent. This is an important task. In the digital era counterintelligence agencies have become adept at intercepting the discreet communications of those who are betraying their nations' secrets, however disguised and buried such communications may be. Classical dead letter drops and meetings that involve an agent avoiding counterintelligence followers are most likely a thing of the past and spy novels. Sheer physical access in such countries as North Korea and Iran is hugely challenging. Contacts are most likely to be made at official functions. The problem even in these situations where Five Eyes operatives have diplomatic status, is that the counterintelligence services of host nations will be fully active. They will be watching, listening, and videoing the activities of their nationals as they have iterations with diplomats, trade negotiators, visiting senior business executives, academic researchers, and so on. A report that was issued in Yahoo News on November 2, 2018 by two capable investigative journalists, Zach Dorman and Jenna McLaughlin, illustrates the above. They discovered that the CIA's internet-based communications system for covert exchanges with overseas agents was compromised. This happened between 2009–2013, with the compromise initiated in Iran. They state: "More than two dozen sources died in China in 2011 and 2012 as a result, according to 11 former intelligence and national security officials," evidently disclosed under the apparent protection of anonymity. They continued: "The issue was that it (the communications system) was working well for too long with too many people. But it was an elementary system." According to their sources Iran succeeded in breaking up a CIA HUMINT network that hampered US intelligence collection against Iran's nuclear program. Dorman and McLaughlin state: "Two former US intelligence officials said that the Iranians cultivated a double agent who led them to the secret CIA communications system." The system was an online system. We are led to believe that once the Iranian double agent revealed to Iran's counterintelligence people the website, the Iranians then scoured the web for other likely operatives, revealing "who in Iran was visiting these sites, and from where, and began to unravel the wider CIA network." In May 2017 the *New York Times* reported the loss of 30 CIA agents in China, and in May 2018 CIA officer Jerry Lee, based in Beijing, was charged with spying for the Chinese. *Foreign Policy* magazine reported that, "Chinese intelligence broke through the firewall separating it (CIA communications system) from the main covert communications system, compromising the CIA's entire asset network in that country."

One may conclude that perhaps China and Iran cooperated in these events. Whatever the accuracy of the above claims, one fact is significant and has been verified. Back in 2008 a defense contractor named John Reidy blew the whistle on various inadequacies and vulnerabilities after his management would not listen to his technical concerns. His complaints were not adequately addressed, and he was fired from his position in November 2011. He had assessed that about 70% of CIA covert operations were compromised. One may speculate that if Reidy's concerns had been addressed early enough then lives could have been saved.

Running Covert Agents

What these unclassified public reports illustrate is simply that running covert agents has never been more difficult than today and in the future, even in the case of the classic "walk-ins" where prospective agents visit Five Eyes diplomatic facilities or make contact with an official in order to start a dialogues of betraying their nations' secrets. Such facilities and overt Five Eyes personnel in sensitive overseas cities such as Moscow, Beijing, Tehran, and Pyongyang are so heavily monitored by multiple surveillance systems and human assets that any individual entering or meeting with a foreign official is likely to be immediately identified. Perhaps long gone are the days when a key MI6 agent from the Cold War, Oleg Gordievsky, a senior KGB official who became head of the KGB (Rezident or station chief) in the London Rezidentura (station) may be recruited by direct contact under the eyes of Soviet counterintelligence. Ben Macintyre's fine book, *The Spy and the Traitor*, spells out in detail how MI6 recruited and ran Gordievsky until he was betrayed by no other than CIA's traitor, Aldrich Ames, as a result of his boss's security complacency and indiscretions. All the above calls into question the future value of HUMINT. The Five Eyes however have enormous combined strategic leverage when it comes to HUMINT, assuming that one avoids the notion that all HUMINT is about covert and clandestine agent-running. The enormous bandwidth of the digital era combined with international travel across every part of human endeavor means that there are new and challenging ways to exploit old-fashioned classical HUMINT. HUMINT is by no means dead, and it will take on new forms based on advanced technology, ingenuity, and innovation for which Bletchley Park forebears would be justly proud. A new generation of original thinkers within the Five Eyes can indeed revolutionize HUMINT in unprecedented ways.

Climate Change

Climate change has to be a Five Eyes concern. The five nations together are spending billions on national defense while our planet is threatened by the undeniable scientific evidence of climate change. The question is, will the international community, and the Five Eyes specifically, be able to mobilize resources to counter this threat. The cascading effects of climate change are predicted to destabilize highly vulnerable regions and tens, and likely hundreds, of millions of people, including for example large centers of urban population in the United States. The United States walked away from the 2015 Paris Climate Agreement, and without United States' leadership and investment in countering the effects of climate change there is a huge international gap, a task that the other Five Eyes need to address. What is the key scientific evidence? The glaciers in Antarctica and the Himalaya mountains are melting and these effects alone will significantly impact our planet. The melting Thwaites Glacier in Antarctica is the size of Florida and if it melts completely scientists estimate that global ocean levels will rise by 2 feet. January 2019 was the hottest month ever recorded in Australia, with 2017 and 2018 the hottest years ever recorded. Rising temperatures are estimated to melt one third of the glaciers in the Hindu Kush region of the Himalayas.[20]

National security and climate change are inextricably linked. Within the Five Eyes the US Department of Defense includes climate change in its threat data and analytics, while conversely the Trump White House challenged the global scientific community. The White House is at total variance with the United States' Director of National Intelligence who has stated that, "Global environmental and ecological degradation, as well as climate change, are likely to fuel competition for resources, economic distress, and social discontent." The US military and intelligence community has been responsible. Not so the Trump White House. What is clearly required is international commitment and agreement, and for the Five Eyes to make a stand through technical intelligence support and do what the late Carl Sagan advocated, to stand together and, "Preserve and cherish the pale blue dot, the only home we've ever known." Drastic change will be needed, and the Five Eyes will become critical by using their vast array of technical intelligence tools to collect and analyze data in the service of the planet. A Five Eyes summit will have to continuously monitor and address how each nation can contribute to economic intelligence collection and analysis, together with the impact of climate change.

CHAPTER 8

The Five Eyes Community in the 21st Century

The world events since September 11, 2011 have shaken the resolve of many nations, particularly within NATO, where member nations have witnessed and become somewhat disenchanted with out -of-area operations and commitments to operations that have gone sadly and strategically out of kilter. Iraq, Afghanistan and Libya come immediately to mind, and each of these emphasize above all, the lack of wide-ranging strategic thinking not just about the how and what, but the why. For example, vast cultural differences and huge sectarian rifts that have spanned the centuries within the Moslem world, with their critical ethnic, religious and regional affinities, were largely ignored in a somewhat heedless and headlong dash to seek reprisal for the events of 9/11, for what initially was a small terrorist organization, manned largely by Saudi nationals, not Iraqis or Iranians, with limited funds and resources. Lessons learned from the past, if applied judiciously, may prove invaluable. The institutional memory of the Five Eyes community has at times been blunted by the sheer passage of time and generation changes during which technical and operational tradecraft were not passed on. What will be required is something bigger than just UK–US extended bilateral agreements, but "A Five Eyes Cooperative Strategy for 21st Century Intelligence Collection and Analysis," supported by all agencies and their political leadership. The combined strength of Five Eyes intelligence has to be a formidable instrument of strategic power in the service of the security of the collective nations. This predicates the need for a "Shared Five Eyes Intelligence Vision."

Intelligence is only valuable to the user if it provides reliable, timely, and actionable information that is superior to normal open-source information, and that provides both clear benefits for decision makers and advantages in terms of insight into and knowledge of the particular subject matter. Ultimately the "game of intelligence," as played out for instance during the Cold War by the various HUMINT services of the main international protagonists, is not relevant unless there is real hard-core information emanating from that process. Pitting one secret intelligence service against another may be the subject of spy fiction but it is irrelevant to the essence of providing actionable classified information of real value.

We have already seen that the pace and quality of technological change has accelerated drastically in the last decade. Five Eyes governments have tended to be behind the curve in responding to technological change, with outmoded contracting systems and timelines from R&D phases to initial operational capability (IOC) woefully slow and ponderous, with the result that the commercial, non-defense intelligence world is far more ahead of the technical game because of the ability to innovate quickly and effectively. Small start-up incubator companies have become the name of the commercial game not just in Silicon Valley but across the whole Five Eyes industrial and scientific base. Five Eyes governments have tried to step up the pace, but have not succeeded to date, with post-DARPA-esque organizations such as the United States DIU (Defense Innovation Unit) failing to deliver for a host of bureaucratic, funding, and political reasons. We noted earlier that large defense and aerospace companies with massive multi-year contracts that seriously influence their bottom lines and annual shareholder returns are chastened by the possibility of small start-ups that can well negate the value of the very programs that are their financial life blood. This aspect is a problem that has to be addressed. There are solutions for all parties. For example, the more systems of whatever technical nature, are open architecture, with the ability to introduce major innovative changes without starting from scratch. In this environment radical innovations can be quickly implemented without the costly multi-year cycle of typical procurements within the defense and intelligence sectors. Intelligence has a massive technical component.

All the Five Eyes key agencies that both cost most in annual budgets and employ most people are at the leading edge of technology. They live and breathe, and one may conjecture possibly die in the future, by being one or more steps ahead technologically than the threat. To fall behind is to fail. At the heart of this issue is, simply, people, and very smart people. The Five Eyes will have to increasingly search for, recruit, and train the next generation, and most of all allow for innovation to occur at the grass roots, just as the pressures and exigencies of war and survival forced the British to recruit the finest minds to Bletchley Park, SOE, and the Double Cross system. Across the Five Eyes community there will need to be a "Brains Trust" of the best and the brightest to keep the community ahead. Greater cooperation and sharing will become more critical within closely guarded compartmented programs, very much along the lines of the US Navy–Royal Navy special intelligence collection and analysis programs. The non-military customers' requirements of the Five Eyes may on the surface look very different from those of the military services but on close inspection there is in fact considerable similarity and overlap, where in the 21st century the digital communications revolution affects for instance foreign policy decision making that overlap with understanding and countering threat weapon systems. The intelligence products, and uses to which they are put, may be different but the essence of the collection sources, methods, and analysis may be very similar in an increasingly artificial intelligence-oriented world in which data sources bear no resemblance to the days of the Cold War. This will require a restructuring of Five Eyes intelligence education and training, requiring experts with proven successful track records to design and implement courses that inspire innovation.

A Brave New World of Next Generation Technologies

The "5G" international technical race has been running for some time. The companies that will win this race will have unprecedented commercial power, and therefore from an intelligence perspective it is critical that both the US and the UK and their Five Eyes partners are 100 per cent not just well informed but also planning how they will interact with what will be a further revolution in global telecommunications. For those not well versed in telecommunications you may ask what is 5G and what will be its impact? 5G is a disruptive technology that will make current use of our cell phones and other digital telecommunications devices look like dinosaurs, because they will in fact be dinosaurs. They will be the fifth generation of systems. 5G devices will be at least one hundred times faster than what you have today in 2020. They will use ultra-low energy, will have extreme broadband (your data rates will boggle the mind), high reliability, flawless mobility (where and when you use), with ultra-low latency, and deep coverage globally and, most of all, low cost. Latency is where battery life is extended without affecting performance, and data is processed at much higher rates. There is therefore a technical challenge to achieve increased processing power while conserving energy. Whoever comes out on top in this race will have a huge commercial gain.

From an intelligence perspective understanding and knowing the technical complexities, and exploitation of 5G systems and the global telecommunications architectures that will support it is paramount. It will require the best of the best in technical intelligence know-how to exploit. Who then are the key players? They may be divided for convenience sake into "Big Boys" and "Little Boys." The former are the top telecommunications carriers and manufacturers: Huawei, ZTE, Ericsson, Nokia, and Samsung. The latter are: Deutsche Telecom, Sprint, Orange, SK Telecom, Korea Telecom, T-Mobile, AT&T, Verizon, and US Cellular. There may be others that join the race in due course. It is a strategic imperative that the Five Eyes anticipate every technical dimension of this race and who does what, where, and how. The exploitation strategy must be designed and implemented well in advance of these systems and the telecommunications architectures of the main players reaching the global marketplace.

The question of what the next generation after 5G will look like, is a strategic issue for the Five Eyes to address, anticipate, and plan for. One of the characteristics of Five Eyes intelligence and procurement systems has been the linear extrapolation of technology, rather than innovative step changes. The natural business cycle between Five Eyes contractors and their government agencies has been to improve on the last system. This makes absolute sense at one level. If you can make an intelligence collection system or an analytical tool better than this makes absolute sense. The downside is that the whole technical and procurement system tends towards conservative change. DARPA in the US has a history to a certain extent of avoiding this pitfall and supporting leading edge, even over the top high risk, innovation. However, even DARPA programs have life spans that are extraordinarily lengthy before they eventually transition to a real-world application, so that in many cases they are no longer innovative and may indeed be costly dinosaurs. I worked on one highly classified DARPA program that was years in the gestation and although its output was technically innovative, by the time it could be integrated as an operational system it had lost its edge and was excessively costly. The science behind it was outstanding, but the US government simply could not convert to an operational system in the right timeline. Winston Churchill had a simple phrase when he issued a direct order saying make something happen immediately: "Action This Day!" It may seem antiquated to reinvent this particular Churchillian aphorism, but on close inspection it really is not. Catastrophic cyber-attacks will require in the coming decades the same degree of instant action, anticipating and mitigating the threats by well-prepared and rapidly implemented counterstrokes. The latter is what may be termed the "Golden Eggs" syndrome. In other words, for the Five Eyes to have in their intelligence basket a whole collection of golden eggs that have not just anticipated the threats' challenges but have at the ready effective means to counter and deceptively negate the enemy's capabilities by highly secure covert means.

This resilience is essential for the Five Eyes in the coming generation. It will take cooperation and the willingness to share intellectual property in the most secure ways. The vetting of participants must be rigorous and new security systems to obviate the worst kind of internal treachery must be in place. The latter requires a whole new systems and technology base. For example, if another Edward Snowden began to interrogate highly classified data and then download to thumb drives, new systems would not only immediately alert, track, and interrogate such actions, but also prevent access in the first place by the most rigorous AI applications. If system denial comes up on the screen, then the user will have to justify access to a superior.

We know that the ocean floor in 2016 had about 300 major transoceanic submarine cables carrying approximately $4 trillion worth of banking, commercial, and personal transactions of one sort or another, in addition to about 95% of the world's voice and internet traffic.[1] In 2020 these numbers have increased exponentially and from an intelligence perspective, 95% of the world's key data and communications pass through undersea fiber-optic cables. An examination of who laid these cables, who owns them, who operates and maintains them clearly raises key questions about their intelligence value. Shades of Blinker Hall? Well, yes, is the simple answer. Much of the data, voice, and imagery will be heavily encrypted and passing in discreet transmission modes. In those cables, together with space-based communications systems, landline systems, and microwave tower-based transmissions lay intelligence nuggets. The sheer volume of traffic alone is a great technical challenge for Five Eyes intelligence. It will require the most sophisticated AI tools to interrogate such data, provided the Five Eyes can collectively retrieve data in a timely manner. If we re-examine how quickly and efficiently Blinker Hall's team intercepted and decrypted the Zimmermann Telegram and then compare the similar tasks of the 2020s and beyond it will be appreciated just how things have changed and the intellectual challenge ahead. The good news is that what human beings invent, design, engineer, and implement can likewise be understood and countered. The inventiveness and intellectual prowess of the Five Eyes will have to be married to new forms of deception and technical artfulness that is sustained by highly resilient systems.

Internally the Five Eyes will require more and more back-ups, and across-the-board power sources and power distribution protection, communications resiliency, discreet standalone cyber detection systems, and ways to mitigate threat access by clever use of new electronic deception tools. Classical Cold War electronic jamming will seem old hat compared to the demands of ensuring GPS systems and transmissions survivability and durability as the 2020s pass into the 2030s. Surprises are never welcome in the Five Eyes intelligence community, whether it is warnings and indicators against, for example, a Chinese surprise attack against Taiwan, or new and insidious ways for threat nations and their surrogates to undermine the Five Eyes and their allies and friendly nations in maintaining critical infrastructure and, in the case of the military, the resupply and transport of military personnel and equipment in a timely and effective way to threat areas.

The worst-case technological surprise scenario is likely to come from the realm of quantum resistant cryptography, a domain in which the Five Eyes must pool their brain power and resources to avoid a bombshell like impact on communications, security, and the ability of the Five Eyes to remain electronically dominant. Encryption is vital for the Five Eyes for internal security and, conversely, the ability to break others encryption is the other side of the coin. There is a current concern that high-capacity quantum computers will be able to break the most sophisticated current encryptions, presenting unacceptable vulnerabilities from a Five Eyes perspective. The current sophisticated human-created algorithms that supposedly are randomly generated numbers, but in fact are not, will be solvable by quantum computers. The latter are a step change in technology, using photons, neutrons, protons, and electrons to execute hugely sophisticated calculations versus ones and zeros. Quantum computers will be the new super computers of the 2030s and beyond. The Five Eyes must ensure that this critical pillar of information security, encryption, is both not undermined and at the same time a lead must be made in striking out technically against adversaries using that very capability. The goal will be for the Five Eyes to create mutual technology that will be "Quantum Resistant" while exploiting the capability to decrypt others' transmissions.

New forms of technical deception can provide bulwarks against invasive attacks on all forms of civilian, military, political, and commercial infrastructure and operations. The great strength of the Five Eyes is the natural distribution of its many and varied global intelligence assets. Sharing data has to be top of the list, underscored by personnel exchanges, and with highly compartmented security arrangements. The most significant differentiator of the 2020s from the post-World War II era is that the civilian world in peacetime is as equally vulnerable to a wide range of electronic attack that was not technically possible earlier. Individuals, banks, the international financial structure, transport, and all other forms of critical infrastructure from power and water supply to communications and the media are subject to state-sponsored cyber-attacks, and those of state-sponsored surrogates, criminal organizations, and malicious hackers.

Next generation technologies have to be not only anticipated and worked on in terms of basic R&D by the collective Five Eyes, they have to be ahead in both capability and timescale of not just current threats but those predicted over the next ten to twenty years. The Five Eyes are challenged in both the civilian and military sectors. These encompass anti-access, area denial weapons and non-kinetic systems, cyber warfare and the wider electronic warfare spectrum, together with what are now a vast range of information threats, and a range of asymmetric threats. The latter cover not just the Five Eyes military but their civilian populations and those of their allies and friendly nations with whom they trade. ISIS is not at all dead. It is proliferating in Africa and Asia in unprecedented ways. In themselves the advanced technologies under review, such as big data analytics, artificial intelligence, autonomous systems, robotics, directed energy, hypersonic, biotechnology, and advanced space and airborne surveillance systems and sensors (including drones, UAVs, and UCASs), are not enough. The Five Eyes will have to integrate these technologies into tactical and strategic operational systems across the breadth and depth of all Five Eyes countries in the most highly secure and compartmented ways with internal threat security systems of the highest order. Cooperation is essential. No one country can monopolize crucial technology. We witnessed how intelligence sharing in World War II helped save the day. To support these developments the Five Eyes will have to develop together the necessary planning and training for joint implementation. The bottom line is that these developments must be shown to impact decision-making to justify Five Eyes intelligence investment.

Education within the Five Eyes intelligence community is critical, with both the scientific and technical intelligence directorates working alongside operational intelligence personnel, to ensure that not just the most effective programs are pursued but also that training courses are designed on an across-the-board basis so that American, British, Canadian, Australian, and New Zealand personnel share training under a common umbrella. We know from past experience that the camaraderie and cross fertilization of ideas between the nations' intelligence communities yield huge dividends. It is recommended that civilians and military personnel are mixed so that there is mutual exposure to threats, needs, and solutions, together with the incubation of new tradecraft, sources, methods, and analysis. The Five Eyes can collectively develop from this process new intelligence doctrine and operational plans, and commit these to policy agreements as add-ons to existing agreements, and kept highly secure. The above is predicated, as always, on good visionary leadership. Historically, the lead nation in terms of investment and global sources and methods has been the United States. However, for the above to be successful the United States will have to be open and sharing within strict compartmented intelligence parameters. In parallel each of the Five Eyes' military schools and war colleges should be drawn into this process, both in terms of inputs and also training and education. There has to be more dialogue between these five communities. Intelligence training schools and the war colleges need more synergism. We have learned since World War II that nothing encourages this more than personnel exchange programs, so that not just ideas and information are exchanged and developed but most of all personal relationships are developed that can be bedrock for the rest of people's careers. The benefits in a crisis are legion. I remember well at the height of the Cold War regularly picking up the secure phone and calling my opposite numbers in each of the Five Eyes nations and almost daily on some occasions leaving my office to visit various intelligence personnel in either the London embassies or in various UK exchange locations. We never, ever, failed and, in the words of Admiral William McRaven, formerly Commander of Naval Special Warfare and Commander of Special Operations Command, spoken at the University of Texas Class of 2014 Commencement Ceremony in June 2014, "We never, ever, rang the Bell!" We stood together in the spirit of Five Eyes cooperation and although at times we may not always have agreed on whatever, we never stopped working together in the spirit of total committed cooperation.

Russia has used social media disinformation to attack the western media and sow doubt and dissension amongst all levels of society from intellectual elites to the less educated. This divisiveness strategy is difficult to measure in terms of overall effects, but the intelligence objectives are clear cut, namely, to create political and social divisions within and between the key democracies. Disinformation is a formidable weapon in the deception armory. Scare tactics using false information confuse and dissemble otherwise stable and fair-minded people. The Kremlin has directly driven these tactics. Its goals are to shape public opinion over a wide range of events, issues, and policies. These include, for examples, the 2016 US election, BREXIT, the Khashoggi murder, the downing with Russian missiles of flight MH-17, the poisoning of the Skripals in Salisbury, England, chemical attacks by the Assad regime in Syria, Russia's de facto invasions of eastern Ukraine and the illegal annexation of the Crimea, and many other social media disinformation campaigns. The Five Eyes has extraordinary talent to not just counter these attacks but turn them around against the Russian regime. The Five Eyes have enormous potential capabilities to counter using, for one unclassified example, AI. The opposition will use AI as much as the Five Eyes. The latter have to be many steps ahead, all the time. Project Maven in the US was under contract in two months and a capability was delivered in six months.[2] Maven (also known as Algorithmic Warfare Cross Functional Team) uses advanced secure AI algorithms to analyze in real-time key data from multiple sources and methods. Vladimir Putin fully understands AI's value. Speaking in 2017 he said, "It comes with colossal opportunities, but also threats that are difficult to predict. Whoever becomes the leader in this sphere will become the ruler of the world."[3] The Five Eyes need to be way ahead all the time as Putin's Foundation for Advanced Studies (a DARPA-like equivalent) seeks equivalency and terrorists use social network mapping, AI-enabled drones, and social engineering attacks to both recruit and undermine stable populations. Counterterrorism intelligence within the UK–US and wider Five Eyes community will need to concentrate joint resources in identifying in real time and eliminating from the worldwide web such terrorist material. Radicalization and extremism are growing, not diminishing. The Five Eyes will have to collectively extend current public–private technical partnerships to stay ahead of the threat and undermine it before it has effect. Similarly, with international hostage taking and kidnapping, where UK–US intelligence can use AI-based systems and technology to detect, locate, track, and eliminate criminal and politically inspired hostage and kidnap entities.

On the military side it will be possible using AI-based technologies with various discreet advanced sensors and guidance systems to use lethal autonomous weapons by the Five Eyes nations and their key allies in real-time situations against terrorist targets, in ways that were impossible with earlier systems like Hellfire missiles on various UAVs, such as Reaper and Global Hawk. The ability to process massive amounts of discreet intelligence data and make accurate real-time decisions beyond normal human operating speeds will change the rules of the game in the counterterrorist fight. The US National Cyber Strategy and the US Defense Department's Cyber Strategy released in September 2018, call for defense of the homeland, to protect American prosperity, deter, detect and punish malicious actors, and with allies push for an "open, interoperable, reliable, and secure internet," and also protecting US space assets simultaneously. Russia and China are clearly identified as adversaries, with China "eroding US military overmatch and is persistently exfiltrating sensitive information from the US public and private sector." In a contested public, private, and military–political cyberspace environment the Five Eyes clearly need to be not just one step ahead but many, so that high-level policy documents such as the one quoted above have real flesh on the bones of what are somewhat obvious goals to even the less knowledgeable layperson. Five Eyes collaboration is paramount. The

US cannot go it alone and most pleasingly the Pentagon has stated its objective to "strengthen the capacity of allies and partners and increase DOD's ability to leverage its partners' unique skills, resources, capabilities, and perspectives." At one level this may be seen by the Five Eyes community as US patronage. However, given the strong historic bonds the younger generation in the US Department of Defense, with little or no knowledge of the Five Eyes' historic record, will need to be both educated and inducted into the Five Eyes community.

One key solution lies in the huge historic bedrock experience of UK–US intelligence in deception. Deception helped win World War II and certainly shortened it, and in the assessment made by Sir Harry Hinsley, the official historian of British intelligence in World War II, may have shortened the war with the combined strengths of ENIGMA and the MAGIC by as much as two years. Cyberspace offers myriad ways for the Five Eyes to cooperatively outthink, outmaneuver, and overwhelm both peer level threats and also low-level terrorist groups and criminal hackers and their paymasters. Classification naturally prohibits disclosure. Suffice to say that the US and the UK together with the other three Five Eyes nations have enormous resources and intellectual pedigree to outflank any of the threats referenced earlier.

Reaching a major conflict zone, staying there successfully and accomplishing various missions, is now not as easy as it was even ten years ago in 2010. To sustain persistent forward presence say in the Pacific and particularly the South China Sea and adjacent sea areas, the US has the weapons and overall force structure to accomplish various missions laid down in national strategic plans in the event of various threat scenarios. However, intelligence shows that peer military adversaries could attempt to block, interrupt, and worst case kinetically challenge US presence and intervention. In this increasingly complex environment Deception, with a very big "D," becomes essential. The threat must never know what it doesn't know and be made to believe a whole host of conflicting informational aspects, while denied, deceived, and disrupted by the most subtle and egregious means. The threat must have zero knowledge of what the Five Eyes are both doing, and could expand as situations deteriorate. Various silver bullets need to be preserved for the ultimate threats, kept under the most secure wraps until needed. Winston Churchill and Franklin Roosevelt, and their key top military commanders, are excellent role models in this regard. They preserved and protected their most secret deception plans and technologies, and only employed them when the timing was just right.

The Five Eyes have the brains, the technology, the cultural and social adhesiveness, plus the binding agreements of decades, to work against several adversaries who have nothing like the cohesiveness of the Five Eyes. In parallel to the big "D" are other technological advances, from robotic operating systems on the land, the sea surface, underwater, and in the air, with unmanned systems, embedded and mobile sensors enhanced by onboard data processing systems, with AI dominant, so that operators are assisted in decision making functions, rather than being overwhelmed by saturated information. The Five Eyes can empower commanders with critical decision-making information, coupled with advances in AI-focused space-based systems that provide resiliency in contested environments so that Five Eyes space-based communications remain secure and intact. All the above will need integration with planned advances in high energy lasers, hypersonic vehicles and weapons, and the hypersonic propulsion systems that carry them. In due course the Five Eyes will have the ability to challenge most threats in ways that were inconceivable less than a decade ago. The problems that have been very eruditely analyzed by Jonathan Ward in his paper, "Sino-Indian Competition in the Maritime Domain"[4] may hopefully not come to pass if all the above becomes increasingly clear to peer competitors, as a major deterrent to aggressive action that may precipitate crisis. The wise words of former US Navy Secretary Richard Danzig may indeed come to pass, that "promoting innovation and enhancing lethality should become a higher priority than acquiring additional ships."[5] *Time* magazine in its June 4, 2018 edition discussed with and analyzed various intelligence related aspects with then Director of National Intelligence Dan Coats. The article indicated that Director Coats, with a background on the US Senate Select Intelligence Committee, and Ambassador to Germany 2001–2005, has solid credentials, but caveated that he may not be able to convince his President of the value of the US intelligence community's intelligence assessments over issues, for example, relating to Iranian nuclear weapon development compliance.

In this environment the Five Eyes become ever more critical as a collective mouthpiece of intelligence credibility, standing firm on well-reasoned analysis based on thorough and accurate sources and methods. In this context the Five Eyes and their political oversight and leadership assume a new dimensional role. This became self-evident in the August 2019 with the resignation of Director Coats, followed shortly afterwards by his Principal Deputy Director, Susan M. Gordon, emphasizing that good unvarnished non-politically-oriented intelligence can only serve the national interest if there is independence from political influence, a hugely different concept from political oversight.

What has evolved from the above discussion is the need for a Five Eyes "Grand Strategy" based on one key notion that intelligence is a dynamic living process and is never static. A biannual "summit" of all the key players from all the Five Eyes intelligence departments and agencies could take place rotationally in each of the five capitals. During the intervening two years working groups and round tables from the many and varied specialist intelligence communities can work on the issues of the day and those predicted in the future, and deliver the most important issues for resolution at the summit. Regularity of meetings is essential in an era when the nature of all the threats that we have addressed, and many than none of us can ever foresee or anticipate, demands meetings of the minds. Such summits can agree on threats, consolidate solutions, initiate joint technology and operational cooperation, with the necessary planning and budgets. The summit members can have their best national advisors present, with one key objective of agreeing on the next phase in the technological revolution and its impact on intelligence collection and analysis. From a security perspective the Five Eyes summit will need to compartmentalize special programs and lay down security guidelines. In the wider security context, it is important that the Five Eyes have agreed ways to uniformly address the insider threat, to mitigate the worst of internal treachery. The Five Eyes should not be hesitant in sharing systems and technology that undermine those who betray the Five Eyes internally. Given good compartmentalization it does not follow that one bad apple will ruin the whole barrel, but nonetheless one bad apple can create enormous damage. We saw historically what Philby did in the UK and the Walkers in the US.

One increasingly strategic issue that such summits must face is the civilian–commercial world interface with government. Cyber threats to every level of society and activity, and attacks on critical commercial intellectual property and defense and security technology require new approaches to educating and training the Five Eyes public and businesses in countering these pervasive threats. Exfiltration of intellectual property is a massive economic and security threat. This applies to not just cyber threats but also physical and personnel security.

Part of the summit process will likely be a domain that is neglected at least from the public's perspective. This is economic intelligence. We tend to concentrate so much on all the other "INTs" and the many threats that confront us that we can easily forget many of the global economic issues that may well be transformed into threat scenarios. Most are aware of the impact of oil and gas issues that have driven foreign and commercial policies for decades and how protection of oil and gas flow to the economies of the democracies has been paramount. None of this will change. However other equally pervasive economic issues may constitute compelling threats in the future. Water rights and water supply issues may become more and more serious. An analysis of all the critical minerals that make up electronic components and whole systems, such as vehicles and aircraft, let alone domestic products, reveals the delicate international economic balance regarding which countries have which minerals and their commercial destinations. In the 21st century the global economic heartland may well be predicated on what minerals are needed for which industries and products and their location and supply chain.

For these summits to be successful and indeed for the whole Five Eyes community to be successful for the foreseeable future, we must have a clear and well-articulated statement of what "Five Eyes Strategy" is. Grand intelligence strategy is not about "how" and "what" all these various entities do and their fine products. It is, very simply, "why" they do what they do at any moment in time. The "what" and "how" come later, as implementation. There is one overriding element that determines the "why." *These are the vital national interests of each of the Five Eyes, and their combined collective interests. These interests drive the "Why." They drive the Five Eyes intelligence community machinery that will provide the vital security for modern society now and for the foreseeable future.*

Without clear definitions of what are these vital national interests, and indeed these will change over time as the global situation changes in its many and varied forms, the great historic intelligence traditions of the Five Eyes as a whole will be grasping at straws. On August 10, 1941 Winston Churchill and Franklin Roosevelt met on board HMS *Prince of Wales* in Placentia Bay, off Newfoundland. The President had sailed from Washington DC in USS *Augusta*. At that meeting these two great men agreed one fundamental thing, grand strategy to defeat Nazism, and this strategy was predicated on one key basic tenet, the vital national interests of the United Kingdom and the United States. The Five Eyes will have to continuously address the changing global scene and adjust their intelligence operations, technology, sources, methods, and analysis to those vital national interests defined by their political leadership.

The history of the Five Eyes is an incredible history of cooperation and dedication. The heart and soul of the Five Eyes is at the working level, the intelligence specialists from the United States, the United Kingdom, Canada, Australia, and New Zealand that have greatly served this extraordinary community. They have and will continue to serve with great distinction. I have been hugely privileged over a 50-year period to have participated in this great community, my roles minuscule as they were in the truly great scheme of things, but like all of us who lived and worked in this community during this turbulent and challenging 50 years, the sum of all the efforts, dedication, hard work, and sacrifice of everyone made a massive difference. I really believe that this international intelligence community reflects and represents the core strengths and values of these five great democracies, epitomizing the ability of each and every country to stay the course, not to waiver, and be steadfastly consistent and loyal in the darkest hours as well as the bright moments of triumph.

The Five Eyes Enduring Culture

What occurred within the Five Eyes community, in retrospect, is quite remarkable. Governments for the past 75 years since 1945 have come and gone, but the Five Eyes have survived without any serious threat to their existence. There have been challenges, but on the whole the abiding professional loyalty that has bound the large number of individuals together, past and present, is emblematic of something much deeper and more sustainable than political change. At one level the Five Eyes have defined the strength of the values and commitment that underpin the essence of each nation's sense of democracy and freedom in a very uncertain world.

There have been political variances within the Five Eyes political hierarchies over issues associated with, for example, the Suez campaign by the British and the war in Vietnam by the United States, but none of these issues have ever undermined the bedrock relationships. The Five Eyes stood together when North Korea invaded

South Korea on June 25, 1950, and fought alongside each other, sharing intelligence, until the war ended on July 27, 1953 with an armistice agreement. The UK fought a successful counterinsurgency campaign in Malaysia and received maximum support from its Commonwealth Five Eyes members. The British supported the US clandestinely in East Asia during the Vietnam War, and the US came headlong in support of the British in the 1982 Falklands campaign. Whatever the political differences over the Middle East foreign policies of the US and Britain, with the other three nations tending to play out their international political roles via the United Nations, the intelligence process based on the core relationships at the working level has endured.

APPENDIX

Influential Individuals and Mentors

Royal Navy Admiral Sir Reginald "Blinker" Hall

The Zimmermann Telegram was one of the greatest intelligence triumphs of British history. Its centenary was commemorated in 2017—and it is most important to recognize the continuity of events since 1917. The Royal Navy Admiral Sir Reginald "Blinker" Hall was the architect of this most famous intelligence coup of all time. He was called "Blinker" because of a permanent facial twitch that he exploited with characteristic aplomb. Hall's genius lay in his early and extraordinarily successful exploitation of radio telegraphy and its cryptologic underpinnings. Hall did not know this at the time, but his actions and those of his key subordinates set the stage for arguably saving the civilized world from tyranny in the Nazi era as a result of critical intelligence cooperation and sharing of the most sensitive secrets. The Five Eyes owe much to Admiral Sir Reginald Blinker Hall. Without the foundations built by him and the maintenance of inter-war capabilities, in spite of the financial downturn caused by the Great Depression, it is difficult to see how the British would have established by 1939 at Bletchley Park what would become a highly secret war-winning organization, working in total cooperation with the US Office of Naval Intelligence.

Blinker Hall was the son of the first director of British Naval Intelligence, William Henry Hall, so intelligence was in his blood when he entered the Royal Navy in 1884. As a captain, Blinker Hall was the DNI throughout World War I, and because of his huge successes he was promoted to rear admiral in 1917, after the Zimmermann Telegram. Later he became vice admiral, 1922, and admiral, 1926.

The British Naval Intelligence Department (NID) was created in 1887, with mainly the defense of British imperial trade interests as a primary driver. In 1887 there were a mere ten staff officers with a budget of about 5,000 pounds a year. Many in the Royal Navy leadership were against such a staff, with senior officers such as Admiral Fisher disclaiming in no uncertain terms that a staff would, "convert splendid sea officers into very indifferent clerks."

When Hall became the DNI, and war was declared in August 1914 he faced much intransigence characterized by a combination of prejudice and ignorance. Operational intelligence as we understand it today was primitive to nonexistent. Hall took one extraordinary step that was to revolutionize naval warfare and which, with the benefit of hindsight today, may seem obvious, but in 1914 was clouded in fog. Hall realized that exploitation of wireless telegraphy and its cryptography could be war winners, what modern parlance would characterize as technical game changers. Hall built wisely on the work of Sir Alfred Ewing, a professor of Mechanical Engineering at Cambridge, who was brought into the Admiralty as the Director of Naval Education and then created the first ever cipher team. Hall's "Room 40" became the heart and soul of naval intelligence in World War I, building on Ewing's foundations, to create a cadre of first-class cryptographers. Hall's single biggest problem was interfacing with the Operations Division of the Admiralty where there was institutional bias against new and mainly civilian technical experts advising operators on key intelligence from wireless intercepts. The issue was clear to Hall: the operators did not wish to share their operational data with Room 40 civilian cryptographers and the latter were deprived of the key opportunity to both analyze and interpret cryptographic intelligence in light of current and planned British naval operations and, most of all, their German adversaries. This failure to make the wise use of such intelligence reached its nadir at Jutland, a subject that has been much underrated in understanding why Jutland was not the success that the Royal Navy wanted and the country expected.

So, what did Hall get up to between January and March 1917 that will forever live in the annals of any intelligence organization worldwide and provided a blueprint for Five Eyes intelligence much later? First, the overall political–military context in which Hall and his Room 40 team were operating. The United States was not in the war in January 1917. The Germans were planning on restarting unrestricted U-boat warfare from February 1, 1917 in an attempt to bring the British economy to its knees by attacking its most vital national interest, seaborne trade. This one fact could be the tipping point for the American President to convince his people to join the war on the Allied side, remembering that in the United States in 1917 anti-British sentiment ran high, with a volatile and outspoken Irish-American and German-American population. Second, on January 11, 1917, the German Foreign Minister, Arthur Zimmermann, presented an encoded telegram to the US Ambassador in Berlin, James W. Gerard, who agreed to transmit the telegram in its coded form. The American Embassy transmitted this telegram on January 16, 1917, five days later.

Why would the German Foreign Ministry be using the American Embassy to send its messages, in this case (the Zimmermann Telegram) via Washington DC to the German Ambassador in Mexico City, Heinrich von Eckhardt? Hall and his staff had realized very early on that undersea communications cables could provide the source of great intelligence and also that by denying their use by cable cutting, an enemy could be deprived of vital communications. The British had cut the German transatlantic cable at the beginning of the war in 1914. The US was neutral in 1914 and permitted Germany limited use of its Europe to US transatlantic cable mainly because President Woodrow Wilson was encouraging peace talks and wanted to ensure that Berlin could talk with the US diplomatically. Zimmermann's telegram was instructing the German Ambassador in Mexico City to inform the Mexican President, Carranza, that if the US entered the war against Germany then Germany would support Mexico financially in fighting a war against the US to regain territory lost to Mexico in the wars with the United States, a bombshell of enormous proportions if made aware to the US government and people.

Hall's Room 40 was reading all the American traffic (that ran via cable from the US embassy in Denmark), including all German traffic, encrypted or otherwise, that was forwarded from the US Embassy in Berlin. The US cable went via the UK, and the intercept point was at a relay station at Porthcurno, near Land's End. Hall's civilian cryptographers Nigel de Grey and William Montgomery brilliantly decrypted the Zimmermann telegram the following day after interception by the British on January 17, 1917. Why was this so speedy and efficient? Hall and his team had also pulled off two critical earlier coups. Room 40 had captured secretly during the Mesopotamian campaign the German Diplomatic Cipher 13040 and, as a result of very good clandestine relations with the Russians, Hall obtained the critical German Naval Cipher 0075 (the 007 part will not be lost on readers). The Russians had obtained this from the German cruiser *Magdeburg* after it was wrecked. Hall had secretly nursed Russian relations.

The genius of Hall was what he did and did not do next. The Americans may well think that this was all a devious British plot to bring the United States into the war. The telegram was brutally explicit in two regards: on February 1, 1917 the Germans would resume unrestricted U-boat warfare, and a German–Mexican military alliance was proposed, with Germany as the funding source. Hall needed a cover story for his knowledge of the German codes and to avoid the Americans knowing that Room 40 was reading their and others' mail, while at the same time convincing Woodrow Wilson and his government that the telegram was real, not a British forgery. Hall never once consulted anyone in the British Foreign Office or within the Admiralty Staff. He acted with his staff alone. He then decided on his "deception plan." This was the real genius of this extraordinary brilliant work by Hall and his team. Hall knew one key fact: the German Embassy in Washington DC, once it received the telegram, would have to transmit it to the German Embassy in Mexico City. Hall knew that they used a commercial telegraph company. NID agents bribed a Mexican telegraph employee to yield the cipher, thereby enabling Hall to inform the Americans that this had come directly from the Mexican Telegraph company from Washington DC. Simple, but brilliant. Hall also, in parallel, took another quite remarkable action, by great timing, by doing nothing until the Germans announced unrestricted U-Boar warfare on February 1, 1917, after which the US broke off diplomatic relations with Germany on February 3, 1917. Hall then did two key things. He only informed the British Foreign Secretary on February 5, 1017 with an emphatic request that the British Foreign Office delay all diplomatic moves with the US until Hall himself took various actions.

With Foreign Office knowledge, Hall then met with the Secretary of the US Embassy in London, Edward Bell, on February 19, 1917, and the following day Hall met with the US Ambassador to the Court of St. James, Walter Hines Page, and handed him the telegram. Three days later Ambassador Page met with the British Foreign Secretary, Arthur Balfour, and on Hall's quite emphatic advice he gave the American ambassador a copy of the stolen Mexican cipher text and the English translation of the full Zimmermann telegram. After some analysis and discussion in Washington, President Wilson was convinced. He went ahead and released the telegram to the US press on February 28, 1917, and this immediately inflamed American public opinion against both Germany and Mexico. Wilson and his top aides realized also that they had to protect the British "Mexican cipher" and British code-breaking capabilities. Herein lay the foundations of what became years later the beginning of what Humphrey Bogart, playing Rick Blaine, said at the very end of the 1942 movie *Casablanca* to Claude Rains, playing the cynical French police chief Captain Louis Renault: "Louis, I think this is the beginning of a beautiful friendship." The American protection of Britain's secrets was indeed the beginning of a very special relationship.

Further positive news for Hall and his Room 40 team was that the Mexican President had been advised that German funding was unreliable, and that a successful war with the United States was unlikely. President Venustiano Carranza was also advised that even if German funding did materialize their sister South American nations, Argentina, Brazil, and Chile, from whom Mexico would purchase arms, would likely be unsupportive of a Mexican alliance with Germany and a war with the United States. Nonetheless the Mexican government did not enforce an embargo against Germany, much to the chagrin of the United States, and Mexico continued to do business with Germany throughout World War I. However, Mexico did not repeat history in World War II, declaring war on the Axis Powers on May 22, 1942.

The final coup de grace was delivered by none other than Arthur Zimmermann himself, who rashly announced on March 3, 1917, in a press conference, that the telegram was in fact true. He then very naively followed this with a statement in the Reichstag on March 29, 1917 that his plan had been for Germany to fund Mexico only if the Americans declared war on Germany. The United States Congress declared war on Germany on April 6, 1917, President Wilson having asked for this declaration on April 2, 1917.

Hall and his Room 40 team had triumphed, and Hall was promoted to Rear Admiral shortly thereafter.

The significance of Hall's achievements and relationship with his American counterparts has to be put in context, 103 years later in 2020. The US Ambassador in London, Walter Hines Page (August 15, 1855–December 21, 1918) described Blinker Hall as the single most influential person, indeed genius, of World War I. There is a memorial plaque in honor of Walter Hines Page in Westminster Abbey, in Westminster, London. He and Hall had a special relationship that bound both the United Kingdom and the United States forever in sharing sensitive intelligence.

Sir Michael Howard

After school at Wellington College and Christ Church, Oxford, Michael Howard (1922–2019) served in the Coldstream Guards in the Italian campaign, winning the Military Cross for gallantry at the first battle of Monte Cassino in 1944. He founded the Department of War Studies at King's College London, as a lowly assistant lecturer and by the sheer weight of outstanding research and teaching, plus energetic and persistent leadership, grew a formidable but in those days a small department. He left, just as I joined King's, to become successively at Oxford the Chichele Professor of the History of War and, from 1980–1989, the ultimate accolade of Regius Professor of Modern History, succeeding Professor Hugh Trevor-Roper (later Lord Dacre), the famous author of the best-selling *The Last Days of Hitler*. Michael Howard completed his active academic career in the United States, as the Robert A. Lovett Professor of Military and Naval History at Yale from 1989 to 1993. As a schoolboy at Bablake I had read his *The Franco-Prussian War of 1870–71* and even then at a young age I had appreciated his mastery of not just detail but the exquisite nature of his analysis and language. As I started research at King's the turnover was in progress with his successor, Professor Sir Laurence Martin (born 1928), who had studied at Christ's College, Cambridge, and Yale University. He spent ten years at King's before becoming Vice Chancellor of Newcastle University in 1978 and then Director of Chatham House, the Royal Institute of International Affairs, in 1991. I got on very well with Laurence Martin. I liked his "American approach" to defense and intelligence and as my research took shape he rapidly realized, as did I, that others needed to become closely involved.

Bryan Ranft

I first had contact with Professor Bryan Ranft at the Royal Naval College, Greenwich, where he was head of Naval History and International Affairs. Bryan was a World War II veteran like Michael Howard, a Manchester Grammar School and Balliol College, Oxford, graduate before World War II broke out. At Balliol he was a contemporary of Denis Healey (1917–2015) who became Secretary of State for Defence, 1964–1970, Chancellor of the Exchequer, 1974–1979, and finally Deputy Leader of the Labor Party from 1980–1983. Like Ranft, Healey served in the British Army in World War II from 1940–1945, reaching the rank of major in the Royal Engineers in the North Africa Campaign, Italian Campaign, and at the battle of Anzio. Healey came from modest beginnings and won a scholarship to Balliol College from Bradford Grammar School. At Oxford, Healey was a member of the Communist Party from 1937–1940, leaving the party when France fell to the Nazis. Healey was an outstanding Oxford scholar, gaining a "Double First" degree in 1940. At Balliol, besides Bryan Ranft, he became a lifelong friend and political rival of the future Conservative Prime Minister, Edward Heath, whom he succeeded as President of the Balliol Junior Common Room. Bryan Ranft's Oxford DPhil thesis had been on the protection of seaborne trade, a brilliant study that traced the early origins in fine detail of how Britain had successively pursued a maritime strategy primarily focused on the defense of trade.

Ranft and Healey came to serious intellectual blows during Healey's tenure of the Ministry of Defence, with Healey laying the grounds for the serious reduction in the size, shape, capabilities, and deployment of the Royal Navy. He canceled the aircraft carrier replacement program, thus ending effectively Royal Navy fixed-wing aviation once the last of the fleet carriers was decommissioned. Overseas bases were to be closed and the Royal Navy was to be withdrawn from persistent forward presence in the Far East and Mediterranean to become a North-East Atlantic Navy. There were serious budgetary issues that Healey faced, but Ranft argued that strategically his policies were unbalanced, with over emphasis on the British Army of the Rhine commitments to the Central Front in Europe that many naval experts argued was unnecessary given the massive commitment by the US Army and the US Air Force, and underpinned by NATO's ability (read the United States) to use tactical nuclear weapons if the Red Army and its Warsaw Pact allies attempted to cross the FEBA (Forward Edge of the Battle Area). Ranft stated in several eloquently argued papers that Soviet expansionism and aggressive posturing was happening at sea, with Soviet Admiral Sergey Gorshkov (1910–1988) supported by the Soviet leadership following a classical maritime strategy to pursue the vital national interests of the Soviet Union. Time would prove Ranft completely correct, but it was too late to undo the severe damage that Healey did to the force structure and therefore deployability of the Royal Navy.

Bryan Ranft rapidly realized that my research interests had polarized on a major unexplored topic in the late 1960s, which may seem unusual today with the total benefit of hindsight. I had been inspired and energized by both my work on the Nazi era and also my intense interest in naval warfare and how intelligence had played a crucial role in the allied victory at sea in Europe and the Pacific. Bryan Ranft was indeed a wonderfully kindly man and generous human being.

Sir Harry Hinsley

Hinsley was born in Walsall in the English Midlands November 26, 1918, and died in Cambridge on February 16, 1998, aged 79, from lung cancer. He came from modest beginnings and was clearly gifted intellectually. Contrary to popular misconceptions of lack of opportunity for working-class children in the 1930s in what is often characterized as a class-ridden society, the young Harry won a place at Queen Mary's Grammar School in Walsall. In 1937 Hinsley won a distinguished scholarship to read History at St. John's College, Cambridge. He was an outstanding scholar at Cambridge, rewarded years later in 1985 by his election to a Fellowship of the British Academy (FBA). When war was declared by Neville Chamberlain on September 3, 1939 after the September 1, 1939 invasion of Poland by Nazi Germany, the Government Code and Cipher School at Bletchley Park was seeking the best and brightest minds to meet the Nazi challenge. He was interviewed by the Director of Bletchley Park, the legendary Commander Alexander "Alastair" Deniston, Royal Navy (December 1, 1881–January 1, 1961) and was very soon thereafter working in "Hut 4," a location that decades later, not until the late 1970s/early 1980s in fact, would become synonymous with war-winning code breaking. Hut 4 provided the keys to critical successful operations against the Nazis and their allies, particularly in the hugely successful fight against the U-boats and helping the winning of the battle of the Atlantic by the most secretive clandestine means. Winston Churchill knew that without the maintenance of seaborne trade between the United States and the United Kingdom the British war effort could die a painful death. His wartime speeches reflect this harsh reality. At Bletchley Hinsley became intimately involved in parallel efforts in the United States, and particularly with the US Office of Naval Intelligence (ONI). Deniston recognized Hinsley's intellectual talent, together with other Bletchley luminaries such as Alan Turing and Gordon Welchman. In late 1943 Hinsley was in Washington DC, still a relatively young man, negotiating a highly classified SIGINT agreement with the United States.

Towards the end of the war he was working for Sir Edward Travis, KCMG, CBE, (September 24, 1888–April 23, 1956), who was the operational head of Bletchley Park during World War II and later the head of Bletchley's successor, GCHQ. Travis was a critical person at Bletchley. He had joined the Royal Navy in 1906 as a Paymaster officer and served in HMS *Iron Duke*. Between 1916–1918 he worked in the famous Room 40 under Captain Blinker Hall. In 1925 Travis became Denniston's Deputy at the GC&CS. During World War II Travis became a critical player at Bletchley Park, about which much has been written in multiple books. Travis was instrumental in the signing of the 1943 UK–US BRUSA Agreement and the subsequent 1946 highly classified secret intelligence agreement, cementing the special relationship in the post-war period and laying the way for the creation of the Five Eyes intelligence agreements and the longest lasting intelligence cooperation in history. Travis was knighted in June 1944, though the reasons for his knighthood were cloaked in disarming secrecy. On paper it looked as if he was rewarded for diplomatic services which, at one level, he indeed had been.

By war's end, after distinguished work, for which he was made an Officer of the Order of the British Empire (OBE) in 1946, and having married the lady who he met at Bletchley Park, Hilary Brett-Smith, Harry Hinsley was back at Cambridge, elected as a Fellow of St. John's College in 1945. In 1969, when I began work with him, he had recently been elected Professor of International Relations, having published earlier in 1962 his major work, *Power and the Pursuit of Peace*[1] that was acclaimed internationally and sealed his academic reputation.

His work on the official history of British intelligence in World War II changed dramatically the world view of historians, analysts, the media, current intelligence agencies and their employees, and the retired and serving military. His 1985 knighthood was justly deserved. He enjoyed the fruits of his labors and retirement from 1989, when he retired as Master of St. John's College, Cambridge, until his passing in February 1998, at age 79. The one accolade I sought came on December 6, 1972 when I was awarded the degree of Doctor of Philosophy by the University of London, King's College.[2]

Harry Hinsley, Sir Edward Travis, and John Titman in Washington DC in November 1945. (US National Archives)

Vice Admiral Sir Norman "Ned" Denning

One of the finest people that I was privileged to meet on a regular basis was retired Vice Admiral Sir Norman "Ned" Denning (1904–1979). He had been a member of the famous "Room 39" during World War II, and later in his career Director of Naval Intelligence (1960–1964), Deputy Chief of the Defense Staff for Intelligence (1964–1967), and earlier 1956–1958 he held a senior position at Greenwich. I first met Admiral Denning through Bryan Ranft after the admiral had retired and was head of the famous "Defense and Security Media Advisory Board" or better known as the "D Notices Committee." The latter was the key committee that ensured that the British media did not unwittingly betray the UK's secrets via inadvertent news media. It meant that Admiral Denning had daily direct working relations with all the Fleet Street newspaper editors, the heads of the independent TV networks and the BBC, together with any other source that may give away information detrimental to national security. I met with Admiral Denning regularly. He gave me unfettered access to his incredible experience and memory bank, that was truly prodigious. His career had spanned the greatest war in the history of our planet through to the Cold War. I soaked up his stories, his insights, his anecdotes, and most of all his wisdom. We would meet for about two hours at a time, often followed by lunch. It was a huge privilege.

Admiral Denning was also the brother of Lord Justice Alfred Thompson "Tom" Denning (1899–1999), the Master of the Rolls (1962–1982), who Margaret Thatcher described as, "Probably the greatest English judge of modern times." Lord Denning joined Lincoln's Inn in 1921, and was called to the Bar in June 1923, a distinguished graduate of Magdalen College, Oxford. I have been a barrister of Lincoln's Inn, called in November 1980, almost 40 years ago at the time of writing, so by a wonderful quirk or irony of fate I was privileged to know both of these brothers, who came from modest beginnings and ascended to the highest offices in the UK, belying any notion that Britain was a class-ridden society in the early and mid-20th century.

James McConnell

During my second year at Greenwich, my colleagues and I, both uniformed teaching personnel and civilian academics, welcomed an American who came to us from the US National Security Agency and the US Navy's key think tank, the Center for Naval Analyses, or CNA for short. This gentleman was James "Jamie" McConnell, an extraordinarily capable and well-established Soviet Union intelligence analyst, and a specialist on all things Soviet Navy. Jamie was a Columbia University graduate in Russian. He was now the only person at Greenwich who not only spoke fluent Russian, and could read the subtle nuances of Soviet military and strategic thought, he was the ultimate expert on Russian open sources and knew in great detail what these were, how to obtain them, and most of all to interpret these sources against the highly classified intelligence sources, particularly SIGINT and HUMINT. He was a most welcome addition to Bryan Ranft's staff. He and I became not only close-working colleagues, we also became friends for life. Jamie McConnell was very much in the forefront of why I would be appointed to Washington DC in 1976, a career-changing event for me. I learned an enormous amount from Jamie about Russian sources and methods, and understanding their strategic thinking and how this devolved to their construction programs, operational deployments, and the use of naval power in pursuit of Soviet goals. He was immersed in Soviet military literature and thought. All this brushed off on me. I soaked up all that I could learn from someone who was the finest independent thinker, who did not and would not accept conventional wisdom as gospel.

This great attribute was to pay dividends for the United States Navy, the UK, and their allies in the years from the early 1970s to the demise of the Soviet Union. In due course he and others, and I became one of them, would challenge various US intelligence assessments for both their accuracy and the data on which they were based. He had chosen to base himself at Greenwich rather than become attached to say the CIA Chief of Station's staff in the US Embassy in London, or work as a Defence Intelligence or Naval Intelligence analyst in the UK Ministry of Defence. He wanted intellectual independence and the freedom to move around those parts of the UK community that had a solid intellectual base to its work on the Soviet Union. This would include academia as well as the defense and intelligence community. He shared with me his seminal thinking on the direction in which the Soviet Union was moving in terms of the role and mission, and the detailed tactical deployment, of their key naval nuclear deterrent assets, their SSBNs, the equivalent in the early 1970s to the UK–US Polaris submarines. He began to postulate what was to become an incredibly accurate rendition of Soviet naval strategic thinking, embodied in what he termed a "Withholding Strategy," that Soviet SSBNs were the fallback second-strike nuclear assets after initial nuclear Armageddon commenced, and that the Soviet would seek to protect them and keep them sacrosanct in what he called "bastions." The latter were going to be under the Arctic ice cap, with the Soviets seeking locations near polynyas, or thin ice covers above the Arctic Ocean, from which submarine-launched nuclear ballistic missiles could be launched as a second strike against the United States and its allies. This would entail the Soviets ice hardening their submarines and using the Arctic as the key bastion, others being defined as those sea areas within a defendable perimeter in the northern Norwegian Sea and the Barents Sea. These bastions would be fully protected by multiple tactical assets. This represented not just new and innovative thinking and assessment, it challenged conventional reports, analyses, and most all US National Intelligence Assessments (NIEs). The difference lay in the delta between strictly conventional intelligence sources and methods, the analytical product derived from these, and the McConnell approach that married these data sources with Soviet open sources. The latter was not easily available to Western sources and was more often than not obtained by surreptitious means. They were not often available for public use in the Soviet Union and although not classified as such was nonetheless restricted in distribution. Added to these more discreet Soviet open sources were the technical papers that Soviet scientists and engineers published within their specialist communities, again not classified but nonetheless with restrictive access. McConnell used these sources in spades and to great analytical effect. They were highly reliable and if read beside the highly classified UK–US intelligence sources a new view could emerge of Soviet intentions. I immersed myself in his output, while realizing that we were all poor relations insofar as we could at best speak a few paltry words of Russian. McConnell was in a league of his own and the UK benefited not just from his time at Greenwich but as a result key British personnel became familiar with his methodology and product, learning greatly from him over the ensuing decades.

The Honorable Professor Alastair Buchan

I recall well in the early 1970s being notified that I had been selected together with one Royal Marine officer, two Army officers, and two Royal Air Force officers to attend a specially tailored course at Oxford University that was designed and led by the Honorable Professor Alastair Buchan (September 1918–February 1976, son of the famous author John Buchan and a former Governor General of Canada), the Montague Burton Professor of International Relations at Oxford. Prior to Oxford he had been Director of the International Institute of Strategic Studies and Commandant of the Imperial Defense College. He had fought in World War II in the Canadian Army. The course was demanding and an inspiration. I was the only one to have a full career in intelligence, but the relationships that I built were enduring, and what I learned from Alastair Buchan and my other mentors in the 1960s, I have, very subconsciously and subliminally, used in writing this book.

David Kahn

Through my intelligence and academic associations I was very familiar with the American, David Kahn (born 1930) author of *The Codebreakers—The Story of Secret Writing*, a very fine description and analysis of the history of cryptography from ancient Egypt through to the time of publication in 1967. I had studied David Kahn's work during my doctoral research, so when he came to St. Antony's College, Oxford as a research scholar, I planned to meet with him. David Kahn was awarded an Oxford DPhil in 1974 under the supervision of the Regius Professor of Modern History, Hugh Trevor-Roper, on modern German history. I was naturally keen to make his personal acquaintance. I visited him at Oxford during my many visits to the other Oxford luminaries mentioned earlier. I was intrigued by some of the difficulties that he experienced in publishing his book, with the US NSA wanting his publisher to redact various parts, even though he had used open sources. I gained much insight into his cryptologic research and how he had managed to amass such a monumental and magnificent data set. I regard David Kahn highly and his work has in my opinion been unsurpassed. He later in life donated all his key research papers and personal documents to the NSA archives. From the earlier differences with the US government David Kahn became a benefactor and much respected historian of the cryptologic arts and sciences that the NSA community embraced as one of their own.

Peter Jay

Peter Jay (1937–), had been commissioned in the Royal Navy, had also worked as a civil servant in the Treasury, and then moved to journalism, becoming for ten years the economics editor of the *Times*. Peter Jay was clearly intellectually gifted, having gained a "First" in PPE at Christ Church, Oxford, where he was also President of the Oxford Union. Peter Jay was the son of Douglas Jay (later Baron Jay), a Labour Party politician.

He was a most capable and popular lecturer. He knew his subject extremely well and expounded with great clarity and humor. He answered questions on the British and world economies with consummate skill. I thought no more of this until one day I was summoned to the Admiral President's office. Rear Admiral "Teddy" Ellis was a delightful man, in his last post in the service before retirement. I knew his son well, who was also a Royal Navy officer close in seniority to myself. The admiral said he wanted me to do him a favor. I was intrigued naturally. He said that he could not order me to do what he was going to request, but clearly hoped that I would concur. He said that he was aware that I knew Peter Jay through his visits to lecture and, here was the rub, he was the son-in-law of James Callaghan. The admiral explained that Peter Jay planned to sail this boat across the Atlantic to the United States. This was a time when there was no global positioning technology (GPS), and sail boats did not have Decca navigators or LORAN, a system that permitted ships to electronically plot their positions using radio bearings if they were in range of the LORAN transmitters. Peter Jay had let the Admiral President know that he very much wanted instruction on how to do astro-navigation and could he help find the right person to teach him. As it turned out, I was the only navigation instructor then on the college staff. Would I instruct him? "Yes, Sir, delighted to do so," rolled off my tongue. The admiral was delighted, and I left his office with a few extra points to my credit. I dutifully obeyed and to be very frank I thoroughly enjoyed the interaction. Peter Jay was exceptionally bright and I taught him the necessary skills to help him navigate safely across the Atlantic.

Little did I realize that I was training the future Ambassador to the United States and that his father-in-law would become Prime Minister. In Washington DC a few years later, at the British Embassy, this would cause me a modicum of difficulty and explanation to my superiors, that is my relationship with the new Ambassador, who succeeded a distinguished and much-loved career diplomat, Sir Peter Ramsbotham (Ambassador 1974–1977), who was also very highly respected by the Americans and was a favorite of all the Embassy staff. On becoming Prime Minister in 1979 Margaret Thatcher was quick to ensure Peter Jay's departure from the British Embassy in Washington, replacing him with another career diplomat, Sir Nicholas Henderson.

Admiral Sir Nicholas Hunt and Admiral Sir James Eberle

Two senior Royal Navy officers during these years at sea were to have an abiding impact on my career and thinking. I had considerable respect for their leadership skills and their fine intellects. Both would in due course become four-star admirals and knighted for their services. The first was my captain in HMS *Intrepid*, Captain Nicholas Hunt (1930–2013; Commander-in-Chief Fleet, and Allied Commander-in-Chief Channel and Eastern Atlantic, 1985–1987), father of the young boy that I knew at this time who became the British Minister of Health and then Foreign Secretary until his resignation in 2019, Jeremy Hunt, MP (born 1966).

While I was serving with Captain Hunt in HMS *Intrepid*, Rear Admiral James Eberle, a World War II veteran, was the Flag Officer Carriers and Amphibious Ships (1927–2018; Commander-in-Chief Fleet, 1979–1981; Commander-in-Chief Naval Home Command, 1981–1982; in retirement Director of the Royal Institute for International Affairs, 1984–1990).

Both these officers influenced my thinking as well as my leadership skills, and I would remain in touch with both for the rest of my naval career and, in the case of Admiral Hunt, after I returned to the United States permanently in 1983. They were thinkers and both nurtured my own naval and strategic thinking. I owe them both a debt of gratitude for taking an interest in my career development. They set a wonderful example.

Daniel Patrick O'Connell

1973 was the 100th anniversary of the Royal Naval College, Greenwich (RNC Greenwich closed in 1998 when British higher military education was consolidated for all services in one location at a Joint Services Command and Staff College in Watchfield, Oxfordshire). Today this historic site is managed by the Greenwich Foundation for the Old Royal Naval College. I was privileged to be on the staff during this celebratory year, culminating in visit and dinner with Queen Elizabeth and other senior signatories. One key symposium-cum-conference that we held was I believe the first ever major gathering relating to the "Law of the Sea." As the junior member of the staff, at least by age, I was directed by the Admiral President to run all the logistics for the conference. The good news was that this allowed me interface with all the guest speakers and conferees, and of these one stood out above all others, and he became the single most important contributor, giving a series of outstanding addresses. This was Professor Daniel Patrick O'Connell (1924–1979), a New Zealander, born in Auckland, who was the Chichele Professor of Public International Law at Oxford, from 1972 until he died in 1979 in Oxford, and the author of what I regard as still the major works on the law of the sea: *The Influence of Law on Sea Power* and *The International Law of the Sea* (published posthumously).[3] The latter is a definitive work. Through O'Connell's seminal work and the publication of the Conference Records there was much impetus given through British government and naval channels to what became the United Nations Convention on the Law of the Sea (UNCLOS for short), signed on December 10, 1982 by 157 signatory nations, with an effective date of November 16, 1994. Because of my logistics tasking I interacted with Professor O'Connell and he became very interested in our joint ideas on the intersection of intelligence with the law of the sea as he envisaged it in preserving international order, not simply on the high seas per se, but in the wider ramifications for international peace and order. I made several subsequent visits to Oxford to develop these ideas. My visits to Professor O'Connell also enabled me to renew the close associations developed with both Professor Buchan and Professor Trevor-Roper. It was an illuminating intellectual experience to see the coalescence of law, intelligence, and recent modern history coupled to their prognoses for the Cold War and dealing with the Soviet Union and its Warsaw pact allies.

My involvement in the law of the sea through Professor O'Connell encouraged me to take a much wider and more detailed look at legal issues that much later would stand me in good stead when addressing international terrorism and the role of the sea, gun running, human trafficking, the international trade in dugs via the oceans of the world, and illegal weapons shipment. Today Chinese encroachments in the South China Sea and a Ruling by the International Court of Arbitration in The Hague against China continue my focus on not just the intelligence implications but the intertwined legal aspects. I became so involved intellectually in the law of the sea aspects that on July 29, 1975, while I was at sea in one of my next appointments after Greenwich, I was admitted to Lincoln's Inn, one of the four Inns of Court, to become in due course a British barrister.

Admiral Sir Herbert Richmond

The Greenwich academic staff had a private dining club that was only open to established academics in the key domains of naval strategy, plans, intelligence, and operations, and the whole panoply of current international relations and politics that underscored all the above. It was a select few and I was privileged to join the "Herbert Richmond Dining Club," named after Admiral Sir Herbert Richmond (1871–1946) who led, with others, the founding of *The Naval Review* in October 1912 with the following goal, "To promote the advancement and spreading within the Service (the Royal Navy) of knowledge relevant to the higher aspects of the Naval Profession." *The Naval Review* to this day is a vital source of high-quality thinking and discourse on all matters relevant to maritime strategy and operations and the myriad associated political–economic–social–diplomatic and historical factors. Richmond was not just a highly successful sea-going commander he was a distinguished intellectual, becoming after his retirement as a four-star admiral the Vere Harmsworth Professor of Imperial and Naval History from 1934–1936 and the Master of Downing College, Cambridge University from 1934–1946. He has been described as "perhaps the most brilliant naval officer of his generation," and as a first-class naval historian he was called the "British Mahan." He was successively in charge of the Senior Officers Course and then the Admiral President of the Royal Naval College, Greenwich 1920–1922. After retirement from the Royal Navy he had the foresight very early on to see the impact of the emerging Japanese threat and what the British government should do to counteract what he saw would become Japanese expansionism.

Vice Admiral Sir Roy "Gus" Halliday

When I served in Washington DC in the mid-1970s my reporting chain would be via Op-96 in the Office of the Chief of Naval Operations in the Pentagon to the British Naval Attaché, Rear Admiral Roy "Gus" Halliday (1923–2007). Admiral Halliday was a distinguished World War II veteran who won the Distinguished Service Cross (DSC) flying from HMS *Illustrious* and HMS *Victorious* against the Japanese from the British Pacific Fleet. He had been shot down and was rescued by HMS *Whelp*, whose First Lieutenant was Lieutenant Prince Philip of Greece, who lent Halliday a spare uniform and later the two of them celebrated on a "run ashore" in Fremantle. Halliday was back on-board HMS *Victorious* in time to take part in the raids on the airfields on the Sakishima Islands in March to May 1945. He was awarded the DSC for his courageous efforts and he also received a "Mention in Dispatches" for his flying during Operation *Meridian*. After the Japanese surrender he learned that his cabin-mate, Ken Burrenston, had been shot down over Palembang, captured by the Japanese and then beheaded at the notorious

Changi prisoner-of-war camp two days after the Japanese surrender, a heinous war crime. After a distinguished post-war career he was appointed Head of Naval Intelligence in 1973 (the DNI position had been abolished as part of the 1967 centralization initiated by Minister of Defence Denis Healey) as a Commodore, from which post he was promoted to Rear Admiral in 1975 and appointed Naval Attaché and Commander of the British Navy Staff in Washington DC. In 1978 now Vice Admiral Halliday became the Deputy Chief of the Defence Staff (Intelligence), and on retirement from the Royal Navy in 1981 he was made the Director-General Intelligence at the Ministry of Defence from 1981–1984. I was privileged to both work for Admiral Halliday in his various roles and appointments, and he became a significant champion of my interests and career development during and after my tour in Washington DC.

Admiral Carlisle "Carl" Trost

My American naval report in Washington DC in the mid-1970s was Rear Admiral Carlisle Trost, Op-96 (born April 24, 1930). He has always been known as Carl. From Illinois, Admiral Trost graduated first in the US Naval Academy class of 1953. He became a submariner and had an extraordinarily successful career; illustrious

USS *Bainbridge* (CGN 25). (Wikimedia Commons, US Navy)

would be a much better description. In May 1986 he was nominated by President Ronald Reagan to succeed Admiral James Watkins as Chief of Naval Operations (CNO). Admiral Trost served as CNO from July 1986 to June 1990. I was therefore unbelievably fortunate to have as my US Naval direct report the officer would in due course become the CNO. Between Admiral Halliday and Admiral Trost who could ever expect to have such fine leaders with such distinguished careers both behind and ahead of them.

Vice Admiral Samuel L. Gravely Jr.

My finale during my appointment in Washington DC in the mid-1970s was actual sea time, in the nuclear-powered cruiser USS *Bainbridge* (CGN 25) in Third Fleet, US Pacific Fleet. I deployed for Exercise Varsity Sprint in the Pacific, sailing from San Diego. This was an enormous eye opener for me on just how prodigious the capabilities of the US Navy were. *Bainbridge* had recently fitted the Naval Tactical Data System (NTDS), by far the most advanced system of its kind in the world. I gained enormous hands-on experience on board *Bainbridge*.

Vice Admiral Samuel Gravely, United States Navy. (Arlington Cemetery)

The Commander of the Third Fleet, Vice Admiral Samuel L. Gravely Jr. (1922–2004) was a remarkable and truly wonderful person and leader. I got to know him well during my time on *Bainbridge*. He was the first African American to serve aboard a fighting ship as an officer, the first to command a US Navy ship, the first to become a flag officer, and the first to command a numbered fleet, a hugely remarkable achievement for his generation. He and I interacted on many subjects, not least naturally the ongoing Sea War '85 project, Soviet intelligence matters, and comparisons and contrasts between the US Navy and the Royal Navy. He invited me to stand with him regularly on *Bainbridge*'s bridge wings as we conducted various evolutions. During Varsity Sprint *Bainbridge* demonstrated just how powerful a tool the NTDS was when coupled to the Terrier missile system. I transferred by helicopter to several other ships for short visits, including the battle group's aircraft carriers. It was a happy time, a great learning experience, and I hope that in my own small ways I contributed.

I stayed in touch with Admiral Gravely after I returned to the UK, corresponding by private letter. He retired in 1980, and I was most upset when my schedule back in London would not permit me to attend his retirement ceremony at the Defense Communications Agency, where he was director. I regard him to this day as one of the finest people that I have been privileged to know.

Glossary

ACINT	Acoustic Intelligence
AIS	Automatic Identification System
ASIO	Australia Security and Intelligence Organization
ASIS	Australia Secret Intelligence Service
C	The initial designating the Director of the British Secret Intelligence Service (The first Director of SIS was Captain Sir Mansfield Cumming, Royal Navy, who signed his documents with just the letter "C")
CIA	Central Intelligence Agency
CinCPac	Commander-in-Chief US Pacific Command
CinCPacFleet	Commander-in-Chief US Pacific Fleet
CinCUSNavEur	Commander-in-Chief US Naval Forces Europe
CJCS	Chairman of the Joint Chiefs of Staff
CNO	Chief of Naval Operations
CNA	Center for Naval Analyses
COMINT	Communications Intelligence
COMSUBPAC	Commander Submarine Forces US Pacific Fleet
CONOPS	Concepts of Operation
CSE	Communications Security Establishment
DARPA	Defense Advanced Research Projects Agency
DIA	Defense Intelligence Agency
DIS	Defence Intelligence Staff (later DI—Defence Intelligence)
DNA	Deoxyribonucleic Acid
DNI	Director of Naval Intelligence (UK and US) and Director of National Intelligence (US)
DOE	Department of Energy (US)
ELECTRO-OPINT	Electro-Optical Intelligence
ELINT	Electronic Intelligence
FBE	Fleet Battle Experiment
FBI	Federal Bureau of Investigation
FEBA	Forward Edge of the Battle Area
FISC	Foreign Intelligence Surveillance Court
FSB	Federal Security Service (Russia)
GC&CS	Government Code and Cypher School
GCHQ	Government Communications Headquarters
GCSB	New Zealand Government Communications Security Bureau
GEOINT	Geospatial Intelligence
GRU	Intelligence Directorate of the General Staff of the Armed Forces of the former Soviet Union and currently of the Russian Federation
HASC	House Armed Services Committee

HPSCI	House Permanent Select Committee on Intelligence
IAEA	International Atomic Energy Authority
IMINT	Imagery Intelligence
IOC	Initial Operational Capability
ISIS	Islamic State in Iraq and Syria
I&W	Indicators and Warning
JIC	Joint Intelligence Committee
KGB	The Committee for State Security was the main security agency of the Soviet Union from March 1954 until December 1991
LASINT	Laser Intelligence
LOE	Limited Objective Experiment
MAD	Mutual Assured Destruction
MAD	Magnetic Anomaly Detector
MASINT	Measurement and Signature Intelligence
MI5	British Security Service
MI6	British Secret Intelligence Service (SIS)
NAB	New Zealand National Assessment Bureau
NATO	North Atlantic Treaty Organization
NCSC	National Cyber Security Center
NCTC	National Counterterrorism Center
NGA	National Geospatial Agency
NID	Naval Intelligence Department
NRO	National Reconnaissance Office
NSA	National Security Agency
NSC	National Security Council (UK and US)
NUCINT	Nuclear Intelligence
NZSIS	New Zealand Secret Intelligence Service
ONI	Office of Naval Intelligence
PFIAB	President's Foreign Intelligence Advisory Board
RADINT	Radar Intelligence
RCMP	Royal Canadian Mounted Police
RDA	R&D Associates
RF/EMPINT	Radio Frequency and Electromagnetic Pulse Intelligence
RINT	Radiation Intelligence
SEAL	US Navy Sea Air Land Special Force Operator
SIGINT	Signals Intelligence
SOSUS	Sound Surveillance System
SSBN	Nuclear-powered ballistic missile Submarine
SSGN	Nuclear-powered guided missile Submarine
SSK	Non-nuclear-powered diesel or air independent propulsion submarine
SSN	Nuclear Powered attack Submarine
TTPs	Tactics Techniques and Procedures
UAV	Unmanned Aerial Vehicle
UCAV	Unmanned Combat Aerial Vehicle
UNCLOS	United Nations Convention on the Law of the Sea
UNO	United Nations Organization
UUV	Unmanned Underwater Vehicle
WMD	Weapon(s) of Mass Destruction

Endnotes

Chapter 1

1 The volumes were published in 1979, 1981, 1984, 1988, and 1990.
2 The Old Royal Naval College is today a World Heritage site, designed by Christopher Wren and built between 1696–1712.

Chapter 2

1 The unclassified product from this work may be read in Bradford Dismukes and James McConnell's, editors, *Soviet Naval Diplomacy* (New York, NY: Pergamon Press, 1979).
2 Readers can find details of the work begun by Admiral Moorer and his board of the USS Liberty Alliance on the Library of Congress website, usslibertydocumentcenter.org, September 2013.
3 The detail is on the Library of Congress website and for just the non-intelligence aspects of the attack on the USS *Liberty* the best book in my opinion is undoubtedly James Scott's *The Attack on the Liberty. The Untold Story of Israel's Deadly 1967 Assault on a US Spy Ship* (New York, NY: Simon & Schuster, 2009).
4 A forward deployment of a military unit is one in which the unit in question is placed such that it is expected to be the first unit to make contact with the enemy or be a lead unit in movement to battle.

Chapter 4

1 Executive Order Number 12333.
2 All figures from *The World Factbook 2018* (Washington, D.C.: Central Intelligence Agency, 2018)

Chapter 5

1 J. Risen and E. Lichtblau, "Bush Lets U.S. Spy on Callers Without Courts," *New York Times*, December 16, 2005.
2 J. Robertson, "Bush-Era Documents Show Official Misled Congress About NSA Spying" Bloomberg, April 25, 2015.
3 Anthony Wells, "Soviet Submarine Warfare Strategy Assessment and Future US Submarine and Anti-Submarine Warfare Technologies," Defense Advanced Research Projects Agency, March 1988, US Department of Defense.

Chapter 6

1 Readers should note that the US does recognize the UNCLOS as a code of customary international law, though it has not ratified the actual treaty.

2 Trump's statement is available online: https://www.whitehouse.gov/briefings-statements/remarks-president-trump-joint-comprehensive-plan-action/ (accessed April 23, 2020).

3 *The World Factbook 2019* (Washington, D.C.: Central Intelligence Agency, 2019)

4 Ellen Nakashima and Paul Sonne, "China hacked a Navy contractor and secured a trove of highly sensitive data on submarine warfare," *The Washington Post*, June 8, 2018.

5 Statement available at https://docs.house.gov/meetings/IG/IG00/20180517/108298/HHRG-115-IG00-Wstate-FanellJ-20180517.pdf (accessed April 23, 2020)

6 House of Commons records, February 27, 1984, Debate 55107, pp. 37–38.

7 Gustav Bertrand, *Enigma ou la plus grande enigma de la guerre 1939–1945* (Paris: Plon Publishing House, 1973), 256.

8 There is an excellent record of these key operations in Desmond Ball and D. M. Horner's *Breaking the Codes: Australia's KGB Network, 1944–1950* (Sydney: Allen & Unwin, 1998).

9 Cunningham Diary, entry for November 21, 1945, British Library, MSS 52578.

10 These words are taken from a Report of the British Joint Intelligence Committee, dated October 29, 1947 (JIC 1947, number 65, "Summary of Principal External Factors Affecting Commonwealth Security," The National Archives).

Chapter 7

1 Cray Inc. was an American supercomputer company located in Seattle, Washington State. The company was originally Cray Research, Inc.

2 Nippon Denki Kabushiki Gaisha is a Japanese multinational information technology company headquartered in Minato, Tokyo, Japan. The company was known as the Nippon Electric Company Limited before rebranding in 1983 as just NEC. NEC is a member of the Sumitomo Group.

3 More details may be found at www.coastguardfoundation.org.

4 See his paper, "Computing Machinery and Intelligence," University of Manchester, 1950, p. 460.

5 Andrew and Leslie Cockburn, *Dangerous Liaison: The Inside Story of the US–Israel Covert Relationship* (London: Harper Collins, 1991).

6 A dhow is a one- or two-masted Arab sailing vessel.

7 Efraim Halevy, *Man in the Shadows: Inside the Middle East Crisis with a Man Who Led the Mossad* (New York: St Martin's Press, 2006) 278.

8 Ibid., 44.

9 Ibid., 270.

10 Ibid., 277.

11 Umar, also spelled Omar, was one of the most powerful and influential Muslim caliphs in history. He was a senior companion of the Islamic prophet Muhammad. He succeeded Abu Bakr as the second caliph of the Rashidun Caliphate on 23 August 634.

12 State Council Information Office of the People's Republic of China, "China's National Defense in the New Era", (Beijing: Foreign Languages Press Co. Ltd., 2019), available http://english.www.gov.cn/archive/whitepaper/201907/24/content_WS5d3941ddc6d08408f502283d.html

13 Statement available at https://docs.house.gov/meetings/IG/IG00/20180517/108298/HHRG-115-IG00-Wstate-FanellJ-20180517.pdf (accessed April 23, 2020).

14 Ibid.

15 USC, #1292 (2017).

16 *The World Factbook 2019* (Washington, D.C.: Central Intelligence Agency, 2019)
17 *The World Factbook 2019* (Washington, D.C.: Central Intelligence Agency, 2019)
18 Andropov was the KGB Director 1967–1982
19 The details above were reported by CBS New York on August 9, 2013.
20 *The World Factbook 2019* (Washington, D.C.: Central Intelligence Agency, 2019)

Chapter 8

1 Bryan Clark, "Undersea cables and the future of submarine competition," *Bulletin of the Atomic Scientists*, June 15, 2016.
2 Kari Bingen, Deputy Secretary of Defense for Intelligence, stated at the Intelligence and National Security Summit hosted by INSA and AFCEA, September 2018, reported by Mark Pomerleau.
3 Quoted by James Vincent in *The Verge*, September 4, 2017, and reported by CNBC.
4 J. Ward, "Sino-Indo Competition in the Maritim Domain," The Jamestown Foundation, Global Research and Analysis, February 2, 2017.
5 R. Danzig, "Former Navy Leader Warns About Fleet Expansion," *National Defense,* January 9, 2018.

Appendix

1 Harry Hinsley, *Power and the Pursuit of Peace: Theory and Practice in the History of Relations Between States* (Cambridge: Cambridge University Press, 1962).
2 Anthony Wells, "Studies in British Naval Intelligence, 1880–1945" (D. Phil thesis, King's College, University of London, 1972).
3 D. P. O'Connell, *The Influence of Law on Sea Power* (Manchester: Manchester University Press, 1975); D. P. O'Connell, *The International Law of the Sea* Vol 1 (Oxford: Oxford University Press, 1982).

Bibliography

Abshagen, K. H. *Canaris*. Translated by A. H. Brodrick. London: Hutchinson, 1956.

Admiralty British. Fuhrer Conference on Naval Affairs. Admiralty 1947. London: Her Majesty's Stationery Office.

Aid, M. *Secret Sentry: The Untold History of the National Security Agency*. New York: Bloomsbury, 2009.

Aldrich, R. J. Editor. *British Intelligence, Strategy, and the Cold War. 1945–1951*. London: Routledge, 1992.

Aldrich, R. J. Editor. *Espionage, Security, and Intelligence in Britain, 1945–1970*. Manchester: Manchester University Press, 1998.

Aldrich R. J. *Intelligence and the war against Japan: Britain, America and the Politics of Secret Service*. Cambridge: Cambridge University Press, 1999.

Aldrich R. J. *The Hidden Hand: Britain, America, and Cold War Secret Intelligence*. London: John Murray, 2001.

Aldrich R. J., G. Rawnsley and M. Y. Rawnsley, eds. *The Clandestine Cold War in Asia 1945–1965*. London: Frank Cass, 1999.

Aldrich R. J. and M. F Hopkins, eds. *Intelligence, Defense, and Diplomacy: British Policy in the Post War World*. London: Frank Cass, 1994.

Aldrich, Richard J. *GCHQ The Uncensored Story of Britain's Most Secret Intelligence Agency*. London: Harper Press, 2010.

Alsop, Stewart and Braden, Thomas. *Sub Rosa. The OSS and American Espionage*. New York: Reynal and Hitchcock, 1946.

Andrew, C. M. *Secret Service: The Making of the British Intelligence Community*. London: Heinemann, 1985.

Andrew, C. M. *For the President's Eyes Only: Secret Intelligence and the American Presidency from Washington to Bush*. London: Harper Collins, 1995.

Andrew, C. M. *Defense of the Realm. The Official History of the Security Service*. London: Allen Lane, 2009.

Andrew, C. M. and D. Dilks, eds. *The Missing Dimension: Governments and Intelligence Communities in the Twentieth Century*. London: Macmillan, 1982.

Andrew, C. M. and O. Gordievsky. *KGB: The Inside Story*. London: Hodder and Stoughton, 1990.

Andrew, C. M. and V. Mitrokhin. *The Sword and the Shield: The Mitrokhin Archive and the Secret History of the KGB*. New York: Basic Books, 1999.

Arnold, H. *Global Mission. Chief of the Army Air Forces 1938–1946*. New York: Harper,1949.

Assman, K. *Deutsche Seestrategie in Zwei Welkriegen*. Vowinckel. Heidelberg: Heidelberg Press, 1959.

Aston, Sir George. *Secret Service*. London: Faber and Faber, 1939.

Bamford, J. *The Puzzle Palace: America's National Security Agency and its Special Relationship with GCHQ*. London: Sidgwick and Jackson, 1983.

Bamford, J. *Body of Secrets: How NSA and Britain's GCHQ Eavesdrop on the World*. New York: Doubleday, 2001.

Bamford, J. *The Shadow Factory: The Ultra-Secret NSA from 9/11 to Eavesdropping on America*. New York: Doubleday, 2008.

Barrass, Gordon S. *The Great Cold War: A Journey Through the Hall of Mirrors*. Stanford, California: Stanford University, 2009.

Barry and Creasy. *Attacks on the Tirpitz by Midget Submarines*. September 1943. *London Gazette*, July 3, 1947.

Beardon, Milton, and James Risen. *The Main Enemy: The Inside Story of the CIA's Final Showdown with the KGB*. London: Penguin Random House, 2003.

Bedell Smith, W. *Eisenhower's Six Great Decisions*. London: Longmans, 1956.

Bennett, G. *Churchill's Man of Mystery: Desmond Morton and the World of Intelligence*. London: Routledge, 2007.

Bennett, R. *Ultra in the West: The Normandy Campaign of 1944–1945*. London: Hutchinson, 1979.

Blackburn, D. and W. Caddell. *Secret Service in South Africa*. London: Cassell and Company London, 1911.

Belot, R. *The Struggle for the Mediterranean 1939–1945*. Oxford: Oxford University Press, 1951.

Benjamin, R. *Five Lives in One. An Insider's View of the Defence and Intelligence World*. Tunbridge Wells: Parapress, 1996.

Benson, R. L. and R. Warner. *Venona: Soviet Espionage and the American Response, 1939–1957. Menlo Park.* California: Aegean Park Press, 1997.

Bilton, M. and P. Kosminksy. *Speaking Out: Untold Stories from the Falklands War*. Grafton: Grafton, 1987.

Booth, K. *Navies and Foreign Policy.* New York: Croom Helm, 1977.

Borovik, Genrikh. *The Philby Files: The Secret Life of Master Spy Kim Philby—KGB Archives Revealed*. London: Little Brown, 1994.

Brodie, Bernard. *Strategy in the Missile Age*. Princeton: Princeton University Press, 1959.

Brodie, Bernard. *The Future of Deterrence in U.S. Strategy*. California: University of California Press, 1968.

Brodie, Bernard. *War and Politics*. London: Macmillan, 1973.

Buchan, Alastair. *War in Modern Society*. Oxford: Oxford University, 1966

Buchan, Alastair. *The End of the Postwar Era: A New Balance of World Power*. Oxford: Oxford University, 1974.

Cable, James. *Britain's Naval Future*. Annapolis, Maryland: US Naval Institute Press, 1983.

Calvocoressi, P. *Top Secret Ultra*. London: Cassell and Company London, 1980.

Carrington, Lord. *Reflect on Things Past. The Memoirs of Lord Carrington*. London: Collins, 1988.

Carl, Leo D. *The International Dictionary of Intelligence*. Virginia: McLean, 1990.

Carter, Miranda. *Anthony Blunt: His Lives*. London: Farrar, Straus, & Giroux, 2001.

Cater, D. *The Fourth Branch of Government*. Boston: Houghton Mifflin, 1959.

Cavendish, A. *Inside Intelligence*. London: Harper Collins, 1990.

Cherkashin, A. *Spy Handler. Memoirs of a KGB Officer*. New York: Basic Books, 2005.

China. The State Council Information Office of the People's Republic of China: In the New Era. July 2019. This is an open source Chinese government official publication and policy statement.

Clayton, A. *The Enemy is Listening: The Story of the Y Service*. London: Hutchinson, 1980.

Cockburn, Andrew and Leslie: *Dangerous Liaison. The Inside Story of the US-Israeli Covert Relationship*. Place: Harper Collins, 1991.

Cocker, M. P. *Royal Navy Submarines 1901–1982*. London: Frederick Warre Publications, 1982.

Cole, D. J. *Geoffrey Prime: The Imperfect Spy*. London: Robert Hale, 1998.

Colvin, I. *Chief of Intelligence*. London: Gollanz, 1951.

Colomb J. C. R. "Naval Intelligence and the Protection of Shipping in War," *RUSI Journal*, vol. 25 (1882): 553–590.

Compton-Hall, Richard. *Subs versus Subs. The Tactical Technology of Underwater Warfare*. London: David and Charles Publishers, 1988.

Copeland, B. J. *Colossus: The Secrets of Bletchley Park's Code-Breaking Computers*. Oxford: Oxford University Press, 2006.

Corera, Gordon. *MI6: Life and Death in the British Secret Service*. London: Harper Collins, 2012.

Dalein, D. J. *Soviet Espionage*. Oxford: Oxford University Press, 1955.

Deacon, R. *A History of the British Secret Service*. London: Muller, 1969.

De Silva, P. *Sub Rosa: The CIA and the Use of Intelligence*. New York: Times Books, 1978.

Dismukes, B. and McConnell J. *Soviet Naval Diplomacy*. New York: Pergamon Press, 1979.

Driberg, T. *Guy Burgess*. London: Weidenfeld and Nicholson, 1956.

Dulles, Allen. *The Craft of Intelligence*. New York: Harper and Row, 1963.

Dumbrell, J. *Special Relationship: Anglo-American Relations from the Cold War to Iraq*. London: Palgrave, 2006.

Earley, Peter. *Confessions of a Spy: The Real Story of Aldrich Ames*. New York: Putnam & Son, 1997.

Elliott, G. and H. Shukman. *Secret Classrooms. An untold story of the Cold War*. London: St. Ermin's Press, 2002.

Everitt, Nicholas. *British Secret Service during the Great War*. London: Hutchinson, 1920.

Ewing, A. W. *The Man of Room 40. The Life of Sir Alfred Ewing*. London: Hutchinson, 1939.

Fahey, J. A. *Licensed to Spy*. Annapolis, Maryland: US Naval Institute Press, 2002.

Falconer, D. *First into Action: A Dramatic Personal Account of Life in the SBS*. London: Little Brown, 2001.

Fanell, James. "China's Worldwide Military Expansion." Testimony and Statement for the Record. US House of Representatives Permanent Select Committee on Intelligence. Hearing, May 15, 2018. Rayburn Building, Washington DC.

Fishman, Charles. *One Giant Leap. The Impossible Mission that Flew us to the Moon*. New York: Simon and Schuster, 2019.

Fitzgerald, P. and M. Leopold. *Strangers on the Line: A Secret History of Phone-Tapping*. London: Bodley Head, 1987.

Freedman, Sir Lawrence. *Strategy*. Oxford: Oxford University Press, 2013.

Freedman, Sir Lawrence. *Official History of the Falklands Campaign. Volumes 1 and 2*. London: Routledge, 2005.

Freedman, Sir Lawrence and Gamba-Stonehouse, V. *Signals of War: The Falklands Conflict of 1982*. Princeton: Princeton University Press, 1991.

Freedman, Sir Lawrence. *A Choice of Enemies: America Confronts the Middle East*. Oxford: Oxford University Press, 2008.

Friedman, Norman. *Submarine Design and Development. Conway Maritime Press*. London: Conway, 1984.

Friedman, Norman. *The Fifty-Year Conflict: Conflict and Strategy in the Cold War*. Annapolis. Maryland: Naval Institute Press, 2007.

Foote, A. *Handbook for Spies*. London: Museum Press, 1949.

Foot, M. R. D. *SOE in France*. London: Her Majesty's Stationery Office, 1964.

Friedman, W. F. and C. J. Mendelsohn. *The Zimmermann Telegram of January 16, 1917 and its cryptographic background*. US War department, Office of the Chief Signal Officer. Washington DC: US Government Printing Office, 1938.

Frost, M. *Spyworld: Inside the Canadian and American Intelligence Establishments*. Toronto: Doubleday, 1994.

Fuchida, Mitsuo and Okumiya Masutake. Edited by Roger Pineau and Clarke Kawakami. *Midway, The Battle that Doomed Japan. The Japanese Navy's Story*. Annapolis, Maryland: Blue Jacket, 1955.

Gaddis, John Lewis. *The Cold War*. London: 2007.

Ganguly, Sumit and Chris Mason. "An Unnatural Partnership? The Future of US-India Strategic Cooperation. Strategic Studies Institute." US Army War College. May 2019.

Gates, Robert. *From the Shadows: The Ultimate Insider's Story of Five Presidents and How They Won the Cold War*. New York: Simon & Schuster, 2006.

George, James, ed. *The Soviet and Other Communist Navies*. Annapolis, Maryland: US Naval Institute Press, 1986.

Godfrey, Vice Admiral John. *Naval Memoirs*. London: National Maritime Museum Greenwich, 1965.

Goodman, M. S. *Spying on the Nuclear Bear: Anglo-American Intelligence and the Soviet Bomb*. Stanford, California: Stanford University Press, 2007.

Gordievsky, Oleg. *Next Stop Execution: The Autobiography of Oleg Gordievsky*. London: Whole Story, 1995.

Graham, G. S. *The Politics of Naval Supremacy*. Cambridge: Cambridge University Press, 1965.

Grant, R. M. *U-Boat Intelligence, 1914–1918*. Connecticut: Hamden, 1969.

Grayson, W. C. *Chicksands. A Millennium History*. London: Shefford Press, 1992.

Grimes, Sandra, and Jeanne Vertefeuille. *Circle of Treason: A CIA Account of Traitor Aldrich Ames and the Men He Betrayed*. Annapolis, Maryland: Naval Institute Press, 2012.

Halevy, Efraim. *Man in the Shadows. Inside the Middle East Crisis with a man who led the Mossad*. London: Weidenfeld and Nicholson, 2006.

Harper, Stephen. *Capturing Enigma. How HMS Petard Seized the German Naval Codes*. London: The History Press, 2008.

Hastings, Max with Simon Jenkins. *The Battle for the Falklands*. New York: W.W. Norton and Company, 1983.

Healey, D. *The Time of My Life*. London: Michael Joseph, 1989.

Helms, Richard. *A Look over My Shoulder: A Life in the Central Intelligence Agency*. New York: Random House, 2003.

Hendrick, B. J. *The Life and Letters of Walter H. Page*. Garden City, New York: Yale University Press, 1922.

Herman, M. *Intelligence Power in Peace and War*. Cambridge: Cambridge University Press, 1992.

Herman, M. *Intelligence Services in the Information Age*. London: Cassell and Company London, 2001.

Higham, R. *Armed Forces in Peacetime. Britain 1918–1940. A Case Study*. London: Foulis Press, 1963.

Hill, Rear Admiral J. R. *Anti-Submarine Warfare*. United States Naval Institute Press. Annapolis, Maryland. 1985.

Hill, Rear Admiral J. R., ed. *Oxford Illustrated History of the Royal Navy*. Oxford: Oxford University Press, 1995.

Hill, Rear Admiral J. R. *Lewin of Greenwich. The Authorized Biography of Admiral of the Fleet Lord Lewin*. London: Cassell and Company London, 2000.

Hillsman, Roger. *Strategic Intelligence and National Decisions*. Cambridge: Cambridge University Press, 1956.

Hinsley, F. H. *British Intelligence in the Second World War*. London: Her Majesty's Stationery Office, 1979–1990.

Hinsley, F. H. *Hitler's Strategy*. Cambridge: Cambridge University Press, 1951.

Hinsley, F. H. and A. Stripp, eds. *Code-Breakers: The Inside Story of Bletchley Park*. Oxford: Oxford University Press, 1993.

Hoffman, David E. *The Billion Dollar Spy: A True Story of Cold War Espionage and Betrayal*. New York: Penguin Random House, 2015.

Hollander, Paul. *Political Will and Personal Belief: The Decline and Fall of Soviet Communism*. New Haven, Connecticut: Yale University, 1999.

Howard, Sir Michael. *Captain Professor: A Life in War and Peace*. New York: Continuum Press, 2006.

Howard, Sir Michael. *Liberation or Catastrophe: Reflections on the History of the 20th Century*. London: A and C Black, 2007.

Howe, Geoffrey. *Conflict of Loyalty*. London: Macmillan, 1994.

Hunt, Sir David. *A Don at War*. London: Harper Collins, 1966.

International Institute for Strategic Studies (IISS). *The Military Balance Collection*. London: IISS, 2020.

Ireland, Bernard. With Eric Grove. *War at Sea 1897–1997*. London: Harper Collins and Janes, 1997.

James, Admiral Sir William. "The Eyes of the Navy. Room 40." *Edinburgh University Journal*, no. 22 (Spring 1965): 50–54.

Janes Fighting Ships. London: Janes Publishing, 1960–2015.

Jeffery, Keith. *MI6: The History of the Secret Intelligence Service, 1909–1949*. London: Penguin Random House, 2010.

Jenkins, R. *Life at the Centre*. London: Macmillan, 1991.

Johnson, Adrian L., ed. *Wars in Peace*. London: Royal United Service Institution, 2014.

Johnson, T. R. *American Cryptology during the Cold War, 1945–1989*. Volumes 1–4. United States National Security Agency. Declassified in 2009.

Jones, Nate, ed. *Able Archer '83: The Secret History of the NATO Exercise that Almost Triggered Nuclear War*. New York: The New Press, 2016.

Jones, R. V. *Most Secret War*. London: Hamish Hamilton Limited, 1978.

Kagan, Neil and Stephen G. Hyslop. *The Secret History of World War 2*. Washington DC: National Geographic.

Kahn, David. *The Codebreakers*. London: Weidenfeld & Nicholson, 1966.

Kalugin, O. and F. Montaigne. *The First Directorate: My First 32 years in intelligence and espionage against the West—the ultimate memoirs of a Master Spy*. New York: St. Martin's Press, 1994.

Kendall, W. "The Functions of Intelligence." *World Politics*, no. 4, vol. 1 (July 1949): 542–552.

Kegan, John. *Intelligence in War*. New York: Vintage Books & Random House, 2002

Kendall, Bridget. *The Cold War: A New Oral History of Life Between East and West*. London: Penguin Books, 2018.

Kent, S. *Strategic Intelligence for American World Policy*. Oxford: Oxford University Press, 1949.
Korbel, J. *The Communist Subversion of Czechoslovakia, 1938–1948*. Oxford: Oxford University Press, 1959.
Kot, S. *Conversations with the Kremlin and Dispatches from Russia*. Oxford: Oxford University Press, 1963.
Krupakar, Jayanna. "Chinese Naval Base in the Indian Ocean. Signs of a Maritime Grand Strategy." *Strategic Analysis*, no. 3, vol. 41 (2017): 207–222
Lamphere, R. J. and T. Shachtman. *The FBI-KGB war: A Special Agent's Story*. London: W. H. Allen, 1986.
Lewis, Norman. *The Honoured Society*. London: Collins, 1964
Liddell-Hart, Sir B. H. *Strategy—the Indirect Approach*. London: Faber & Faber, 1954.
Liddell-Hart, Sir B. H. *The Other Side of the Hill*. London: Cassell, 1951.
Liddell-Hart, Sir B. H. *Memoirs in Two Volumes*. London: Cassell, 1965.
Liddell-Hart, Sir B. H. *The Real War, 1914–1918*. Boston: Little Brown & Company, 1930.
Lockhart, Sir Robert Bruce. *Memories of a British Agent*. London: Putnam, 1932.
Lockhart, Robin. *The Ace of Spies*. London: Hodder & Stoughton, 1967.
Lyubimov, Mikhail. *Notes of a Ne'er-Do-Well Rezident or Will-o'-the-Wisp*. Moscow: 1995.
Lyubimov, Mikhail. *Spies I Love and Hate*. Moscow: AST Olimp, 1997.
Macintyre, Ben. *The Spy and the Traitor*. London: Crown Publishing Group, 2018.
Marder, A. J. *From the Dreadnought to Scapa Flow*. 5 Volumes. Oxford: Oxford University Press, 1940.
Marder, A. J. *The Anatomy of British Sea Power*. New York: Alfred Knopf, 1940.
Martin, Sir Laurence. *Arms and Strategy*. London: Weidenfeld & Nicholson, 1973.
Mathams, R. H. *Sub-Rosa: Memoirs of an Australian Intelligence Analyst*. Sydney: Allen & Unwin, 1982.
McGehee, R. W. *Deadly Deceit: My 25 Years in the CIA*. New York: Sheridan Square, 1983.
McKay, Sinclair. *The Secret Life of Bletchley Park*. London: Aurum Press Limited, 2010.
McKay, Sinclair. *The Lost World of Bletchley Park*. London: Aurum Press Limited, 2013.
McKay, Sinclair. *The Secret Listeners*. London: Aurum Press Limited, 2013.
McKnight, D. *Australia's Spies and Their Secrets*. London: University College London Press, 1994.
McLachlan, Donald. *Room 39. Naval Intelligence in Action, 1939–1945*. London: Weidenfeld & Nicholson, 1968.
Mikesh, R. C. B-57: *Canberra at War*. London: Ian Allan, 1980.
Mitchell, M. and T. Mitchell. *The Spy Who Tried to Stop a War: Katharine Gun and the Secret Plot to Sanction the Iraq Invasion*. London: Polipoint Press, 2008.
Monat, P. *Spy in the US*. New York: Harper & Row, 1961.
Montagu, E. E. S. *The Man Who Never Was*. London: Evans Brothers, 1953.
Montgomery Hyde, H. *George Blake: Superspy*. London: Futura, 1987.
Moore, Charles. *Margaret Thatcher: The Authorized Biography. Volume 2. Everything She Wants*. London: Allen Lane, 2015.
Moorehead, A. *The Traitors*. London: Hamish Hamilton, 1952.
Morley, Jefferson. *The Ghost: The Secret Life of CIA Spymaster James Jesus Angleton*. London: St. Martin's Press, 2017.
Murphy, D. E., S. A. Kondrashev and G. Bailey. *Battleground Berlin: CIA vs. KGB in the Cold War*. New Haven: Yale University Press, 1997.
Nicolai, Colonel W. *The German Secret Service*. Translated by G. Renwick. Frankfurt am Main: Fischer, 2007.
Nott, J. *Here Today Gone Tomorrow: Recollections of an Errant Politician*. London: Politico's, 2002.
Oberdorfer, Don. *From the Cold War to a New Era: The United States and the Soviet Union, 1983–1991*. Baltimore, Maryland: John Hopkins University Press, 1998.
Orlov, Alexander. *Handbook of Intelligence and Guerrilla Warfare*. London: Cresset Press, 1963.
Packard, W. *A Century of Naval Intelligence*. Washington DC: Office of Naval Intelligence, 1996.
Parrish, T. *The Ultra Americans: The US Role in Breaking Nazi Codes*. New York: Stein and Day, 1986.
Parker, Philip, Editor. *The Cold War Spy Pocket Manual*. Oxford: Pool of London Press, 2015.
Paterson, M. *Voices of the Codebreakers: Personal Accounts of the Secret Heroes of World War Two*. Newton Abbot: David and Charles, 2007.

Pavlov, V. *Memoirs of a Spymaster: My Fifty Years in the KGB*. New York: Carroll and Graf., 1994.
Pawle, G. *The Secret War*. London: Harrap, 1972
Pearson, John. *The Life of Ian Fleming*. London: Jonathan Cape, 1966.
Petter, G. S. *The Future of American Secret Intelligence*. Washington DC: Hoover Press, 1946.
Petrov, Vladimir and Evdokia. *Empires of Fear*. London: Andre Deutsch, 1956.
Philby, Kim. *My Silent War*. New York: Grove Press, 1968.
Pincher, C. *Too Secret Too Long*. London: Sidgwick and Jackson, 1984.
Pincher, C. *Traitors: Labyrinths of Treason*. London: Sidgwick and Jackson, 1987.
Pincher, Chapman. *Treachery: Betrayals, Blunders, and Cover Ups: Six Decades of Espionage*. Edinburgh: Mainstream Publishing, 2012.
Polmar, Norman. *The Ships and Aircraft of the US Fleet*. Volumes. Annapolis, Maryland: United States Naval Institute Press, 1984.
Powers, T. *The Man who Kept the Secrets: Richard Helms and the CIA*. London: Weidenfeld and Nicholson, 1979.
Pratt, F. *Secret and Urgent. The Story of Codes and Ciphers*. London: Robert Hale, 1939.
Primakov, Yevgeny. *Russian Crossroads: Toward the New Millennium*. New Haven, Connecticut: Yale, 2004.
Prime, R. *Time of Trial: The Personal Story Behind the Cheltenham Spy Scandal*. London: Hodder & Stoughton, 1984.
Raeder, E. *Struggle for the Sea*. Translated by Edward Fitzgerald. London: Kimber, 1959.
Ramsay, Sir Bertram Home. "The Evacuation from Dunkirk, May–June 1940," *The London Gazette*, July 17, 1947.
Ramsay, Sir Bertram Home. "Assault Phases of the Normandy Landings, June 1944," *The London Gazette*, October 30, 1947.
Ranft, Bryan, ed. *Technical Change and British Naval Policy 1860–1939*. London: Hodder and Stoughton, 1977.
Ranelagh, J. *The Agency: The Rise and Decline of the CIA*. New York: Simon and Shuster, 1986.
Ranft, Bryan. "The Naval Defense of British Sea-Borne Trade, 1860–1905." D.Phil thesis, Balliol College, Oxford University, 1967.
Ransom, H. H. *Central Intelligence and the National Security*. Oxford: Oxford University Press, 1958.
Ratcliffe, P. *Eye of the Storm: Twenty-Five Years in Action with the SAS*. London: Michael O'Mara, 2000.
Rej, Abhijnan. "How India's Defense Policy Complicates US-India Military Cooperation." US Army War College. February 26, 2019. https://warroom.armywarcollege.edu/articles/indias-defense-policy-and-us/
Richelson, J. *A Century of Spies: Intelligence in the Twentieth Century*. Oxford: Oxford University Press, 1995.
Richelson, J. *The US Intelligence Community*. New York: Ballinger, 1989.
Richelson, J. *The Wizards of Langley: Inside the CIA's Directorate of Science and Technology*. Boulder, Colorado: Westview Press, 2001.
Richelson, J. and D. Ball. *Ties that Bind: Intelligence Cooperation Between the UKUSA Countries*. Boston: Allen and Unwin, 1985.
Report of the Security Commission, May 1983. Cmnd 8876. Her Majesty's Stationery Office, 1983
Report of the Security Commission, October 1986. Cmnd 9923. Her Majesty's Stationery Office, 1986.
Rintelen, Captain Franz Von. *The Dark Invader*. London: Peter Davis, 1933.
Roberts, Captain Jerry. *Lorenz. Breaking Hitler's Top Secret Code at Bletchley Park*. Cheltenham: The History Press, 2017.
Roskill, S. W. *The War at Sea. 1939–1945*. Three Volumes. London: Her Majesty's Stationery Office, 1954–1961.
Roskill, S. W. *Hankey, Man of Secrets*. London: Collins, 1969.
Rowan, R. W. *The Story of Secret Service*. London: Miles, 1938.
Ruge, F. *Sea Warfare 1939–1945. A German Viewpoint*. Translated by M. G. Saunders. London: Cassell, 1957.
Ryan, C. *The Longest Day, June 6, 1944*. New York: Simon & Schuster, 1960.
Sainsbury, A. B. *The Royal Navy Day by Day*. London: Ian Allen Publications, 1993.
Saran, Samir & Verma Richard Rahul. "Strategic Convergence: The United States and India as Major Defense Partners." Observer Research Foundation (ORF), June 25, 2019.

Scott, James. *The Attack on the Liberty. The Untold Story of Israel's Deadly 1967 Assault on a US Spy Ship.* New York: Simon & Schuster, 2009.

Schelling, W. R. *Strategy, Politics, and Defense Budgets.* New York: Columbia University Press, 1962.

Schull, J. *The Far Distant Ships. An Official Account of Canadian Naval Operations in the Second World War.* Ottawa: Ministry of National Defence, 1962.

Schurman, D. M. *The Education of a Navy: The Development of British Naval Strategic Thought, 1867–1914.* Oxford: Oxford University Press, 1966.

Sebag Montefiore, Simon. *Stalin: The Court of the Red Tsar.* London: Vintage, 2003.

Showell, Jak P. Mallmann. *German Naval Code Breakers.* London: Ian Allan Publishing, 2003.

Sides, Hampton. *On Desperate Ground. The Marines at the Reservoir. The Korean War's Greatest Battle.* New York: Doubleday, 2018.

Sillitoe, Sir Percy. "My Answer to Critics of MI5." *The Sunday Times,* November 22, 1953.

Singh, Zorawar Daulet. "Foreign Policy and Sea Power. India's Maritime Role." Center for Policy Research, Delhi. *Journal of Defense Studies,* no. 4, (2017).

Smith, B. F. *The Ultra-Magic Deals and the Most Secret Special Relationship 1940–1946.* Shrewsbury: Airlife Publishing, 1993.

Smith, B. F. *Sharing Secrets with Stalin: How the Allies Traded Intelligence, 1941–1945.* Kansas: University of Kansas Press, 1996.

Smith, M. *New Cloak. Old Dagger: How Britain's spies came in from the cold.* London: Victor Gollanz, 1996.

Smith, M. *Station X: The Code-Breakers of Bletchley Park.* London: Channel Four Books, 1998.

Smith, M. *The Emperor's Codes: Bletchley Park and the Breaking of Japan's Secret Ciphers.* London: Bantam, 2000.

Smith, M. *The Spying Game: A Secret History of British Espionage.* London: Politico's, 2003.

Smith, M. *Killer Elite: The Inside Story of America's Most Secret Operations Team.* New York: St. Martin's Press, 2007.

Smith, M. and R. Erskine, eds. *Action this Day: Bletchley Park from the breaking of the Enigma Code to the Birth of the Modern Computer.* London: Bantam, 2001.

Sontag, S. and Drew, C. *Blind Man's Bluff: The Untold Story of American Submarine Espionage.* New York: Public Affairs, 1998.

Stafford, D. *Spies Beneath Berlin.* Second Edition. London: John Murray, 2002.

Stein, H., ed. *American Civil-Military Decisions.* Birmingham, Alabama: University of Alabama Press, 1963.

Steinhauer, G. and Felsted, S. T. *The Kaiser's Master Spy.* London: John Lane, Bodley Head, 1930.

Strip, A. J. *Code Breakers in the Far East.* London: Frank Cass, 1989.

Strong, Major General Sir Kenneth. *Intelligence at the Top.* London: Cassell, 1968.

Sudoplatov, P. *Special Tasks: The Memoirs of an Unwanted Witness—a Soviet Spymaster.* London: Little Brown, 1994.

Sunday Express Magazine, London. *War in the Falklands: The Campaign in Pictures.* London: Weidenfeld & Nicholson Ltd, 1982.

Svendsen, A. *Intelligence Cooperation and the War on terror: Anglo-American Security Relations after 911.* London: Routledge, 2009.

Thakur, Arvind and Michael Padgett. "Time is Now to Advance US-India Defense Cooperation," *National Defense,* May 31, 2018.

Thatcher, M. *The Downing Street Years.* London: Harper Collins, 1993.

Thomas, R. *Espionage and Secrecy: The Official Secrets Act 1911–1989 of the United Kingdom.* London: Routledge, 1991.

Thompson, Julian. *No Picnic. 3 Commando Brigade in the South Atlantic 1982.* New York: Hippocrene Books, 1985.

Thompson, Tommy. "The Kremlinologist. Briefing Book Number 648." George Washington University, November 2018.

Thomson, Sir Basil. *The Story of Scotland Yard.* London: Grayson & Grayson, 1935.

Trento, Joseph J. *The Secret History of the CIA.* Roseville, California: Prima Publishing, 2001.

Tuchman, Barbara W. *The Zimmermann Telegram*. New York: Viking Press, 1958.

Toynbee, A., ed. *Survey of International Relations, 1939–1946*. Oxford: Oxford University Press, 1952.

United States Department of Defense. "Preparedness, Partnerships, and Promoting a Networked Region." Indo-Pacific Strategy Report. Washington DC, June 1, 2019.

United States Department of Defense. Soviet Military Power. An annual publication from September 1981 to September 1990. This series may be obtained from the Superintendent of Documents, US Government Printing Office, Washington DC, 20402. This outstanding series, contains extensive unclassified detail of Soviet: Policies and Global Ambitions; Forces for Nuclear Attack; Strategic Defense and Space Operations; Forces for Theater Operations; Readiness, Mobility, and Sustainability; Research, Development, and Production; Political–Military and Regional Policies; The US response.

United States Department of State. "Intelligence: A Bibliography of its Functions, Methods, and Techniques." Part 1. December 1948. Part 2. April 1949.

Urban, M. *UK Eyes Alpha: The Inside Story of British Intelligence*. London: Faber and Faber, 1996.

Vickers, Philip. *A Clear Case of Genius. Room 40's Code-breaking Pioneer. Autobiography of Admiral Sir Reginald Hall.* Cheltenham: The History Press, 2017.

Vincent. J. *The Culture of Secrecy: Britain 1832–1988*. Oxford: Oxford University Press, 1998.

Waters, D. W. *A Study of the Philosophy and Conduct of Maritime War, 1815–1945*. Parts 1 and 2. Published privately. Copies are in the UK Ministry of Defence Library (Navy), and the National Maritime Museum, London.

Weiner, Tim, David Johnston and Neil A. Lewis. *Betrayal: The Story of Aldrich Ames, an American Spy*. London: Penguin Random House, 1996.

Wells, Anthony. "The 1967 June War: Soviet Naval Diplomacy and the Sixth Fleet—A Reappraisal." Center for Naval Analyses, Professional Paper 204, 1977, Department of the Navy.

Wells, Anthony. "NATO and US Carrier Deployment Policies." Center for Naval Analyses, February 1977, Department of the Navy.

Wells, Anthony. "Sea War '85 Scenario." With Captain John L. Underwood, United States Navy. *Center for Naval Analyses*, April 1977, Department of the Navy.

Wells, Anthony. "NATO and Carrier Deployment Policies: Formation of a new Standing Naval Strike Force in NATO." Center for Naval Analyses, April 1977, Department of the Navy.

Wells, Anthony. "The Application of Drag Reduction and Boundary Layer Control Technologies in an Experimental Program." Report for the Chief Naval Architect, Vickers Shipbuilding and Engineering Ltd, January 1986.

Wells, Anthony. "Preliminary Overview of Soviet Merchant Ships in SSBN Operations and Soviet Merchant Ships and Submarine Masking." SSBN Security Program, Department of the Navy, 1986, US Navy Contract N00016-85-C-0204.

Wells, Anthony. "SSBN Port Egress and the Non-Commercial Activities of the Soviet Merchant Fleet: Concepts of Operation and War Orders for Current and Future Anti-SSBN Operations." SSBN Security program, 1986, Department of the Navy, US Navy Contract N136400.

Wells, Anthony. "Overview Study of the Maritime Aspects of the Nuclear Balance in the European Theater." US Department of Energy Study for the European Conflict Analysis Project, October 1986, US Department of Energy.

Wells, Anthony. "The Soviet Navy in the Arctic and North Atlantic." *National Defense*, February 1986.

Wells, Anthony. "Soviet Submarine Prospects 1985–2000," *The Submarine Review*, January 1986.

Wells, Anthony. "A New Defense Strategy for Britain." *Proceedings of the United States Naval Institute*, March 1987.

Wells, Anthony. "Presence and Military Strategies of the USSR in the Arctic." Quebec Center for International Relations, Laval University Press, 1986.

Wells, Anthony. "Soviet Submarine Warfare Strategy Assessment and Future US Submarine and Anti-Submarine Warfare Technologies." Defense Advanced Research Projects Agency, March 1988, US Department of Defense.

Wells, Anthony. "Operational Factors Associated with the Software Nuclear Analysis for the UGM-109A Tomahawk Submarine-launched Land Attack Cruise Missile Combat Control System Mark 1." Department of the Navy, 1989.

Wells, Anthony. "Real Time Targeting: Myth or Reality." *Proceedings of the United States Naval Institute,* August 2001.

Wells, Anthony. "US Naval Power and the Pursuit of Peace in an Era of International Terrorism and Weapons of Mass Destruction." *The Submarine Review*, October 2002.

Wells, Anthony. "Limited Objective Experiment ZERO." The Naval Air Systems Command, July 2002, Department of the Navy.

Wells, Anthony. "Transformation—Some Insights and Observations for the Royal Navy from Across the Atlantic." *The Naval Review*, August 2003.

Wells, Anthony. "Distributed Data Analysis with Bayesian Networks: A Preliminary Study for the Non-Proliferation of Radioactive Devices." With Dr. Farid Dowla and Dr. G. Larson, December 2003, The Lawrence Livermore National Laboratory.

Wells, Anthony. "Fiber Reinforced Pumice Protective Barriers: To mitigate the effects of suicide and truck bombs." Final Report and recommendations. With Professor Vistasp Kharbari, Professor of Structural Engineering, University of California, San Diego, August 2006. For the Naval Air Systems Command, Department of the Navy. Washington DC.

Wells, Anthony. "Weapon Target Centric Model. Preliminary Modules and Applications. Two Volumes." Principal Executive Officer Submarines, August 2007, Naval Sea Systems Command, Department of the Navy.

Wells, Anthony. "They Did Not Die in Vain. USS Liberty Incident—Some Additional Perspectives." *Proceedings of the United States Naval Institute,* March 2005.

Wells, Anthony. "Royal Navy at the Crossroads: Turn the Strategic Tide. A Way to Implement a Lasting Vision." *The Naval Review*, November 2010.

Wells, Anthony. "The Royal Navy is Key to Britain's Security Strategy." *Proceedings of the United States Naval Institute,* December 2010.

Wells, Anthony. "The Survivability of the Royal Navy and a new Enlightened British Defense Strategy." *The Submarine Review*, January 2011.

Wells, Anthony. "A Strategy in East Asia that can Endure." *Proceedings of the United States Naval Institute*, May 2011. Reprinted in *The Naval Review*, August 2011, by kind permission of the United States Naval Institute.

Wells, Anthony. "Tactical Decision Aid: Multi intelligence capability for National, Theater, and Tactical Intelligence in real time across geographic pace and time." May 2012, Department of the Navy and US National Intelligence community.

Wells, Anthony. "Submarine Industrial Base Model: Key industrial base model for the US Virginia Class nuclear powered attack submarine." With Dr. Carol V. Evans. Principal Executive Officer Submarines, Naval Sea Systems Command, Department of the Navy.

Wells, Anthony. "The United States Navy, Jordan, and a Long-Term Israeli-Palestinian Security Agreement." *The Submarine Review*, Spring 2013.

Wells, Anthony. "Admiral Sir Herbert Richmond: What would he think, write and action today?" *The Naval Review Centenary Edition*, February 2013.

Wells, Anthony. "Jordan, Israel, and US Need to cooperate for Missile Defense." *United States Naval Institute News*, March 2013.

Wells, Anthony. "A Tribute to Admiral Sir John 'Sandy' Woodward." *United States Naval Institute News,* August 2013.

Wells, Anthony. "USS Liberty Document Center." Edited with Thomas Schaaf. A document web site produced by SiteWhirks, Warrenton, Virginia. September 2013. This site was transferred to the United States Library of Congress in April 2018, to be maintained in perpetuity for the benefit of scholars, analysts, and historians. USSLibertyDocumentCenter.org.

Wells, Anthony. "The Future of ISIS: A Joint US–Russian Assessment." With Dr. Andrey Chuprygin. *The Naval Review*, May 2015.

Wells, Anthony. *A Tale of Two Navies. Geopolitics, Technology, and Strategy in the United States Navy and the Royal Navy, 1960–2015*. Annapolis, Maryland: United States Naval Institute Press, 2017.

Wells, Anthony & Phillips, James W, Captain US Navy (retired). "Put the Guns in a Box." *Proceedings of the United States Naval Institute*, Annapolis, Maryland, June 2018.

Wemyss, D. E. G. *Walker's Group in the Western Approaches*. Liverpool: Liverpool Post and Echo, 1948.

Werner, H. A. *Iron Coffin. A Personal Account of German U-boat Battles of World War Two*. London: Arthur Barker, 1969.

West, N. *A Matter of Trust: MI5 1945–1972*. London: Weidenfeld and Nicholson, 1982.

West, N. *GCHQ: The Secret Wireless War, 1900–1986*. London: Weidenfeld and Nicholson, 1986.

West, N. *The Secret War for the Falklands*. London: Little Brown, 1997.

West, N. *Venona*. London: Harper Collins, 1999.

West, N. *At Her Majesty's Secret Service: The Chiefs of Britain's Intelligence Agency, MI6*. London: Greenhill Books, 2006.

Westad, Odd Arne. *The Cold War: A World History*. Oxford: Oxford University Press, 2017.

Wheatley, R. *Operation Sea Lion. German Plans for the Invasion of England, 1939–1942*. Oxford: Clarendon Press, 1958.

Wilkinson, N. *Secrecy and the Media: The Official History of the UK's D-Notice System*. London: Routledge, 2009.

Wilmot, C. *The Struggle for Europe*. London: Harper Collins, 1952.

Wilson, H. *The Labour Government 1964–1970: A Personal Record*. London: Michael Joseph, 1971.

Winterbotham, F. *The Ultra Secret*. London: Weidenfeld & Nicholson, 1974.

Wohlstetter, R. *Pearl Harbor, Warning and Decision*. London: Methuen, 1957.

Wolin, S. and R. M. Slusser. *The Soviet Secret Police*. London: Methuen, 1957.

Womack, Helen, ed. *Undercover Lives: Soviet Spies in the Cities of the World*. London: Orion Publishing Company, 1998.

Wood, D. and D. Dempster. *The Narrow Margin*. London: Hutchinson, 1961.

Woodward, Admiral Sir John "Sandy." *One Hundred Days. The Memoirs of the Falklands Battle Group Commander*. With Patrick Robinson. Annapolis, Maryland: United States Naval Institute Press, 1992.

Woodward, L. *My Life as a Spy*. London: Macmillan, 2005.

Wright, P, with Greengrass, Paul. *Spycatcher. The Candid Autobiography of a Senior Intelligence Officer*. New York: Viking, 1987.

Wylde, N., ed. *The Story of Brixmis, 1946–1990*. Arundel: Brixmis Association, 1993.

Young, J. and J. Kent. *International Relations Since 1945*. Oxford: Oxford University Press, 2004.

Young, J. W. *The Labour Governments, 1964–1970: International Policy*. Manchester: Manchester University Press, 2003.

Zimmerman, B. *France, 1944. The Fatal Decisions*. London: Michael Joseph, 1956.

Index

References to images are in *italics*.